Miller, Sheldon.

Stealth management.

$27.95

DATE			

STEALTH
MANAGEMENT

*"With shared goals
they will hardly know
you are leading them"*

Sheldon Miller

Stealth Management Institute
Tulsa, Oklahoma

Published by
Stealth Management Institute
15 West 6th Street
Suite 1608
Tulsa, OK 74119

Manufactured in the U.S.

ISBN: 0-9635316-0-3
Library of Congress Catalog Card Number: 92-90895

CONTENTS

FOREWORD

Key issues for most businesses are improving productivity, maintaining quality, and technology development. Success or failure in these vital areas depend on the development of professional management. Winners in the productivity race distinguish themselves from losers because they understand this fact. Every operational area must be improved continually, from strategic planning to the organization of people. It requires dedication and cooperation from all employees.

Our company is currently in the process of applying the management style described herein. Changing from an entrepreneurial to a professional management style is not easy. It requires dedication to vision, persistence, and a good practical "road map." This book serves as that "road map." The positive response from our employees to the process has been so beneficial that actual achievement of planned goals will be but "icing on the cake." If you want to develop an atmosphere that stimulates learning, creative thinking, and productivity, Stealth Management is for you!

Sheldon Miller has done a superb job of putting together a practical training manual for the small to medium sized company that seeks to improve its competitive posture through employee motivation, good communication, and job satisfaction. This book addresses all fundamental issues underlying productivity improvement. Step by step, it takes you through the process of developing, cultivating, and motivating the team and provides answers to many questions you might have along the way. The anecdotes are personal and help to broaden the perspective of the areas addressed.

Stealth Management is a resource that can be referred to again and again.

Mark J. Tomer
President
Enardo Manufacturing Company

GLOSSARY
OF TERMS

Stealth Management — a management style in which all involved are encouraged to participate after which the leader announces a decision. This management style accents the proper use of interpersonal skills and is implemented in such manner as to maximize achievement toward well chosen goals, both short and long term. It embodies all the precepts of professional management.

Hierarchy — in management, this refers to a group in authority who manage so as to accent their superiority and provide special "perks" available only to those at the top.

Information Technology — the art of utilizing communication and information to maximize organizational achievement.

Leadership — the ability to generate commitment, confidence, and excitement in the pursuit of a cause or goal.

Management by Objective — a management style which primarily accents achievement of specified goals without necessarily requiring broad based consultation.

Participative Management — a management style in which all are encouraged to contribute their thinking.

Planning — the process of establishing a plan for selecting and achieving long range organizational goals.

Professional Management — Professional management is leading people in a manner that maximizes achievement toward well chosen goals, both short and long term.

Strategic Planning — that portion of the planning process that deals with response to external influences not within our control, particularly those that are long range in nature.

Organizational Culture — the personality of the organization, or the psychological climate within which the members function. It includes the values and motivating influences that make the organization different.

AUTHOR'S "BRAINTRUST"

During the writing of this book, I have been blessed by constructive suggestions received from many reviewers. Some have had large business background, some small business background. They have included a banker, a psychologist, a publisher, a newspaper writer with previous large corporate experience, a human resource manager, a merchandising executive, a management consultant, a manufacturing company president, a corporate planning coordinator, and the best lecturer on the subject of management I have known. Each of them has influenced me to make changes and they have my sincere gratitude.

Among them are the following:

Richard Bednar — former senior manager for a major accounting firm

Dean DeVore — formerly president of medium sized manufacturing company, a management consultant, and now a managing director of a career consulting service company

Anthony J. Eccles — Director of the Sloan Programme, London Graduate School of Business

Dr. John W. Bonge — professor in the school of management, Lehigh University

Joseph Cristiano — a dynamic lecturer who refers to himself as a management exorcist. He urges business leaders to exorcise bad management practices from their organizations

9

Gene Engleman — a successful banker and businessman who, in the spirit of helping American business, has given generously of his time as a lecturer for the American Management Assn.

Dr. Nancy G. Feldman — a former professor and management consultant

Louis Gelfand — formerly Director of Corp. Relations for a Fortune 100 company, a published author, and ombudsman of a metropolitan newspaper

Professor Benjamin Litt — professor in the school of management, Lehigh University

Martin Mazner — former Director of Marketing for Ashton Tate Corp. and subsequently a group publisher for Ziff-Davis Publishing Co.

Dr. Bruce Merrifield — Asst. Sec'y for Productivity, Technology, and Innovation, U.S. Dept. of Commerce

Donald R. Newlun — A former manufacturing company executive, now a Professor in the Technology Department of a state university

F.G. "Buck" Rodgers — Former Corporate V.P. of I.B.M. in charge of world-wide marketing

Carol Rorschach — manager of a small electronics manufacturing company who also has had considerable experience in technical writing

H.T. Sears, Jr. — former vice-pres. of a major oil company. He took early retirement and now is the C.E.O. of a small manufacturing co.

Desmond Sides — formerly in the managerial services dept. of a "big eight" acctg. firm, now comptroller and office mgr. of a large non-profit organization

Richard Silverman — former manager of human resources for a Fortune 100 company and now a management consultant

Jack Stack — President of Springfield ReManufacturing Corp. His success and management style prompted Inc. magazine to name him C.E.O of their management "dream team".

George Stone — formerly vice-president of a large department store chain and now a management consultant

PREFACE

Those who attend good schools of management should acquire a fairly sophisticated understanding of professional management. A few years ago, however, when such schools were teaching profit enhancement via case studies, often this was not so. Managers of most small to medium-sized businesses have not had management training, however, and this book is primarily written for them.

There are many books and training programs which purport to teach professional management, but I found none to help me in implementing such a management style in my business. This book is meant to fill that void.

You may find portions of the text already within your sphere of knowledge, but being led in recipe-like fashion through the process of implementing professional management may reinforce that knowledge. Although I have chosen to be very specific, your own implementation scenario could be quite different in detail.

Most of the anecdotes are from my experience in the field of manufacturing. Each of them has been included because it accents the pragmatic value of one or more principles in that portion of the text. As you read them, try to dwell on the probable principles being covered. I hope they prove interesting and give added meaning to your reading, regardless of the nature of your business.

Sometimes, the difference between managers who achieve at the highest level and those who merely do *passably well* is difficult to explain — especially when there seems to be little difference in their intelligence, training, or ability. If we would take the time for deeper analysis, however, we would find almost always, that the difference is in their soft skills which have been referred to as *enrichment skills* by Research Recommendations (published by the National Institute of Business Management, Inc.). These include style, self appraisal, worldliness, sensitivity, charisma, and others. You can enhance them over time if you choose to do so. I have attempted to be helpful in that effort.

In the interest of verbal simplicity, I often use the male gender instead of having to say *he or she*.

Section I

TO CHANGE OR
NOT TO CHANGE

---

1 • Changing Concepts

We give of ourselves when we give the gift of words:
encouragement, inspiration, guidance — Wilferd Peterson

The meaning of some words change with time requiring new editions of dictionaries. Such is the case with the word *manager*. The meaning of the word *subordinate* is also in need of change as it is applied to the typical organization chart.

If still working for an organization, the thought that I was being "managed" would not appeal to me, nor, probably, to most people. Yet, we still commonly use the word *manager*. A well trained member of a working "team" can function best when trusted to do the job on his own and in his own way. He does not need to be managed, but often encouragement, inspiration, or guidance is needed and helpful.

The authoritarian manager of old is gradually evolving into an enabler, a facilitator, an organizer, and one who empowers others. In performing these functions, what does a person really do? In each case, that person we now call a manager, is managing information and things — organizing, communicating, explaining or interpreting, responding to questions, scheduling, buying, selling, etc. In no case should he be managing people. People manage themselves, and those who do not manage themselves in a team spirit within the defined mission of the organization should not long be tolerated. With that thinking in mind, **every use of the word manager hereinafter shall mean primarily a manager of information and things — not a manager of people.**

If being referred to as a *subordinate* suggests comparative superiority or inferiority, it would be better not to use it. As will be reiterated later in the book, a leader's power emanates from below. Without the contribution of those at the bottom of an organization a leader has no power, but we still refer to them as subordinates, unfortunately. A machine operator usually is more knowledgeable about the use of his machine than his foreman and can run that machine better than the foreman. If, in management, we think of the words *subordinate* and *superior* as only conveying relative location in terms of being nearer to or farther from the CEO on the organization chart, being a subordinate does not have such negative impact. In this manner, its meaning is evolving to be more appropriate.

The person who performs as an organization's CEO does have to be a leader. As we descend the organization chart, however, those referred to as managers are charged with a lesser degree of leadership responsibility but an increasing responsibility for encouraging, inspiring, and guiding.

These thoughts are considered utopian by most business leaders. They are partially correct in that if all organizations hired only people who could promptly adapt to such concepts, there would be a huge group of unemployables. Our social mores will have to change considerably for such idealism to even approach practicality, but to summarily dismiss them on this basis is also incorrect. Much of what may be considered utopian is practical in today's organizational culture and to the degree that it is applied, productivity will improve and society will reap considerable indirect benefit.

A final thought about words and people's sensitivity to them: if you involve all members of the organization in both the planning and the decision-making process, they will derive a sense of participation that borders on a feeling of ownership. The words or titles used will become less important. Everyone will share the same goals and be part of the same team.

2 • Personal Changes Come First

It can be said, "If you want to change your organization, you usually must change yourself first." Why do we suggest there is need for personal change? If you are civic minded and environmentally conscious, for example, your employees are more apt to be inclined that way. If you are highly ethical, there is less potential for unethical behavior in your company. If you are sensitive to people, they will respond to you in a better manner than were you a strong authoritarian. If you encourage and reward initiative and are not punitive toward people when they make mistakes, they will be more open with their ideas. If you are jumpy and quick tempered, they will spend too much time "protecting their rears." All this being true, you can understand why your organization reflects you. Therefore, it follows, if you want to change or improve your organization, you must first change yourself.

What is meant by "you must first change yourself"? It is not so intimidating a suggestion as one might think — and none of us is perfect. In effect, you should alter your behavior in subtle ways so that all members of the organization perceive you as an individual who has changed for the better, especially those who report to you. Does that mean you are other than a good person now? Of course not! A good leader or manager, however, should be perceived as a caring person, prone to extending recognition and reward for good work, and not hierarchical in management style. He should forgive mistakes and encourage a working atmosphere that promotes shared goals and innovation. These are important traits of a good manager, and to the degree that you may not exhibit these traits in the eyes of others, you have room for personal improvement. None of us is expected to be a paragon of excellence, but if you are perceived as a good manager by your fellow workers, the performance of the organization will be better, and in today's social environment, superior leadership performance without such favorable perception is very difficult. Most managers grossly misjudge how their behavioral traits are perceived by others.

Management is changing rapidly today. The level of productivity necessary to meet competition requires a greater degree of professionalism on the part of business leaders. It is important that managers be leaders not "bosses" — and, that applies to both top and middle managers.

The goals of this book are to:

1. Convince you of the need for professional management
2. Help you learn the precepts of professional management
3. Help you analyze yourself and prepare to be a better leader and manager
4. Show you how to implement the most effective style of professional management in your organization
5. Persuade you to implement these principles of management as soon as possible

If you already use modern management techniques, I hope this book strengthens your philosophy and adds support as you encounter inevitable change. If you are running your business by instinct, even with high intellect and ambition, be aware that maximizing productivity and achieving well-chosen goals usually require a professional management approach. If you are persuaded to adopt such a management style, the improved performance of your organization will soon be evident.

During most of my career, as a small businessman, I did not take the time to study management or even read on the subject. Further, after long hours of work, my span of attention for reading was limited. I almost "blew" it by waiting until there were discretionary funds in our business before seeking training in the art of professional management. By then, it was so late in my career there was barely time to reap the benefit. You may have these same restraints, but I hope you appreciate the need for continuing education, even for business executives at the highest level.

If you have ever attended a management training course, you probably returned to work with a changed outlook toward your job

and your organization but with a feeling of frustration that left you wondering, gnawingly, "How can I put all that theory to actual use?" Before you could answer the question, you again became embroiled in your everyday problems and the knowledge you acquired was set aside. Such is the experience of most business executives who seek improvement in this way. If such training was presented with good managerial perspective and followed by in-depth implementation instructions, you would feel impelled to apply what was learned. Often managers who, in a fragmented manner, are exposed to training in special areas of management have difficulty "putting it all together". Such training can be likened to "treating the symptoms", whereas installing professional management in your organization is "treating the disease". Experience has shown that implementing professional management in a comprehensive manner, before working on specific areas of management, will usually cause most of the ills of poor management to disappear. At a later point, reference is made to the value of training in specific areas of management, but that is after a professional management style is in place.

3 • What Is *Stealth Management*

As we approach the 21st century, we must take into account the changes that have occurred in management. No longer can we motivate people with intimidation except under conditions of severe privation. Even fat paychecks often fail to motivate. Today a leader spends most of his energy in the following areas:

- Good working climate
- Organizational culture
- Mission and values
- Monitoring performance
- Communicating
- Establishing shared goals
- Maintaining good morale
- Assuring conformance to law

A leader should be perceived as a good person and be understanding of people. He should be deeply sensitive in all his actions. He must not appear aggressive or egotistical. The traits of a good manager will be discussed in detail later in the book, but many of them could be included under the term, "aggressive humility". His influence and managerial style should project unobtrusively except under certain circumstances such as crisis management. The title "*Stealth Management*" is derived from these characteristics of a modern manager/leader. He must lead and influence in a manner that permits those who follow him to share the same goals and to feel that they have a part of the decision-making process. All this requires great attention to soft skills as opposed to conventional hard skills.

Because this style of management involves the organization from the bottom up, even in the process of planning and goal setting, all members of the organization wind up sharing the same goals. "They will hardly realize they are being led". It reminds me of the story about a famous military leader back in the 2nd century who was asked how he continually managed to win battles. His answer was, "It's really simple. I lead the troops where they want to go". We can assume, of course, that much discussion and strategic planning took place before such consensus occurred, but obviously when the troops and their leaders all want to achieve the same goals, the job of leadership is much easier.

Stealth Management does not imply furtiveness, however. In all areas, a good manager should treat all members of the organization as members of the team in word and deed. The principles of *Stealth Management* are applicable to the corporate "intrepreneur" and the smaller business owner, chief executive, or entrepreneur.

We all know of the development of the stealth bomber whose approach is difficult to detect. We also know that because our lives depend on well designed and well built aircraft when we are flying passengers, quality is an uppermost goal in aircraft manufacturing — a goal which can be achieved only through good management.

While studying for a degree in engineering, I enrolled in all the aeronautical and navigation courses available to me because of my interest in aviation. In late 1939 I accepted a job with the largest aircraft manufacturer in the United States at the time. The onset of World War II became evident soon thereafter and our company was forced to grow exponentially over the next few years. At age twenty three, I found myself coordinating the work of forty engineers each of whom was a better engineer than I, a condition which should not have been permitted but for the fact that I then had more aircraft training. That experience spawned my rapidly acquiring an appreciation for what I refer to as *aggressive humility*.

One plant I worked at grew, while I was there, from seven hundred employees to over fourteen thousand and its engineering department from five to over fifteen hundred employees — all within two years. Under such conditions, changes in procedure were required almost daily. Usually, these changes were communicated by memo sent through the company mail, from the general manager to all department heads. Sometimes the changes had irritating impact and resulted in morale problems for several days plus decreased motivation. This was never true, however, in the flight test department which had about seventy-five employees.

The chief test pilot, "Red" Frank, always called his people together, read such memos to them, invited comment and endeavored to communicate the probable reason for the policy change. On one occasion, their group firmly decided that the action was not in the best interest of the company and "Red" passed on their feelings to *the front office*. The company retracted the initial memo and revised it accordingly.

"Red" was a fine test pilot and a very good manager. He consulted with his people in the planning of every test flight and the evaluation of data accumulated during the flight. They helped prepare an agenda for the pilot which assured that his in-flight tests for the plane were in proper sequence to minimize danger to the pilot or the plane. They made sure that the airplane was completely ground-checked before flight time. Strategies for response to the unexpected were well developed. "Red" and his fellow pilots realized their success, and possibly their lives, largely depended on their ground crew team. They more than appreciated the team. They caused each member to feel individually responsible for the success of every flight. As a manager, "Red" applied good planning, dedicated responsibility, excellent participative communication, shared goal setting, and control. His management style included all the precepts of *stealth management.*

Perhaps if all managers were to think of themselves as test pilots, with their career lives dependent on their fellow workers, they would be motivated to manage better.

4 • Take The Test !

As you may know, and as will be noted in other portions of this text, most managers do not change as a result of their taking management training, regardless of the form in which it is presented. This topic is therefore devoted to persuading you to manage in a professional manner.

Recently I participated in a brainstorming session on the subject of "How can we persuade managers to agree to change — agree to become professional managers?" One of our group, who is a popular lecturer on management, is adamant in his belief that the head of a company is the key to what extent good training can help the organization. He says, "If the C.E.O. does not have a *passion* for optimizing the performance of the entire organization, including top management, the company will continue to drift along in the same old manner."

It is easy to assume that you, the reader, are the C.E.O. of your company and that, therefore, you must have *passion* for improving productivity, but the gnawing question still is there: "How can you be convinced?" What is there about your company that could motivate you to become a professional manager if but you were aware? Our brainstorming effort has produced the following list of characteristics that are prevalent in the typically company that we are trying to benefit:

- Employees do not feel motivated
- Employees do not derive satisfaction from their jobs
- Employees regard top management as being haughty
- Top managers do not realize how they are perceived by others in the organization
- There is poor communication

- It is the rare employee who leaves work with the thought "I did a good job today"

As a C.E.O., because you do not knowingly encourage any of the foregoing problems in your company, it is natural for you to believe they do not exist. We observe that they are prevalent in most organizations. Do not merely ask one or more of those who report to you, "Do we suffer from any of those problems?" They will give you the answers they think you want to hear. The people at the bottom of the organization chart will give you the truth, if permitted to do so with assured privacy.

To prove us wrong (or correct), as far as your own company is concerned, included at the back of this text are two tests for you to apply. Test number 1 is designed to evaluate employee attitude toward the company and its management. It should and can be administered so as to afford privacy to the employee and thereby give the employee an opportunity to voice feelings and opinions that may have harbored for some time. If the results reflect overall satisfaction, yours is an exemplary organization. If the results indicate less than satisfaction, would you not then agree that changes are called for? It is our hope that the results of this test will persuade you to value our overall *Stealth Management* program enough to choose to utilize it. We are of the belief that you will not overlook any prevailing dissatisfaction within your company.

5 · About My Friend Hank

The following story is about my friend Hank, a good person who failed to achieve his potential because he did not acquire the managerial training which might have permitted him to do so.

It was a beautiful day, and I walked seven blocks from my office to attend the funeral of my friend Hank in May of 1990. Because we both had been manufacturers in the same city, I saw many familiar faces there to pay their respects. The eulogy caught the essence of Hank's personality and character, reminding me of what a fine person he had been.

During the service, while thinking of my relationship with him, I became aware that Hank had been a major influence on my business career. In many ways he had been the typical small business person who usually does a good job of solving problems and meeting short range goals but does not apply long-range planning or goal-setting within his company. He was a good person but unaware of his managerial shortcomings. He had difficulty delegating, and many of the right business decisions he made were for the wrong reason. He worked long hours and had unusual tenacity when faced with tough problems. The trouble was that he was not trained to be a *professional* businessman. I hope that many readers can easily identify with him and see a need for changing their management style as a result.

I first met Hank in the mid 1940's while interviewing him on behalf of our chamber of commerce. We were surveying area manufacturers as to their potential need for malleable castings in an attempt to lure a large foundry to our city. He was only one year older than I, but I soon was in awe of him. He already had his own business — a contract machine shop filled with relatively new machinery. He was a natty dresser and had his two door Cadillac parked in front of the office. He met me garbed in tan coveralls. He loved machines and never let another employee use a newly acquired machine until he had "broken it in" and learned all of its idiosyncrasies. He rarely let another employee machine a part of any complexity until he had mastered the procedure first. His temper could be aroused easily, although he rarely directed it toward individuals and it usually was of short duration. There were a few new employees who almost quit due to Hank's temper, but older employees knew that it would be forgotten by next day. He looked younger than his age and enjoyed that attribute throughout his life. He had a sense of humor, and usually was quite friendly. His management style was largely instinctive and did not include long range planning.

In spite of management characteristics which perhaps limited his progress, his company did grow and did enjoy a cadre of loyal customers. After his business was twenty years old, he needed additional space and took a big "plunge", considering his financial strength. He acquired three acres of choice industrial land and built an impressive manufacturing facility. It had over 20,000 square feet of space in which he employed fewer than twenty-five people. From what I have said about him, you might think he was a consummate egotist who delighted in putting on a big front. Such was not the case. He truly loved machinery, his manufacturing plant, good clothes, and a hi-performance car — not because of the impression they would make on others, but because they appealed to his own sensibilities. For example, he delighted in the *purr* of a powerful automobile engine as well as its quick response. In retrospect, *catering to his own sensibilities* was a big limitation — it considerably reduced his potential for achievement. Many small business managers seem to suffer from this same shortcoming. **Their management styles cater excessively to personal sensibilities as opposed to instilling shared goals throughout their organizations.**

I went to visit Hank at his new facility. He was dressed in his usual coveralls and escorted me into his office. It was nicely furnished, in living-room fashion, without a desk or filing cabinets. His secretary would bring data needed to his office when so requested, but he spent most of his time in the shop area. When visiting him, the receptionist would give me permission to go into the manufacturing area and look for him. After finishing what could not easily be interrupted he would turn off his machine and greet me.

Before experiencing slow business in 1983, his employment exceeded 100 and he had gone through two building expansions. The last expansion added a new office building which provided excess office space that he rented to others.

What can we say about Hank, and why is he typical of many managers of small to medium sized businesses? The things to be said about him as a business manager would include the following:

Positive attributes:

- Cared about people
- Provided his employees a pleasant physical work environment
- Was dedicated to his work
- Was customer oriented
- Was not afraid to be different

- Overall, he treated his employees well
- Did not ask others to do what he was unwilling to do himself
- Was not hierarchical in his management style
- Was very energetic
- Was a *hands-on* type of manager

Negative attributes — typical of most untrained managers:

- Did not provide his company the benefits of long-range planning
- Was task oriented
- Was only involved with short term goals
- His life was excessively centered in his company to the exclusion of outside interests
- Did not give his employees a sense of involvement
- Managed primarily by instinct
- Required his entire organization to revolve about him

Through the years, I envied his "image of success" because I constantly had to manage my company's money very conservatively and often could not afford to do the good things for our company that Hank was able to do for his. It was revealed later that in the early years he had a financial backer, a convenience I did not enjoy. Nevertheless, his construction of a new facility, which apparently enhanced his progress, influenced my building a new factory a few years later that turned out to be a very positive move for my company. It located us closer to our principle customer, enhanced our image among our customers, and substantially improved employee morale.

I next learned from observing Hank's operations that applying color dynamics to machines and a factory's interior would result in improved productivity. We applied this knowledge in our facility and our employees responded with improved morale and an increased desire for neatness in the workplace.

A few years later, we were having difficulty maintaining consistent quality in the manufacture of a line of check valves. Hank suggested that acquiring a numerically controlled machining center would be a big help. After careful consideration, and at a cost of one hundred thousand dollars, we acquired such a machine. We were told by its manufacturer that we were the smallest company ever to purchase a machine of that type from them. Hank had warned me that such machines were a boon to productivity and quality, but they all had "bugs" and required that the operator learn to compensate for inherent idiosyncrasies. Sure enough, even though we had been assured by the manufacturer that their newer models were not that way, we did have a serious problem. How a valued employee solved that problem will be told later.

After we had been using our new machine for several months, Hank helped to further reduce our valve costs by acquainting me with what was then an esoteric machining technique in which cutting-oil is pumped through a hole drilled through the center of a cutting-tool. Very few manufacturers, regardless of size, had yet incorporated such sophistication into their machining procedures. By keeping the tool cutting edge cool and well lubricated, we could machine much faster. It required a special swivel type of injection fitting at the top of the rotating tool, a device we could not purchase. It was usually incorporated into the basic design of some types of machines. From Hank, we learned how to make such a device "in house". It permitted more than doubling the cutting speed.

As you can see, Hank indeed had been a considerable influence for good in my career. However, having reached a point where progress seemed to be slow and unsatisfying, it seemed to me that there had to be a better way of managing than I could learn on my own or from Hank. Being aware of friends that worked for large companies who occasionally were required to attend management seminars, I decided to *get away* and enroll in a management course. Perhaps there was much for me to learn. What an understatement that proved to be!

Many readers would ask at this point, "What was Hank's level of success?" You could say that he had a good company which was almost always moderately profitable and able to weather the hills and valleys of the business cycle without too much difficulty. He enjoyed a conservative but comfortable life which pleased him, and he was highly regarded by those who knew him. Through the years his company employment grew to a little over one hundred and at the time of his death it was about sixty-five. Yes, in his eyes, he enjoyed success. He desired no more. If the majority of entrepreneurs measure success in this same way, however, our country will continue to tolerate an unambitious level of productivity that bodes ill-tidings for the future. The majority of job creation and innovation stems from small businesses like Hank's. For that reason it is important to our nation that small business managers become more professional. That requires training.

In what follows, I describe my management training and the process of rebuilding my interpersonal skills — skills necessary for a *professional* manager.

6 · On to Acapulco

After investigating the many management training courses available to me, I decided to enroll in The President's Course given by the American Management Association because it was comprehensive, was designed for company presidents, and would only take a week of my time. Although it was offered in many locations, it was most convenient for me to take the course offered in Acapulco, Mexico and combine it with my yearly sales trip to call on customers in Mexico City. I anticipated a leisurely applied study program plus many hours of relaxation. Instead, the training was intense, even extending to after dinner sessions on some days. What was being taught impressed me so much that I decided to implement the professional management style they referred to as *consultative management* into my company as soon as possible.

They indicated, about mid-way through the course, it would be a mistake for us to try to apply what was being taught without help. It would require the guidance of a trained professional. I invited one of the lecturers, an industrial psychologist, to dinner and discussed employing his firm to help us implement professional management in our company. I explained that we were a small company with fewer than 40 employees and had reached but two million in yearly sales. His response impressed me favorably and we hired his company. The following topic tells the story of how they helped us.

7 · *Stealth Management* Worked For Me

In June of 1981 I attended an American Management Association seminar held for a group of businessmen who had previously completed the President's Course. At the outset, each attendee was asked to introduce himself and tell how he had benefited from what he had learned from the course. When my turn came, after introducing myself, I told them that the previous day I had been fired as president of my company. After letting the shock of that true statement sink in for a few seconds, I continued by relating the following story:

While attending the President's Course in 1977, I felt so enlightened by the professional management style being taught, I promptly decided to try to implement that management style into our company. After spending a very expensive $20,000 on consulting industrial psychologists and receiving an estimated $2,000 worth of benefit, I temporarily abandoned the effort for several months to allow my key people to cease laughing at me. Their previous experience had been only with large businesses. Yes, I was the kind of manager who employees felt free to criticize. Because of that, we already had an important part of a good working climate in our organization. Then, beginning on my own and improvising as we went, we proceeded to implement professional management into our company. Fortunately, the process progressed very well, and within three years our company grew over 350% in sales and even more in earnings.

In late 1980, because of my approaching retirement age, we sold the company to a group of entrepreneurs who were starting a new conglomerate to be composed of manufacturing companies of which ours was their first acquisition. That offer was particularly attractive because it provided that I would become a member of their board of directors and probably be involved in their acquisition program. I was excited over a new career and would be reporting to and be working with MBA type business executives who, it would seem, were trained in enlightened management philosophy. Instead, they proved to be closer to a master/slave style of management.

My new boss was soon going around me to effect decisions without me. In early 1981, because some of the assumptions made by our company planning group were no longer valid, I called them together to re-address our plan so that I could bring my new boss up-to-date. It would not be right for him to go to a board of director's meeting the following week without that information. The changes made by our planning group reduced sales projections for the following year to eleven million dollars. Even though the changed sales forecast was still 40% greater than our previous year's sales, incensed at what we had done, he demanded that we return to the original numbers when reporting to the directors. I agreed to be silent if he so requested, but refused to report numbers that disagreed with those of our planning group unless he could convince the group to change them.

He invited two of our managers to the directors meeting with me. After my report indicating the revised figures, one of them volunteered I was wrong. The other one fence-straddled by saying we could "try" for the bigger goal, which of course had nothing to do with planning. Because they had participated in our planning group's decision to revise the projections a few days earlier, they had obviously been pressured to refute my report.

The following Monday, I took those who reported to me to lunch and announced that as of Wednesday I was delegating my entire job to them. That would be better for me than quitting or getting ulcers. I would be in my office reading, available to answer any questions. To alleviate concern for me, I informed them of my love of reading. They had been with me for many years and understood. A few days later I was removed as President and, in accordance with my employment contract, became a part-time consultant for the next four and one half years with a generous pay raise every year. Of course, the new owners never consulted me and made many mistakes that could have been prevented.

At coffee-break time, most of the group were around me indicating interest in my story and had many questions. At lunch, the director of The President's Club asked whether I would consider entering their speakers training program, which I subsequently did. That exposure enriched my knowledge of professional management appreciably and considerably alleviated the emotional impact of leaving so many fine employees who had been with me for many years.

At a management training seminar I subsequently attended, during the first activity, we each were asked to cast two votes among six potential topics that could be accented during the day. Among the six were such topics as people problems, marketing, cash flow, etc. and a sixth blank subject described as "other." My turn finally came, and I rather energetically gave two votes for "other", which had received no votes as yet. I then defined "other" as, "How to implement professional management in a small business." Immediately, the man to my left tapped me on the shoulder and said, "That's what I would have voted for, had it been there." My subject was noted politely, in very small writing, and seemingly ignored by the seminar monitor.

During our lunch get-together, however, so much comment was received indicating common interest in the topic I had suggested, that they returned to it with considerable attention in the afternoon session. Subsequent discussion made it obvious that although everyone there had been exposed to much training in professional management, most had not applied (in their companies) what they had learned. There seemed to an obvious need for a management book that deals with the individual's potential for leadership, that gives more attention to the actual process of implementing professional management, and is more sensitive to small business. This book is my attempt to fill those needs.

Stealth Management worked for me. Why not share it?

Section II

COCKPIT CHARISMA
and
STEALTH MANAGEMENT

8 • Interpersonal Skills

Have you ever travelled on a plane whose captain seemed particularly happy and whose cheerfulness became evident through his light-hearted banter over the intercom? If you have enjoyed such a flight, you probably noticed that the entire crew was happy. So it is with any organization. The demeanor of the leader permeates the whole organization, making all its members happier or less happy. It is important to be perceived as pleasant and caring.

Reflecting upon my training at Acapulco, it was obvious that before changing my management style to make it more attractive to employees, it first would be necessary for me to change myself so that they would be more likely to perceive me as a pleasant and caring person. I would, for example, have to learn to control my feelings and be more alert to the feelings of other people. Such skills are described by behavioral psychologists as interpersonal skills.

Stealth Managers influence rather than command. Just as an airplane pilot keeps his crew and passengers more content by projecting cheerfulness, sensitivity, and honesty, so must a manager. It is not necessary to have the personality of a stand-up entertainer, but being perceived as a good manager or leader requires a reasonable measure of the same attributes. An inconsiderate *sourpuss* will always have trouble with employees.

One reason that managers fail to benefit fully from the reading of management books or management training courses is that, over the short term, no one can change you or me. Each of us must be motivated to want to change. If you are a strong authoritarian type of manager, going to a one week course will not change your approach to management. Suppose the course focused on interpersonal skills and motivated you to "re-frame" your self-image so that the perception others have of you would be improved. There would then be a much higher probability that you would successfully implement what was taught in the course. This process of "re-framing" and self-change, not usually covered in management training, is covered later in this section. The term "re-framing" is fitting in this context, because it suggests changing one's self so as to be viewed differently by others.

Communication modes and behavioral traits are interpersonal skills that we constantly and automatically use in our everyday relationships with other people. Consider my own experience. Applying the management style taught by the President's course at Acapulco required conveying to my employees a sense of participation in our organization's planning and decision making. This mutual involvement would make the company's goals, the employee's goals, and my goals compatible.

Also, our employees would need a working climate that embodies caring, trust, and the freedom to make mistakes without incurring recrimination.

In reflecting on what self-changes would be appropriate, I first decided to try to suppress my inclination to respond with anger at the mistakes of others and instead to dwell on the possible cause of an error. While making this change, I observed that mistakes often could be eliminated by better communications — certainly a better response than anger without constructive discussion. Anger was obviously inappropriate, it ceased being instinctive, and suppressing it soon became unnecessary. Change two: I began asking for evaluation of company-wide communications before issuing them, whereas previously I would issue or post them with an occasional unintended error. Change three: when communicating verbally on important matters, I would ask the other person to paraphrase what I had said in order to assure understanding. This produced another advance in my management style. Many times, this paraphrasing exercise revealed the need for further clarification. Change four: I also began to find the time to offer sincere compliments for a job well-done. I had known, of course, that people appreciated receiving praise for their accomplishments, but more often than was justified, I felt too busy.

Those are but a few examples of change I made in my own behavior. They were easy modifications to make and they became self-motivating because people began responding to me in a more positive manner. It seemed I had discovered a new self-reward system for such improved behavior. Not only was it better than resorting to my former instincts, but it served as a motivating basis for self-improvement of many kinds. Why had the many training courses to which I had been exposed not taught that, I wondered.

9 • What Is Professional Management ?

Professional management is leading people in a manner that maximizes achievement toward well chosen goals, both short and long term. It requires training and experience. It involves the ability to provide direction and incentive to people; to monitor their progress; to provide necessary training; to assure an appropriate working climate; and, to establish and maintain a proper reward system. These and other important facets of management are referred to throughout this text.

Professional management requires a strong belief in the attitude that usually two minds are better than one, three minds are better than two, etc. Consider what can happen on a golf course. Tournaments are often arranged for the players and/or members of most golf clubs. One type of tournament is referred to as a scramble, in which four players form a golf group which play together. Each player hits his first shot.

The best shot of the four is chosen, and everyone then hits a second shot from that position. The best second shot is chosen, and everyone then hits a third shot from that position, and so on. With such a playing approach, very low scores usually are achieved by the foursome — much better than any one of them might enjoy if playing alone.

I once played in a scramble type golf tournament in which the entry fee was pegged higher than usual to permit raising funds for the benefit of our state university golf team. I entered after some persuasion by a friend who was underwriting the tournament. I was teamed with a foursome made up of the golf team coach who was a par shooter, a former team member who had a two handicap, and another person who had a seventeen handicap. I had a miserable handicap of 29.

Our group finished with a score of 12 under par — 12 strokes better than the average score of even a superior golfer. I contributed at least 5 best shots, including one that won a prize for the shot closest to the pin on that hole — I, the truly bad golfer.

This story is evidence that in virtually all endeavors, even the person who seems least capable can and will enhance the group's performance if properly motivated to contribute. Even a professional golfer would not, alone, have so good a score as his team in a scramble.

In business, giving people the opportunity to contribute fully calls for managing in a consultative/participative manner, thereby encouraging maximum performance. I call *it stealth management.*

The majority of top managers (owners or chief executives) have failed to adopt the most effective management techniques. Therefore, their employees are not fully motivated; such managers are perceived as bosses, not leaders. As bosses, they may be getting the job done, but if their employees shared the same goals as the boss, their commitment and performance would be enhanced.

The rapidity of change is very challenging to managers in today's business climate, making it more important than ever for them to be well trained. In manufacturing, the cost of product development is rising dramatically and dynamic change is reducing market life of the average product. Therefore, engineering and development costs must be amortized over a shorter time span.

Too frequently, after going through the painful series of changes referred to as restructuring, management finds its business still not performing as anticipated. Such disappointment usually results from changing things at the top but not changing the organization's culture from the bottom up, a process that takes considerable time. It requires saturating your company with such values as mission, trust, shared goals, and a sense of participation in all its employees.

Peter Drucker, a most highly regarded management professor at Claremont College has said, "In the future, management will have to be considered as both a science and a humanity." It is a science because it depends upon a vast and expanding body of knowledge involving both theory and practice. It is a humanity because it involves aptitudes and skills in working with people.

People are not born to be excellent managers — they become excellent managers through training and experience.

All books and teachings about management need to be modified and adapted to your personality traits and individual goals, as you introduce them to your organization. To a large extent, a manager requires, in addition to energy, attributes such as intuition, creativity, sense of timing, optimism, and perhaps most of all, the ability to share with co-workers the decision-making process and rewards that accrue from achievement. In each organization, management style must be tailored not only to the type of business but also to the people involved. Therefore, if a consultant is hired to help professionalize your management technique, because of limited exposure to your particular activity, he would not simply tell you how to run your business. Instead, he would guide you through an improvement process designed specifically for your organization, eliciting information and recommendations from you and your people.

The management style advocated here has evolved from what previously was called participative management. To many people, the word participative suggested partnership which was not intended. The result was a new term, "consultative management", in which the leader involves his people by consulting with those reporting to him in a manner that leads toward consensus. After this process, the leader makes or announces the final decision. If a true consensus is reached, so much the better, but after everyone has been encouraged to contribute and there are still differences, the manager makes the decision in the interest of keeping the decision-making process from being unduly long. That decision should take cognizance of all feedback and suggestions received, and should be accompanied by valid reasons for the decision being other than what some might have preferred.

Consultative is a word that is relatively difficult to pronounce and apply — another reason for my coining the name *Stealth Management*. When properly applied, *stealth management* produces harmony in an organization. It does so as a result of conveying to its members a sense of "having a piece of the action".

What a person does merely to keep a job is in stark contrast to what that person might do if fully motivated, and it is toward maximizing motivation and high achievement that good management is directed. Given an acceptable level of compensation, psychologists have proven, through statistical studies, that good management will contribute more than any other influence toward maximizing long-range job satisfaction and productivity.

I have omitted the statistical backup data (usually provided in formal management training) that derives from the research of industrial psychologists in favor of being able to concentrate on the actual process of developing good management practices.

There is no intent to minimize the importance of such statistical data, without which the premises from which the theory of enlightened management derives would be unprovable. If such background is desired, a list of recommended reading material will be found at the end of this book. The authors have various backgrounds from which their knowledge is drawn, and one may have greater impact than another because of differences in perspective and style of presentation. In any case, when studying management or industrial psychology, it is important to use only texts that are reasonably current. There are books written by well regarded authors early in their careers which are not in agreement with their current writings.

Frequently the words leader and manager are used interchangeably, but a good leader is not necessarily a good manager, and among managers only a small percentage are good leaders. It seems true that many political leaders are less than good managers; it also seems true that although most successful business managers would make poor politicians, many of them prove to have leadership ability in other kinds of organizations. The characteristic that distinguishes a person as a leader is his ability to generate commitment, confidence, and excitement in the pursuit of a cause or goal. The person with leadership ability does not have to possess a high level of charisma — although it would be helpful. He is less apt to be directly involved with long range planning although he should believe in and support it. He is more apt to be a generalist as opposed to being a specialist; that is, his aptitudes, interests, and knowledge have a broader base. **He induces his followers to want to follow instead of being submissive to his power.** In so doing, he infuses a spirit of team work that affords the group a level of achievement that exceeds the sum of all their individual abilities.

Leadership ability permits a manager to properly balance the many areas of influence in which he continually functions. He senses when it is appropriate to be less participative and more directive. He knows when too much attention is being given to short range goals at the sacrifice of long range achievement. He is more likely to put important external trends and events in proper perspective in terms of their impact on the organization. He senses the correct amount of personal attention to convey to associates without being excessively paternalistic.

In top management positions, these leadership traits are vital but they are not usually exhibited in full measure by managers at lower levels. Leadership ability can be developed through proper training, and in reviewing managers for promotion such characteristics should be taken into account.

Although professional managers should be very participative, it is important for a manager to sense when he must proceed based on his own experience and knowledge rather than taking time for consensus building. When dealing with crisis management, for example, initial steps often must be directive rather than participative. Sometimes, when decisive action is necessary, it could take too long to thoroughly acquaint others of impending change. There also are occasions when they may not have sufficient background in a given area of knowledge to be able to view a problem from the right perspective. Under such circumstances, a good leader will make the necessary decision and advise those who report to him of his intended actions and reasoning, beforehand if possible.

Two basic principles of professional management are: one, the person closest to the action makes the decision; and two, decisions should be made when needed — not delayed until they become less effective.

Imparting the basic principles of professional management for the individual manager is the goal in what follows.

10 • Are You a Good Manager ?

Several years ago a friend of mine sold his business for over three million dollars, a sum far beyond his wildest dreams. He was then a very successful businessman, he thought — rich, and confident of his financial and managerial abilities! He felt too young to retire and decided to invest in a new company, a specialty wire and cable manufacturing business. The new venture operated at a sizable loss for its first three years, during which time he put his personal signature on bank loans for the business that exceeded his financial strength. When the business finally went bankrupt, he had to declare personal bankruptcy. That left him, at an age well past normal retirement, having to take advantage of his many friends and business contacts in looking for employment.

Is the foregoing story unusual? — absolutely not! Does a successful business history necessarily indicate managerial ability? — no, indeed! Why, then, are so many unprofessional business people successful? The answer, as you may suspect, includes such reasons as:

- Moving into a managerial position as a result of "Being in the right place at the right time"
- Becoming a manager during an upbeat portion of a business cycle during which "You can do no wrong"

- Being a good innovator thereby enhancing rapid growth in spite of unbusiness-like management
- Having a likable personality and good friends which can compensate for lack of managerial ability during a period of favorable business climate
- Belonging to a group in which good employees or partners make the enterprise a success

Be assured that in most such situations, the success of the business, given a series of negative influences, is tenuous at best. Bankruptcies are spawned in this manner. With good management, they can usually be prevented.

You are a manager if you are getting things done through other people. There are several types of managers. There are still managers who believe in a virtual master/slave approach, and those who still apply management by fear — an approach that seems to enjoy resurgence during periods of high unemployment. There are many degrees of strong authoritarianism. There is a euphemistic "Golden Rule" approach which really means: "They who have the gold, rule!" That management style has many varieties depending on how you set the rules. There is management by objectives. There is "performance and reward" which varies from simple piecework pay to bonuses earned for achievement of long-term or short-term goals. There are managers who still are influenced excessively by prejudices about people. One very authoritarian manager I know of, formerly with a large department store chain, "needled" his personnel so constantly, that they referred to his management style as his MBA program, "Management by Acupuncture". The list is quite long.

It is the rare person who is a good manager merely because of his or her personal magnetism or charisma, and in most such cases the organization eventually flounders when that person is gone. There is also the entrepreneur who develops something novel, be it a widget or a service that fills a distinct need in the market place. Without training, that kind of manager typically is successful only in a small organization and even then would enjoy enhanced performance through the application of *stealth management*. Furthermore, such success when not accompanied by good management is too often short lived.

11 • You Cannot Do It Alone

As soon as you have one employee you are in a posture of depending on someone else in running your business. The greater the number of employees, the more time you must devote to managing, and the less time you have for other business activities. As this responsibility of managing grows, management techniques and their influence become every bit as important as methods and efficiency on an assembly line. In fact, social, governmental, and environmental restraints have become so complex and changing that, in the future, mature businesses will require professional management in order to compete favorably.

Therefore, as a manager, you are in a position to profit from the philosophy of *stealth management*. The typical personality traits that make for management styles such as management through fear, master and slave, and their many variations will no longer work — at least, not for long. More importantly, there are management techniques which will consistently produce a higher level of productivity, greater job satisfaction, contribute to a better society, and enhance financial achievement. Because this is true, the sooner you adopt such a management style and apply it in your business, the more sure will be your success.

The urgent need for change is accented by the stream of negative financial data with which we have been constantly assailed during the decade preceding this writing. Consider the following:

- The gradual decline of many of our basic industries
- The excessive level of personal debt
- An unsatisfactory level of unemployment
- The negative balance of trade
- A sharp decline in the international value of the dollar
- Our becoming the largest debtor nation in the world
- A productivity growth less than many of the nations in the world with whom we compete

- Our dangerous dependence on other countries for many basic materials
- The orientation of institutions, business, and government, being toward short — rather than long-term goals

These factors are hurting us and will become increasingly detrimental to business if not controlled. It is certainly difficult to assess how our life-style may have to change, but already we can see an increase in the numbers of people living beneath the income level defined by our government as poverty. Large numbers of people are having to learn a new vocation or reduce their economic goals because of involuntary job displacement. Loyalty to an employer is becoming a very scarce value. Good management and the application of good planning techniques can go a long way toward alleviating such problems in our society.

A few years ago I had occasion to teach business management at a local college. The professor, who had to be absent, suggested I dwell on entrepreneurship and had alerted the class to expect me to address that subject. I wanted to be sure that the class, about fourteen in number, all had reasons or objectives for having enrolled in that class. Although at their age that would not have occurred to me, I since had learned that having a reason or objective before any course of action greatly enhances motivation and achievement. Among the fourteen, only two intended someday to become managers. Several had no reason for being in the class except to accumulate credits toward graduation, and some found it was the only available course that fit into their schedule.

Having brought up the subject, I felt obligated to pursue it to a satisfying conclusion, explaining how the study of management had helped me and that management primarily involved getting along with people with whom you shared common goals. I then asked the class if, individually, they had goals and if getting along with people was important to them. With the answers as expected, it was easy to suggest that what might be learned from the study of management could be applied throughout life. I related the following story:

Imagine a manufacturing company large enough to dominate what is often referred to as a *company town*. Because the company is led by well-trained enlightened managers, it is progressing well and the employees are a happy group. The typical employee looks forward to going to work each day, and the townspeople are proud of the company. "What consequences might you expect for that town?" I asked the class, writing each comment on the blackboard. Soon the class caught the idea and the list included the following:

- Families were happier with less divorce
- There was less crime
- Children achieved better in school
- The incidence of mental illness was below average
- Fewer police were needed
- Because of a higher quality of life, there would be less divisiveness between political parties, ethnic groups, or cultural strata

We terminated the list although the suggestions were still coming, and I pointed out to the class that if all those desirable results could come from good management, certainly we all could benefit from its study. ***Good management in business can have important consequences for society.***

We subsequently delved into the assigned subject of entrepreneurship, which was more animated than it otherwise might have been because of the foregoing subject.

12 • Your Personal Qualifications

After most management training seminars, a survey usually is made to ascertain participant evaluation of course quality and effectiveness. Invariably, the responses seem to represent enthusiasm for the training and a desire to apply what was learned as quickly as possible. Were you to survey a group with extensive management training a few years after completion of their training, you would find that most of them had not incorporated into their business very much of what was taught. Were we talking only of second or third level managers, it would be easy to blame top level managers for such lack of response. Unfortunately, it seems true even for them. Perhaps the teaching reinforced a previously held belief or opinion that resulted in a good impression of the course, but failure to implement much of what was taught indicates that they were not motivated to change.

The reasons for such poor results have to do with the individual and an inherent resistance to the precepts of professional management. It may be that his personal goals or traits conflict with those of his business; perhaps he or she is the victim of poor time management. If such conflicts become impediments for you, and you still appreciate the advantages of enlightened management, this section may be especially valuable.

A detailed discussion of management attributes, and personal philosophy could be considered irrelevant by many readers. If you wish to verify their value, ask a few people to differentiate between empathy, sympathy, compassion, and sensitivity. You will get very confusing answers. Yet each is important in how you are perceived as a manager.

Consider these qualities desirable in effective managers:

- Integrity
- Intellectual maturity
- Competence
- Sensitivity
- Ability to communicate
- Intelligence
- Ability to enhance motivation
- Patience

This list is typical of what would be compiled by a group of employees if asked to indicate what qualities they would like in an executive. You may be surprised to know that it is also the same as what executives might like in their fellow managers or what any group of employees might like in their peers. Unfortunately this list is incomplete — as indicated by the fact that many leaders and executives with these qualifications are not very successful. What then must be added to the list to identify more accurately the successful professional manager — one who can change careers and repeat his success? Experience suggests that the above list should also include these qualities relative to executives or people who are in a leadership position:

- Emotional stability
- Ambition and high energy level
- Self esteem
- Optimism
- Perspective
- Flexibility
- Commitment
- Appreciation for *stealth management* style
- Willingness to take and manage risk
- Enjoyment of one's work
- Basic goodness
- Caring about people
- Ability to make decisions when needed
- Ability to make decisions without personal prejudice

To be sure that we have a common understanding of each item in the foregoing lists, let us define and discuss them.

Integrity has broad implications which must include honesty, trustworthiness, and constancy of attitude. It should be accompanied by a well defined sense of values which has become second nature through both practice and thought. Ideally, these are part of a profound philosophy of life, developed from within yourself by your own thought processes. If you have a value system to which you adhere, but do not consider yourself as having a philosophy of life, you might do well to adopt your value system as your philosophy. With experience and thought, you can expand and develop it to include both a mission and goals. Such philosophical thinking ought to be private and always subject to change and maturation. Having a philosophy of life permits people to save much decision making time and to be more easily understood by others; it adds purpose to one's life. Making that statement fully evident could require the writing of another book. Perhaps an example will help:

During most of my career, I met very few fellow employees who had a philosophy of life, but I vividly recall one. His philosophy was well thought out and had matured with time. He was not a "number 2 executive", but on those occasions when we would be entertaining a foreign client, he would be the first employee to whom I would introduce our guest. With confidence, I would even ask him to be our host if I was unavailable. This was true because, as part of his philosophy, he considered all people to be his social equal unless he personally observed reasons for concluding otherwise. He would not think of an Englishman as being haughty, a Mexican as being poorly educated, or the Chinese as being incapable of high-tech thinking — a type of stereotyping of which many people are guilty. I never had to spend time coaching him in such areas. I recall the first time he was invited to lunch by a supplier. Without having to think, he responded, "I'd enjoy having lunch with you. This time is on me and you can be the host next time". He said that without any intent of leaning on an expense account. He had long since realized, as part of his value system, that obligating himself to a supplier might put him in a compromising situation when making a future company decision concerning that supplier.

Intellectual Maturity almost defies definition. Although age and experience certainly contribute to it, we all know people who have more "maturity" than someone else who may be considerably older. It involves perspective, objectivity, social presence, decisiveness, self esteem, and dependability — all of which are enhanced by experience. An intellectually mature person's mind usually is *made up* with regard to life's more basic issues but he or she is willing to change when presented with new ideas.

Competence means having the training and knowledge that permits managing an organization in a particular arena of activity. Were you a military leader, you would have to have military training and experience in sufficient depth to provide the expertise required to lead your troops. If you were managing a retail business, you would require the training and experience to merchandise and finance your store. If you were a manager in a manufacturing business, you would need both knowledge and experience to supervise those people working for you. It certainly is unnecessary that your knowledge or ability, as they might relate to any given task or specific specialized area of the enterprise, exceed that of those working for you. However, your level of expertise in all relevant areas must be sufficient to permit you to communicate well with your co-workers, be able to challenge them appropriately, and evaluate their performance.

Sensitivity is quite often confused with empathy, sympathy, understanding, and perceptivity. In fact, one might still be confused after studying the dictionary for the meanings of these words. I once asked a psychologist who had been lecturing at a management seminar, for a good definition of sensitivity as it applies to management. He defined sensitivity as awareness of the impact on others of your words and/or your actions. That is an excellent definition. Being sensitive, when applying the expression outside the field of interpersonal relationships, has other implications such as being sensitive to cold or to ragweed pollen. After words have been spoken or an action involving people has occurred, making a necessary correction is typically much more trouble than to have prevented the problem by applying appropriate sensitivity beforehand.

The *Ability to communicate* is invaluable. Such talent, however, is not as simple as it is perceived to be, and is often complex because it involves interaction with another person. Frequently the listener, because of poor concentration, inadequate vocabulary, inattentiveness, or other reasons, hears something other than the message you wanted to convey. Sometimes, the words you use do not impart the meaning you intend, or you do not have a clear idea of what you want to communicate. A good definition: *the ability to transmit thought, information, or feeling so that it is understood as intended.*

Intelligence, in this context, requires sufficient mental acuteness to be able to communicate and to reason well with all those with whom you need to relate in the performance of your job. Being the leader of a sophisticated research organization might require a different kind of intellectual capability from being president of a shirt manufacturing company. However, *because all those with whom you need to relate* might include bankers, stockholders, consultants, government officials, etc., each manager's situation is different.

Ability to enhance motivation, in the context of management, involves skill in arousing a desire for achievement in those who report to you. What an employee does to merely keep his job compared to what he or she might do if fully motivated, for example, might be the production of 10 pieces per hour compared to 25 pieces per hour in a manufacturing operation. The contrast could be even greater in terms of beneficial impact if we consider creativity.

Emotional stability usually means being purposeful as opposed to being impulsive. With emotional stability, there is little difference between what you believe and what you do.

Patience is a virtue that can easily be mistaken for benign inaction. In management, it is the ability to wait for planned programs to reach their expected conclusions or for target dates to arrive without upsetting those around you by evidencing impatience. Giving others the required time to do a job is part of simple trust. However, having patience does not preclude your requiring timely interim information on work for which you are responsible, nor does it minimize the need for corrective action when such projects are inexcusably past due.

Having a high energy level means applying your energies so as to set an example of dedication and activity that commands respect as opposed to being lethargic — to lead instead of merely "going with the flow".

Ambition is a necessary part of leadership and the ability to motivate. It is the desire on your part to achieve or progress toward some goal. If you, as a manager, do not have and convey ambition, it is certainly less likely that those you lead will feel motivated.

Self esteem requires assurance and respect for yourself as a person. It does not suggest conceit or a sense of superiority. It does include an appreciation of your emotional stability and confidence in the perception other people have of you. It results principally from repetitive achievement of a satisfying nature. We might call that valuable experience. Such a person does not need to constantly seek confirmation from others.

Optimism is essential. Being optimistic has a positive impact on the outlook of all those around you. Achievement requires taking occasional risks. If you are not optimistic, you are unlikely to take risks. Every successful businessman I have known is an optimist, and risk taking is frequently a necessary element of success.

Perspective is the ability to view things in their true or relative importance, both short-term, long-term, and historically. It also involves the ability to set priorities when faced with the multiple considerations typically involved in decision making. Having perspective minimizes unnecessary worry or concern, permitting you to more effectively direct your energy. In our present political and sociological scene we see too many people and groups who become so oriented to single issues that they dangerously reduce their perspective.

Flexibility is the capacity to adapt to new situations. Because so many influences around us — including environment, politics, and human frailty — are a frequent source of surprise, the need for change is constant.

Commitment involves dedication, and even emotional obligation, to your job, your organization, your associates, and the goals you share with them. It means that you do not give up easily and you will go beyond the call of duty when necessary.

Appreciation for the **Stealth Management** *style* is the largest contributor to maximizing performance. Such management style permits motivating people more effectively and thereby enhances achievement of your own goals. It has been said that the most efficient form of management is benevolent dictatorship. Unfortunately, none of us is so perfect as to make it practical in the management arena.

The **Willingness to Take and Manage Risk** is essential in management today. Because our world is changing so rapidly, we in management are constantly involved in managing change. Change requires decision making and risk. The manager who merely "goes with the flow" will soon be left behind by the competition. Taking and managing risk should not be synonymous with *dice rolling*. Taking business risks should be accompanied by proper planning and monitoring so as to minimize and limit potential loss as well as maximize the probability of success.

If you *enjoy your work,* you derive pleasure from your job and usually look forward to going to work. Of course, this is not always the case — there are unpleasant periods in virtually every job. Because our working hours are a considerable percentage of our lives, those who enjoy their work are very fortunate.

Basic goodness is a quality that cannot be taught. It derives from the sum of all our experience — upbringing, schooling, family, etc. If goodness were measurable it would be appropriate to say that those who may not now enjoy the highest mark can improve over time if they are sufficiently motivated to do so. As a manager, being accepted as a good person by your fellow workers is of distinct advantage. If you are so regarded, you are assumed to have good character and a dependable value system.

To *care about people* is an important trait that is evidenced best by the ability to participate in the feelings of others — sometimes called empathy. If a manager does not have such an attitude, many of his actions will have a *ring of insincerity* to his fellow workers or team members.

Making decisions when needed is obviously an important trait, but one that often is neglected. When decisions are delayed, too frequently the effect of the decision is blunted or even negated.

Freedom from prejudice, insofar as management is concerned, is essential. You should not exhibit or be perceived to possess prejudice having to do with politics, race, religion, age, or gender. Mere modification of your conduct will not mask inherent prejudice. People usually can see through that. Any overt prejudice in your attitude toward these subjects can result in your being perceived as incapable of making objective decisions. Of course, we all have prejudices to varying degrees, but in management they must never be directed toward people. Further, we should be ready to overcome our prejudices based on new evidence or knowledge.

None of us possesses all the foregoing attributes in full measure, but as a manager, you should be aware to what degree you are perceived to possess each of them. You should endeavor to compensate for areas in which you consider yourself weak, not only in the manner of your conduct, but also by delegating to others in a way that reinforces your management effort in those areas of weakness. By being aware of those attributes that make for a good manager, you can do a much better job of delegating and evaluating employees and applicants. In addition, this awareness can motivate you to improve.

It has been suggested that after recognizing the positive attributes of a manager, a list of frequently observable negative characteristics also should be noted. If you exhibit an acceptable level of the positive attributes, however, negative ones become relatively unimportant. This prompts the thought that although it would be difficult, if not inappropriate, to set priorities among such personal qualities, there are at least two of special importance. Without *integrity* or the quality of *caring about people*, it is unlikely that you can be a good manager regardless of how well you may be endowed with all the others.

13 • Your Personal Goals

If you wish to achieve as a manager, you should have personal goals which are harmonious with those of the organization. If this is not the case, you will find it difficult to conform to the goals and the mission of the organization, and such conflict will inhibit performance.

Included in the definition of integrity is a strong recommendation that you have or develop a philosophy of life. It suggests that you begin with your value system, if you do not already have a philosophy of life. Another description for a personal philosophy is "an organization of one's convictions". Such a philosophy should also include your definition of success; this will be invaluable in helping you set goals for yourself. If you have not tried to define success, you will find that defining it for yourself is not easy. For example, if success were to include acquisition of material things, what about the one or two teachers who had a particularly positive impact on you? Are such teachers successful even though they usually do not achieve great financial rewards? Questions of this kind are constructive, especially for teenagers.

Ralph Waldo Emerson's definition of success is an excellent one albeit without the goals we usually associate with management. It does contain many of the elements of human behavior that are respected in a manager. He defined it as follows:

> To laugh often and much; to win the respect of intelligent people and the affection of children; to earn the appreciation of honest critics and endure the betrayal of false friends; to appreciate beauty; to find the best in others; to leave the world a bit better whether by a healthy child, a garden patch, or a redeemed social condition; to know even one life has breathed easier because you have lived. This is to have succeeded.

In the process of arriving at your definition of success, be reminded that there is the externally recognized type of success typified by wealth, fame, and power. There is also the inner success that is best measured by your sense of personal fulfillment. This inner success is certainly more lasting (more likely to result in people remembering good things about you), and more often than not, it will be accompanied by external success. Further, without a sense of personal fulfillment, happiness is unlikely. You will be perceived as a better manager or leader if your personal goals do not overly accent the external manifestations of success and minimize personal fulfillment.

I once made a presentation to the president of a small company in an attempt to gain him as a consulting client. At the outset of our meeting, I gave him a short resume of my training and experience. Then we had a discussion of his business, including its history and trends in the industry served by his company. Next, by discreet questioning to learn about his management style, I determined that he was task-oriented and without long term goals. He made it a point to be able to run their computer and had personally written all the computer programs they were using. He was culturally inclined, an avid reader, very bright, and delighted in what are referred to, usually, as non-material things. He had a few time consuming hobbies and loved to travel. The business, which had been started by his father, had provided him a enjoyable life, but then was having trouble because he had not responded to a changing market-place. I told him that we could cooperate to institute professional management in his company. It would greatly help the company to effectively plan for the future and accommodate to the changes in his business climate that were troubling him. The first step, if he employed me, would be to have an in-depth talk about his personal goals. I indicated that an understanding of himself as a person and what he wanted out of life would help align his expectations and those of his company.

Aware that I was competing with another consulting firm for his business, I realized that prying into his personal thinking could possibly lose me the job — in fact, it did. My competition got the job and worked with him for a year without effecting any apparent improvement in his company or change in his management style. Thus, ignoring the need for compatible personal and career goals, his company continued to flounder.

The foregoing story seems to validate the assertion of Peter Drucker, in an interview published in the Wall Street Journal in 1986, that all management books he had read, including his own, as of that date, were flawed in that they neglected the individual's personality, personal traits, abilities, and goals in the process of teaching professional management.

It certainly follows that you cannot expose strong authoritarians to a course in management and expect that, because of such exposure, their personality will suddenly change. However, if such people are taught enlightened management principles, and are convinced that their previous management techniques require change, progress is likely. If, achieving your desires or goals in life are in the profession of management, and if you have a sufficient measure of the basic abilities required, training will enable you to overcome specific deficiencies and enhance your ability to manage. Remember — *managers are not born, they are the result of training and experience.*

14 • Know Thyself

Knowing yourself is more complex than it might seem. Cervantes, a Spanish writer who lived in the 16th century said, "Make it your business to know yourself, which is the most difficult in the world." To know yourself is to know what physical, psychological, and aptitudinal tools you possess. Awareness of this *tool inventory* is important in your personal planning and can influence greatly your level of achievement. It also gives you a reference base from which you can expand and improve your inventory of such tools. Usually the best way to do this is to submit to an appropriate battery of aptitude and psychological tests and discuss them with the psychologist.

Unfortunately too many of us have neither the time nor the inclination to take advantage of the benefits that can be derived from good psychological testing. Should you fit into that category, rather than completely eliminating such benefit, try the following idea:

Review topic 12 (your personal qualifications), assessing your attributes and goals in comparison to those referred to as being either necessary or desirable. Discuss them with those who are close enough to know you well and are willing to engage in such a personal evaluation. This will require that you consider such *feedback* as constructive and not permit it to affect adversely those close relationships. List your strengths and weaknesses and arrange them by attaching numerical evaluations to each, indicating relative importance in the pursuit of your goals. In making this evaluation, be objective and try to avoid prejudice. Although outside help can be worthwhile, it could have a very intimidating effect upon a friend to ask for this overall evaluation of you. It will be less intimidating if you spread the "job" around by asking several friends or close acquaintances to each evaluate a small portion of such a profile. After each such occasion make appropriate notes, and over a period of time you will accumulate a fair evaluation of how you are perceived by others.

After you have given your strengths and weaknesses adequate consideration, reevaluate the weaknesses with a view toward improving yourself in those areas. Determine how might you go about effecting improvement, and how long a process would such an improvement program be. Are you be able to handle the improvement approach by yourself or should you have help? How will you know whether or not you are improving?

Most important: review your strengths and constantly find ways of using them to enhance your achievement. We all have weaknesses, some inherent and some acquired. The inherent ones should be compensated for and the acquired ones sublimated or eliminated through education and experience so far as possible. In managing people, you will find usually, that constant appreciation for that which is good in a person and minimal attention to weakness will result in improvement much more rapidly than if your attitude is mostly negative. Teachers demonstrate the effectiveness of this principle in the classroom, and good teachers constantly utilize it as a motivational tool. Similarly, constant awareness of your strengths helps you overcome weaknesses by putting them in more accurate perspective.

Early in my career, I interviewed an applicant for the position of office manager. An aptitude test indicated his organizational ability was very low. Believing as I do, that most often weaknesses that are neither genetic nor physical can be overcome via gradual change or compensated for by strengths, and because he impressed me in so many other respects, I hired him. He was superb at his job. His intelligence, good memory, and desire to achieve more than compensated for the lack of organizational ability. I never made him aware of the results of the aptitude test and, in fact, threw them away.

I do not suggest that aptitude tests are not useful. Indeed, they can be very useful when other factors are taken into consideration. Further information on this subject is covered under the topic of Psychological Profiles and Aptitude Testing. Certainly, strong aptitudes and a good attitude will make a weakness much less apparent and much less important as well.

Knowing yourself is important when studying professional management with the aim of introducing such management techniques into your business. Those who teach in this field, unless on a one-on-one basis, cannot modify their teaching to fit you personally in an ideal manner. Therefore, it is to your advantage to be aware of how you must change in order to best adapt that teaching for your benefit.

Such awareness will permit you to proceed with fewer false starts and greater confidence.

The chart below will help you initiate a personal profile using data provided by friends and close acquaintances. Note that the names of suppliers of evaluation data used as an example are purposely omitted.

My Personal Management Profile

Trait	poor	fair	good	excellent	Comment
Ambition			x		*Need to be goal oriented*
Energy level		x			*Medical advice could help*
Emotional stability				x	
Optimism				x	

The foregoing chart contains but a few items out of the many that you would review.

One other aspect of *knowing yourself* concerns your tendency toward emotional *ups and downs*, usually referred to as moods. If your emotional cycle produces abnormal mood swings, there will be times when you have difficulty interacting with people. If your emotional ups and downs are in a normal range, however, you should learn to take advantage of them. Do this by performing those activities you are responsible for that do not involve other people during periods when you are not your most cheerful or optimistic self. Those times when you enjoy a feeling of well-being or a sense of enthusiasm are best for working on those things that require interaction with people. These include such activities as selling, visiting with people, or chairing a meeting. You are not always free to cater to these *moods*, but you would be surprised at how often you can plan your more important unscheduled activities with these considerations in mind.

Once when our company was contemplating expansion we determined that it would be accomplished best by building a new manufacturing facility and moving from our old plant. We had employed an architect who took an automobile tour with me to many of the more desirable building sites in our city, and I had chosen a likely place. In 1966, the site was priced at a cost exceeding our ability to purchase without borrowing the money. Our banker, at the time, was a rather conservative person who was soon to retire. Regulations at the time, intended to minimize excess speculation, would not have permitted him to loan us money to purchase a building site. One day, while at the bank and in a particularly optimistic mood, I discovered that he was on vacation. The president of the bank was a more venturesome person who had been a former business owner himself. Feeling that in his absence, my banker would not interpret my going around him as improper, I went in to see the bank president and negotiated an open-account loan for sufficient funds to purchase the new building site. To many business people this will not seem unusual. However, because of the tight economic conditions, prior to that time all our borrowing required the pledging of collateral. The transaction had to be written up as a non-collateralized loan, since it could not refer to the intended use because of regulations against such real estate borrowing. Within a year, we had moved into our new plant which was ideally designed to house our manufacturing operation and thereby improve our efficiency. It also enhanced our stature with employees and customers and was a major contributing factor to our future success. The *good feeling* impulse paid off. Had I done the same thing on a day when I did not sense such optimism, the results may not have been nearly so beneficial.

15 • Enjoy, Enjoy

The advantage of enjoying what you do includes personal fulfillment and achievement. You have more control over this level of enjoyment than you possibly realize — it is largely a matter of attitude. The following story was told a few years ago by a lecturer at an American Management Association seminar about a street sweeper:

In London, at a time not long ago when street sweepers were people using handbrooms instead of mechanical behemoths with huge rotary brooms, there was one street sweeper who had graduated from college with a masters degree. He was in his mid-thirties, had a pleasant personality, and seemingly enjoyed his job. Having come to the attention of one of London's newspaper editors, a reporter was assigned to interview the man. How could a man with that level of education be content in such a menial un-challenging job?

The street sweeper's story, in short was: "I find my job very interesting, and believe I am the best street sweeper you can find. I am assembling all the statistics that apply to street sweeping and expect to write a manual on the subject very soon. I can tell you when to push the broom directly forward and when to push it at a diagonal to be most efficient; how many strokes you should take or how long you should sweep before picking up the sweepings; when to replace the brush; what type bristles wear best under various conditions; what type exercises make me feel better if done before going to work and after finishing for the day to compensate for the strain on the arms and shoulders from this unusual work; and the effect of all types of weather on how best to sweep and the type brooms used. I am constantly learning new things about my job."

Of course the street sweeper story is most unusual, but it does demonstrate that most jobs can be more interesting than they would otherwise seem if you have a pleasant, even creative, attitude toward your work. Sometimes it merely takes a realization that your present job is but a stepping-stone toward the next assignment which will be more challenging, and that performing it well can be a source of satisfaction. We all experience situations having varying degrees of dissatisfaction from time to time. When such a situation must be tolerated, so that it does not have any lasting negative influence on us, we can ease the dissatisfaction by adopting an attitude of "Enjoy, enjoy".

Do not let such an attitude lull you into complacency. Certainly the street sweeper is not a success in the context of using his native talents to achieve at the maximum level to which he is capable. Success can be thwarted by complacency.

People will achieve more from enhanced productivity and creativity and be less prone to mistakes when they are happy. Therefore, manage people so as to encourage them to be happy.

Section III

— COMMUNICATING —
THE ESSENCE OF
MANAGEMENT

---

16 • Communicating Is An Art

Recently, I had the rare pleasure of being in a small audience when Miss Helen Hayes (at age 88) was speaking on two subjects, theater and the "art of growing old". Reflecting on the importance of communication skills to both subjects, she said, "Is it not a shame that in our society, in which a picture can be electronically transmitted instantaneously to any point in the world, a person next to us is often farther away than a star."

Her observation is particularly apropos of the communication problems in management. It is a more complex art than generally realized. No matter how well you communicate verbally, it will be to little avail if you do not have a good listener or if your audience hears you with a prejudiced ear. It is an aim of this section to improve your communication skills — especially your sensitivity to the impediments and your ability to minimize them.

Virtually all our actions as leaders and managers involve people. Good communicating does not require a big vocabulary or knowledge of Shakespeare. Good communication requires that you say what you mean, mean what you say, and be understood as you intend. Sounds simple, it's not!

The purpose of communication is to create understanding! The ability to communicate well is the essence of management in that it is such an important ingredient of all managerial functions.

If you ever have attended a non-profit organization's board of director's meeting, the following scenario will seem either familiar or readily believable. Imagine twenty-five volunteers who have become board members through the election process or by appointment (all having first established their eligibility by being generous contributors of time and/or money), assembled to make a relatively important decision. A committee, appointed by the president a month earlier has studied the problem in depth and the committee chairperson has been asked to report on their study and make recommendations to the board. While this report is being given over a period of several minutes, the committee members, being familiar with what is being reported, listen with mild boredom except for one who really disagrees with the others. He is debating whether or not to argue for his point of view when the report is complete.

Early, during the report presentation, three other members of the board of directors find themselves in disagreement with one facet of the report and, deliberating how they will subsequently indicate same, fail to listen to most of what the committee chairman is saying. The board president and secretary are deeply occupied in taking minutes or giving consideration to the rest of the meeting agenda. Four other creative people have thought of improvements to the committee's recommendations, are developing their own ideas for presentation, and fail to hear much of the report. Two people are somewhat late for appointments — really did not have time for this meeting and are listening but perfunctorily. One person is still angry because at the last board meeting he felt insulted; the chairperson did not recognize him when he wanted to talk against an action taken. One person is really not feeling very well and naturally is worrying about something else. Two people were not at the last two meetings and have some difficulty putting everything in perspective.

The report has been given, and discussion is invited. By the time a few people have volunteered their thoughts, the committee chairman is beginning to wonder, "Did I give a bad report, or was no one listening?" The board chairman considers much of the discussion inane, but people want to be heard. Finally, sensing a trend toward consensus, he calls for a vote and eight hands go up promptly. A few who have no strong opinion, observing that a good friend is for the motion, also raise their hands. We now have a small majority in favor the motion is going to pass — and five others therefore raise their hands. Two others do not want to be obstructionists and refrain from voting, and with very few "nay" votes the committee's recommendations are accepted.

The foregoing scenario reflects many of the obstacles to good communication and is certainly not uncommon in volunteer organizations. Such a meeting does result in waste and error. With respect for all those devoted people, without whom most charitable organizations could not exist, this somewhat exaggerated story is not intended to be critical. The world is better off because of them. There are, however, ways to communicate more effectively, and better methods for reaching decisions (see subject number 36) that would make such generous efforts much more productive.

In all fairness, it should be pointed out that non-profit organizations can be categorized under at least three descriptions: (1) those that have no operational cashflow — such as some small churches. (2) those that have operational cashflow but still have a dependency on volunteer support, such as hospitals; and (3) those that have little operational cashflow but do have yearly money allocated to them, such as organizations like Red Cross, that belong to United Way. Those in category three usually have performance requirements assigned to them based upon which the following year's allotment could depend. Category two often have performance standards imposed upon them from either internal or external sources. Category one usually has no external performance standards applied and rarely incorporates any professional management into its operations. Some of the more progressive volunteer organizations provide for a professional trainer who teaches communication and decision making skills to members of their board, thus improving performance.

In small business board of directors' meetings the same communication impediments exist, but they occur less frequently because such boards usually have fewer members. Also, in the typical corporate board meeting, in which the chairman occupies much of the time reviewing performance data, he uses visual aids, such as graphs and charts to improve communication.

17 • To Be a Good Listener

Being a good listener can involve many senses, not only the sense of hearing. A given statement can mean different things depending on body language. For example, a deprecating statement made to a friend, as you patted him on the back and while you evidenced a broad smile, would be interpreted differently from the same words addressed to a person you disliked while you were somber-faced or reflecting irritation. A beggar, asking for a hand-out while apparently inebriated, would evoke a different response than the same words from a sober person obviously in need. Yes, we also listen with our hearts. Most of us, while pre-occupied with television or reading material, have failed to hear correctly when being spoken to because we were not listening with our minds.

Prejudice often keeps people from being good listeners. An aunt of mine suffered the loss of her daughter as a result of an automobile accident. The level of alcohol in the blood of the other driver proved to be considerably above what classified him as driving *under the influence.* My aunt's grief is certainly understandable. After gaining control of her emotions, she joined M.A.D.D., *Mothers Against Drunk Drivers,* an influential organization. In her zeal to further the cause of M.A.D.D., however, she virtually shut out all other interests and became over-bearing on the subject. Everyone was judged by whether or not they supported M.A.D.D. If she were a manager, she would have been ineffective during that part of her life because of her single-issue orientation. Managers should not allow their concern for outside causes, regardless of their merit, to affect their attitudes toward those with whom they come in contact in their working environment. Managers should have a reasonably good perspective and be open-minded and flexible — aware that mores and value systems change with time. Now that so much of our business is international, various kinds of prejudice can prevent our understanding other cultures. Such prejudices can be economically as well as ethically detrimental.

You should listen with your ears, your eyes, your heart, and your brain — each available and used as needed. As a manager, you would be well advised to think of yourself as a diagnostician who must apply these listening skills to what you hear. If your attention is divided because of pre-occupation, when being spoken to by a fellow employee, be considerate enough to say so and promise to visit with that person on the subject as soon as possible. That will not leave a bad impression, but seeming lack of concern will.

18 · Paraphrasing

There is a communication game played by several people seated in a circle. One person tells a story to the person to the right; that person then tells the story to the next person and so on until the last person has been told the story. The last person then relates the story he heard after which the first person tells the story that the round began with. Invariably, you find as the story progresses around the group, it changes with each repetition — largely because of the kinds of communication problems described in the story of the board of directors' meeting.

Usually, you can assure that what is heard is what you wanted to convey by asking the listener to paraphrase what he thought you said. If the response differs from what you intended, you can correct the impression. You can also diagnose the cause for misunderstanding. Would it have been correctly understood had you said it in a different way, for example? Or, did you fail to speak in terms with which the listener is familiar? This is often a problem when communicating with children.

Paraphrasing is a technique for improving communication accuracy when there is risk of error and when the subject matter is of importance. It is also helpful when conversing with people from different cultures than yours. It would be interesting, after playing the communicating circle game in the usual manner, to play it again with each person paraphrasing what they heard and receiving correction, as needed, before repeating the story.

19 • The Senses

We are well aware of the physical senses of sight, smell, hearing, taste, and touch. We also are aware that there are many emotional senses, but most of us, and certainly many managers, pay insufficient attention to them. They include such important emotional feelings as a sense of:

- Pride
- Accomplishment
- Belonging
- Charity
- Participation
- Trust
- Intuition
- Imagination
- Value
- Joy
- Sadness
- Challenge
- Superiority
- Purpose

The above list could possibly be much longer, but it is sufficient to indicate how perceptive you must be when, as a manager, you are trying to manage with sensitivity.

A former employee of mine, who we will call Frank, is now manager of foreign sales for a medium sized family-owned chemical company. The owners decided to build a new seven story office building and delegated to Frank the additional duty of administering the move to the new building and coordinating the decorating and furnishing. The owners were lovers of art and supporters of many civic cultural organizations. When the building was completed and occupied, a large soft sculpture was located opposite the elevators on the groundfloor. A soft sculpture is an ob-jet d'art made of compliant materials, usually woven, and has three dimensional character. Its variety of textures and colors all tend to invite the inquisitive viewer to touch and feel the sculpture. Touching became so prevalent that the surface of the soft sculpture was becoming soiled and Frank had to take some corrective action. He placed a sign below it reading, "Do not touch the soft sculpture". That did not help. He then changed the sign to read, "Please do not touch the soft sculpture!". It, too, did not help.

Frank now had a problem. His boss would be most unhappy were he to remove the art from its intended location, yet he could not let the employees continue to literally ruin it. After wracking his brain for an approach that would be heeded, in desperation, he changed the sign to read, "Please try not to touch the soft sculpture!" The new sign worked and received the cooperation of everyone. The question is why did this sign work and previous ones fail.

The apparent reason seems to be that the words *please try* ask for a decision by the viewer. I call this participative communication because it asks the recipient (listener or reader) to participate in a decision or thinking process. In management, the *sense of participation* is one of the more important of the senses, if not the most important. "Participation" will figure in many of the discussions that follow.

In the field of communications, and certainly that includes advertising, with any given effort, the more of the recipients' senses you engage, the greater will be your penetration of his perception and memory. A billboard may have a plain black and white verbal message which gains the viewer's sense of vision and to some degree the sense of awareness. The message may be forgotten shortly and function only through repetition. If the billboard has attractive color and/or design it would also involve our understanding of esthetics, our liking of color, and thus more effectively target the sense of vision. The message with color and good design probably would be remembered longer than the first and have greater advertising value.

I recall once seeing a sign advertising an automobile brand. The sign was about 30% completed and an inanimate model of a sign painter was positioned on a scaffold, supposedly painting the sign. The sign was lighted at night and visible to me as I drove home from work each evening. After a couple of nights I realized that the sign was more complete each day. Obviously that billboard attracted much attention, and even caused traffic to slow down. The number of psychological senses being stimulated were considerable, including humor, curiosity, emotion, vision, and anticipation. As a result, I still remember it.

Sometimes, when preparing to communicate, considerable objectivity is required. What seems appropriate to you, in the case of a television advertisement, may be less than effective because you have not had sufficient experience in that area. A trained advertising person should have greater knowledge of how to best engage the senses of the audience to be addressed than the person untrained in advertising. Perhaps you have observed advertising that receives much exposure but which impresses you negatively. Sometimes an unpleasant impression achieves better results than a pleasant one, and sometimes your sensitivities are not the same as the majority of those to whom the advertising is being directed.

It is also true in management. A high level of sensitivity beforehand of how your actions or communicative effort will affect the intended audience should result in much greater effectiveness.

20 • Emotions Affect Communication

When you are angry, it is difficult to be either a good listener or a good communicator. While suffering emotionally from the loss of someone close to you, immediately after being the recipient of bad news, and sometimes even after being elated by very good news, one's ability to communicate or to be a good listener is diminished. As a manager, when such emotional influences can cause your communicative effort to be less than effective, it often is wise to delay communicating until a more appropriate time. When urgency prohibits delay, communicate as necessary, even under circumstances that are undesirable, but follow up later in a manner that assures the communication is understood as you intended.

If it is necessary that you communicate with an associate at a time when one of you is emotionally low (or high), soon thereafter let the associate know that you were upset at the time (or that you knew he was upset at the time), for which reason you are checking to make sure that you said what you intended and had been properly understood. Paraphrasing can be a useful tool in such a situation.

It is important to emphasize that the good things you may have done all week in your relationships with people can be undone very easily by one sentence spoken late Friday while you or others are tired or suffering from emotional stress of any kind.

21 • How Are You Perceived?

An aggressive attitude can often be perceived negatively and have a detrimental effect on your managerial efforts. It usually helps to function with a degree of humility; on occasion, even a bit of humorous self-deprecation is helpful. Humility of this kind, when accompanied by healthy self-esteem and strong goal orientation, may be thought of as *aggressive humility.*

Many of us are insensitive to the fact that there can be a vast difference between the attitude we wish to convey and how that attitude is interpreted by others. It is very useful for us to reflect on this matter, and even solicit evaluation from others, on occasion, as to how we are *coming across.*

Sometimes I take the opportunity to browse in a bookstore. On one such occasion I observed a book entitled "Business Anecdotes" and chanced to open the book to a story having to do with the subject of perception. It told of a father whose young daughter enjoyed buying candy at a neighborhood candy store. Most of her friends preferred to buy candy at a large shopping mall nearby. When asked why she preferred the smaller neighborhood store, the man's daughter informed him that the small store owner always gave her extra candy. Mothers Day was coming and he decided to investigate his daughter's story. He first took her to the large shopping mall store where they chose a type of candy and asked for a pound. The sales-lady quickly overloaded the scale and then removed candy until the scale read an even pound. They then went to the small store, asked for a pound of a particular candy, and the owner put about half a pound of candy on the scale and then added additional candies until he reached the pound. His daughter was quick to comment, "See he always adds more candy. He likes me." Awareness of the variability of human perception often can be very helpful.

In the early 1980's an employee survey among General Motors hourly employees produced convincing data showing that their view of top management, plant managers up through central executive officers, had the greatest single impact on job attitudes. This survey, conducted by Opinion Research Corporation, has since been proven true even for personnel in the "Big Eight" accounting firms. How the C.E.O. of an organization is perceived by those at lower levels on the organization chart has a vital influence on their attitude and productivity. Since a manager's power to manage comes from those whom he manages, it is important to be thought of as a good person and an efficient manager.

22 • Participative Communication

The previous stories about the soft sculpture and the billboard advertisement are examples of how to obtain reader or viewer participation with the written message. A participative style in verbal communication is also very helpful — especially in management. Suppose you observed that the leaves had accumulated outside your company's building and you wanted them removed. You seek out the person responsible for keeping the grounds and tell him, "Joe, please rake up the leaves". Joe, perhaps being a subservient type, drops whatever he is doing and proceeds to follow your order. Two days later, he completes that nasty chore and then goes back to his normal duties. Meanwhile, during those two days, several items normally taken care of by him are left unattended causing annoyance and even inconvenience to other employees.

If, instead, you had said to him, "Joe, the leaves are nearly through falling, so please try to get them cleaned up when it is convenient". It is then Joe's decision as to when would be a good time to do the job and whether to do it a little at a time or all at once. Not only will Joe have more responsibility and a sense of participation, but there is less likelihood of his other duties being neglected.

Suppose you have an employee whose job is to mold rubber parts in a large mold. Whereas, a former employee on that operation averaged 1200 parts per day, George is producing 1500 parts of equal quality. You walk by George's work station and say, "George, you're doing a great job", and he responds, "Thanks". In contrast, suppose you walk up to George and say, "George, I notice that your production per day is up considerably over normal. What is your secret?" George responds that he felt that with a higher temperature setting, he could reduce the cycle time and increase production. So he got permission for the change from his foreman, who cleared it with engineering, and the improved production was the result. To that you might comment, "George, that's the kind of thinking we need more of". With the second communication, George participated in a discussion that made him proud of his innovative thinking in that now even you, the "top man", knew about it. You and he know each other better and will communicate easier thereafter.

Sales people learn early in their selling experience that it is important to persuade the customer to participate in the presentation process. Conversation that relates to the customer's sphere of interest, encourages participation. Have you ever been in a social situation with one other person, a person you know and consider uninteresting? Ignoring him would be awkward, and finding something to talk about is challenging. In such a situation, try to find out something about that person such as his vocation or hobby — something you can talk about. Usually, the other person when talking about his or her interests becomes a more interesting person and participates actively in conversation from then on.

If you develop a communication style that encourages your listeners to participate in a thinking dialog, you will find it makes people more responsive to you, and your message will be less prone to misinterpretation.

The antithesis of participative communication would be confrontation, which is invariably the wrong way to communicate. Confrontation is often accusatory, at least in a subtle manner, and in the process of becoming defensive, the listener ceases to be a constructive communicator. To minimize this problem, *confront the problem — not the person!* By way of suggestion, consider the following:

- Confront behavior, not personality
- Be observant, not judgmental
- Discuss pertinent ideas rather than giving advice
- Help to find alternatives rather than offering solutions

When you confront a person (a personality), you can initiate many sources of attitude difficulties, not the least of which is anger. When you draw a conclusion, as a manager, too frequently it is accepted as an order, leaving no room for improvement or change. The same is true in making a judgment. It is often accepted as final. Giving advice can also be interpreted as an order.

Because even to a well meaning person our ideas may not seem natural and could be challenging to adopt, it will be helpful to establish the following "Rules of thumb":

- When communicating, think in terms of the impact upon and value to the receiver — not the giver (you)
- Address problems with a problem-solving stance rather than an accusatory or punitive approach. Do not, under any circumstances, avoid problems or delay your response to them.
- No one ever really wins an argument. An argument too often results in a win-lose situation where one person is considered the winner and the other the loser. Settling divergence of thinking through proper discussion usually results in a win-win situation.

Accenting the importance of a participative approach to management and communications, there is a saying, **"Tell me and I may** forget, show me and I may remember, but involve me and I will understand."

23 · Influencing People

You cannot change people

Usually, you cannot cause another person to change. Some people, about to marry, do so with the hope they will be able to change their spouse-to-be. Such hope usually proves futile. So it is with managers who hope to change an employee. **The only way people can change in a meaningful way is for them to want to change themselves.** This is true, for example, as it relates to all debilitating habits — alcoholism, drug abuse, gambling, or eating disorders. It is also true of behavioral patterns such as being poorly organized, lack of ambition, or laziness.

If you cannot change a person, how should you deal with an employee whom you want to change in some regard? Usually, you are well advised to view the whole person and how he relates to the job. Decide if he is an asset or a liability to the organization. Then act accordingly. If the person is deemed to be an overall asset, it would make sense, during a performance review, to point out those areas where improvement or change might enhance his job performance or potential for advancement. Then offer training or counseling toward those ends. If you desire the employee to continue with the company, care should be taken not to criticize in a deprecating manner. It would be much better to improve the employee's self-esteem by praising those areas of performance that are of merit.

Although you can rarely change another person, under the influence of such emotional pressures as fear or peer pressure, a person often decides, because of self-conviction, to change. After being alarmed by a medical report, a person may establish new patterns of eating, drinking, or exercise. Popular conventions sometimes motivate revisions of dress or hair styles. Peer pressure on the job can move a worker to become more conscientious. In each of these examples, note that persuasion may move someone to desire change, but the realization of change only follows self-conviction.

People do change

It is true that you cannot change a person in the short range, but over an extended period we all undergo change. If you are close to someone and there is mutual respect, over the years he will have learned and perhaps changed in some way because of his association with you. You also will have changed because of that association. If this premise is valid, you can, as a leader or manager, influence long range change in other people. To do so constructively, requires sufficient contact and mutual respect, both expected consequences of good management. From this one derives a very important concept: **if, as a leader, you can, over a long period of time, cause people to change, you have a serious responsibility to make that influence constructive.** For example, an employee should not become distrustful of others — or himself — as a result of your management style. He should not become contentious because you have encouraged or permitted a spirit of individual competition to minimize or eliminate group spirit.

There are many rewards available in the field of management, and none is more satisfying than the awareness that during your career you have been a beneficial influence on others. In small business, because you are usually on a more intimate basis with your employees, the potential for beneficially influencing them is certainly greater than it would be in large business. This gratification is very much like that felt by the generous person who performs an anonymous charitable deed which, according to the philosopher Maimonides, is charity at the highest level. Such philosophy, of itself, will not make you a successful manager, but it certainly can enhance your sense of achievement.

24 • The Marshmallow Syndrome

In the practice of management, it is important to encourage employees at all levels to communicate their suggestions and/or criticisms without fear of retribution. Because creativity is such a scarce commodity, it should be encouraged constantly. It can be the difference between success and failure. The first time an employee receives *bad vibes* for having offered constructive criticism or an original idea may very well be the last time he so volunteers. Management can be guilty of extending *bad vibes* by not responding appropriately, or by not being timely with the response — even by not responding at all.

In the smaller organization, such input may be gained via direct solicitation — presenting the problem and asking for suggestions from everyone. In the larger company, a more formal approach, such as a suggestion box and evaluation system, may be used effectively. I say "may be" because suggestion boxes can also have negative effect. (see topic 52) One company had a suggestion box which received many contributions, but virtually no answers or evaluations ever came back. One day, during a coffee break, an employee took some paint and painted on the suggestion box "the marshmallow". The employees, by and large, thought it both appropriate and funny. After all, you could poke things into it and nothing came back. Since learning of that incident, I refer to such a condition — where downward communication is lacking, or very poor — as the *marshmallow syndrome*. Usually, where downward communication is poor, all communication is poor.

Every suggestion, even those considered inane, should receive a serious reply. Those that merit adoption should receive recognition and appreciation. Those that are unacceptable should be evaluated and the contributor thanked. Reasons for rejecting a suggestion should be presented in a manner that will encourage future suggestions. Also be cognizant that an idea that seems impractical in January may be very practical in May.

Section IV

"TURNING ON" YOUR TROOPS

25 • People Have The Same Needs

You need not be a psychologist to be a good manager. When the psychology that should be applied as part of your management style becomes natural to you, it will seem like good common-sense. Sometimes, much training is needed before this "natural style" exists. It is too bad that in the field of management, common-sense is not universally common.

People have the same needs

Understanding *the other person* requires a basic understanding of humanity — especially physiological and psychological needs. Abraham H. Maslow, an eminent psychologist, developed what has become known as *Maslow's Hierarchy of Needs*. He depicted them in a graphic manner with a pyramid-like arrangement in which each group of needs depended on those needs placed at a lower level. Maslow placed *the external environment* at the bottom (therefore most basic) of his hierarchical list of needs. It included freedom, justice, orderliness, and challenge (stimulation) — all of which he called preconditions for need satisfaction. The next level up were the physiological needs of air, water, food, shelter, sleep, and sex. Then he added *safety and security* which he regarded as basic deficiency needs. Next came *love and belongingness*, followed by *high-esteem by others*. At the top of his pyramid are a group of growth needs which he feels are of equal importance; they include truth, goodness, beauty, aliveness, order, individuality, perfection, necessity, completion, simplicity, richness, playfulness, effortlessness, self sufficiency, and meaningfulness.

As managers we must take into account that people all have the same basic *survival* needs, whether they reside in darkest Africa, the country-side of India, or New York City. Such needs include:

- Air, water, and food
- Freedom from pain
- An acceptable environment
- Protection from the elements
- Companionship

In the context of management, we assume that employees have a sufficient measure of survival needs, even though there are an increasing number of people who do not. Aside from the rare exceptions that we face as managers, we normally concern ourselves only with those amenities or influences on living standard that can be affected by management.

When, as managers, we encounter an exception, it is usually a new employee who has suffered serious financial distress prior to employment. Such an employee may need special help for a few months before being able to sustain himself. I can recall an instance of unsatisfactory job performance by a new employee resulting from his having to sleep in his car. In another case, an employee who obviously was not well was found to be suffering from badly infected teeth and unable to afford corrective dental care. In these, and other cases, we usually gambled on the benefit to the company that would result from helping the employee. We used the vehicle of a company loan so that we would not to be involved in preferential treatment. This form of *good samaritanism* was not always appreciated in the long run. However, because of those occasions in which it was appreciated, and the overall effect that such compassionate behavior had on our company image and *esprit de corps*, we never regretted being so paternalistic.

The following is a list of employee needs that a manager should pay heed to:

- Job definition
- Goals and performance standards
- Proper tools for the job
- *Stroking* (nurturing the constant need for recognition and sense of participation)

The above list only includes needs that you must address continually — those that should be *ingrained* in your management style for automatic review and attention.

What people want

What do your employees want? The list includes:

- Job security and opportunity for advancement
- Satisfactory working conditions   .
- Meaningful work
- Working for a progressive company
- A good supervisor and pleasant co-workers
- Good fringe benefits and reasonable hours
- Good pay
- Recognition

The list would be virtually the same regardless of what group of workers compiled it. Certainly individuals might add other wants such as a desire for autonomy, an avenue for creativity, or a sense of belonging. Satisfactory working conditions would have a different definition for the steel erector working on a high building or the casting cleaner working in a hot foundry. In such cases, competitive working conditions that are applicable to a specific job might be substituted for satisfactory working conditions. The list would be ordered differently by different people depending on their background, their previous job experience, or the nature of the particular job. The person who had just left a job where he had a tyrannical boss would find a pleasant supervisor extremely important. The person whose previous job provided no sick leave or vacations might find those benefits of prime importance.

Psychological research has shown repeatedly, however, that given an acceptable life-style, a pay increase is no longer the prime motivator or desire of most employees.

Suppose we consider two companies, each of whom has provided their employees with all their reasonable wants. They both started about the same time and are competitors in the same type business. One *gets along* in a conservative way whereas the other is growing by leaps and bounds, enjoys vastly superior employee morale, and is much more profitable. Why are such differences frequently observable in business? Invariably, the difference is due to management style.

Imagine a regional high school football championship game at which scouts from several colleges are in attendance, seeking football players for their programs. You have an assignment to interview all the seniors on both teams before the game, and ask of each, "Which would you prefer — winning the game in a see-saw battle in which no individual player is particularly outstanding — or, losing the game with you personally having the best football day of your career and receiving an award for being the outstanding player?" What would be the predominant response you might expect? This study has been duplicated many times and usually shows a preference for being the outstanding player and playing for recognition by the scouts. That could be the difference between receiving a college athletic scholarship and not going to college. Psychologically the answer to the question, "What's in it for me?" is all important — not only in the game of football, but also in motivating people generally.

You should not ask an employee to *do something for the good of the company*, but instead show why it benefits the individual to *do it for the company*. Persuasion of this kind should be part of your management style — the **stealth management** style that will give your organization superior performance.

It is interesting to note that a recent poll of male and female managers on the relative satisfaction of career versus home life revealed results that are contrary to commonly held beliefs. Quoting from an article entitled "How Managers Balance Their Life Roles and Responsibilities" in The American Manager magazine, 47% of the males polled received more satisfaction from their home life while 37% received more satisfaction from their career. In contrast, 28% of the women received more satisfaction from their home life while 60% received more satisfaction from their career. Although I do not believe these results are typical of women at large, since they automatically exclude such a high percentage of those who prefer home life (they are not working outside the home), as a manager you will find such statistics interesting.

In the early 1930's, Elton Mayo, a clinical psychologist working at the Harvard business school, conducted a set of memorable experiments having to do with productivity. They were done at a Western Electric Company plant located in Hawthorne, New Jersey and are referred to as the Hawthorne Experiments. Mayo isolated a group of workers who were involved in wire assembly by placing them within a temporary enclosure at the corner of a large manufacturing area. The workers chosen for the experiment were picked at random and were not informed as to the nature of the experiment. The first observation was that after isolating the group, their productivity rose. The level of lighting was turned up and productivity went up. While planning another portion of the experiments, the lighting was returned to its original level and, unexpectedly, productivity went up further. Padding was installed on the chairs and productivity rose. Mayo tried many other changes, with an original intent of developing a working climate that would have maximum influence toward increased productivity. The results were, at first, totally confusing because every change seemed to improve productivity, whether removing amenities or adding amenities. The final conclusion was obvious, however: the worker responds sharply to the condition of being noticed, being given attention, and becoming aware that someone cares.

The "Hawthorne effect" could be rather temporary and is not a basis for expecting long-term benefit from change that is implemented without good reason.

We have become much more sophisticated in the application of industrial psychology since Elton Mayo's work, but his findings are as valid today as ever.

26 • Trust

If an employee feels trusted, he will certainly have a better relationship with all those below and above him, be more apt to enjoy his job, and be proud of his company. Having trust in your employees reduces overhead such as excessive quality control and internal auditing; in government, such cautionary measures are referred to as bureaucracy and red tape. In a commentary on management, Business Week Magazine (July 16, 1981) noted at that time, Ford Motor Co. had 11 layers of management between the factory worker and the chairman, while Toyota had but six. Ford has taken bold steps to improve in this regard. All of them involve increased trust in their employees.

Controlling overhead in small business necessitates having a minimum of management layers. Because of that, it is easier to convey a sense of trust in a small company.

In the United States, management traditionally believes a manager should not have more than seven people reporting to him except at the bottom supervisory level. In Japan, you sometimes find 10 or more people reporting to a vice-president. This is practical there because Japanese managers inherently have a high level of trust. Usually an employee feels sure that those above, below, or around him all have the company's best interest at heart. They each have goals with pre-determined benchmarks to reach. Not reaching them calls for investigation and change with a report to all concerned, but only under unusual circumstances would less than planned performance be a basis for mistrust.

Creativity is much enhanced by conveying a sense of trust within your organization. To convince yourself of this, ask the question, "would I feel like experimenting with new ideas if I did not feel trusted or sensed someone looking over my shoulder trying to catch me in an error?"

27 · Mistakes will be made

As a manager, your attitude toward mistakes will have a marked impact on employee performance. If you view mistakes with scorn or derision, an employee will become defensive in his approach toward his job. He will spend an excess amount of energy trying to reduce the chance of being caught in an error rather than performing in a more constructive manner. This negative defensive posture is prevalent in our society, particularly in service oriented professions such as medicine, accounting, and law. As a result, the client has to pay much higher fees and sometimes receives lower quality service. The high cost of insurance, brought about by what many consider an excessive tendency to settle dissatisfaction by suing, is having considerable negative impact on those who indirectly bear the cost of such litigation. We compare unfavorably in this regard throughout the rest of the Western World. Do not inadvertently increase your cost of doing business, along with stifling creativity, by mishandling mistakes.

Certainly mistakes are undesirable and minimizing their frequency through the use of proper planning, adequate training, and subsequent monitoring is extremely important. It would be better for a mistake to be revealed as soon as possible in order to permit early corrective action. Permitting people the freedom to make mistakes facilitates disclosure. However, an employee who makes an excessive number of mistakes or who makes mistakes because of poor training or poor planning clearly has a problem that needs to be addressed. This is true whether they are mistakes of omission or mistakes of commission. Good monitoring should include diagnosing the cause of mistakes to prevent recurrence — not primarily to assign personal blame.

When you are in a position of having to deal with mistake of some magnitude on the part of an employee, unless you have reason to take punitive action, it is important that you do not tarnish your relationship with that employee. I once had an employee accidentally damage a very sophisticated cable assembly we had completed for the Navy by hitting it with a fork lift truck. The cable could not be repaired and was already embarrassingly late in delivery. It was the first of a series of such assemblies, and we had customer purchasing and quality control people all over our plant. The loss was in the $15,000 range, but the embarrassment was inestimable. I waited a few hours for my emotions to subside and then walked over to the employee and said, "Paul, you had a bad morning". He actually started crying and was unable to communicate for a few seconds. During that time, I let him know that we were aware that he felt more sorry for the accident than anyone, and that there was no benefit in our *crying over spilled milk*. Subsequently, with his superior, we devised a handling technique that would prevent the same type accident in the future. Over the next several years, he was an exemplary employee in every respect, but had the incident been handled with any type of recrimination, we could have, in effect, lost a good employee.

As an aftermath, we learned much later that other employees also acquired a deeper respect for the company because of the manner in which we handled the Navy cable accident. Several months later, I learned that even our customer, a sub-contractor to the Navy, also thought well of us because of our treatment of this employee. While visiting the customer, and in a purchasing supervisor's office, the director of purchasing came into the office and referred to our incident with the damaged cable in a friendly manner. I was able to interpret his comments as a compliment to our company's usual attitude toward mistakes when they invited me to lunch (as opposed to my inviting them). They extended us another order soon after.

Recently, while visiting a friend at his office, I noticed a plaque on his wall entitled "Lincoln's Failure". It read as follows:

"When Abraham Lincoln was a young man he ran for the legislature of Illinois and was badly swamped. He next entered business, failed, and spent 17 years of his life paying up the debts of a worthless partner. He fell in love with a beautiful young woman to whom he became engaged — then she died. Entering politics, he ran for congress and was badly defeated. He then tried to get an appointment to the United States Land Office and failed. He became a candidate for the United States senate and was badly defeated. In 1856, he became a candidate for the Vice-Presidency and was again defeated by Douglas. But! — in the face of all this defeat and failure, he eventually achieved the highest success attainable in life and undying fame to the end of time."

I would not necessarily classify Mr. Lincoln's failures as mistakes. However, the story seems appropriate when trying to put into perspective how sometimes too much importance can be attached to mistakes. We have all heard the saying "A person who does not make mistakes is not doing anything!" In this era of change, some companies find that following a mistake, a pat on the back for having tried is a positive influence in increasing creativity and innovation.

28 · People motivate themselves

How do you define creativity? In his book, *Managing Group Creativity*, Arthur Van Gundy defines creativity as: "the drive that impels people to achieve a goal." **Just as you cannot change anyone — he has to change himself, so it is that you cannot motivate anyone — he must motivate himself.** Indirectly, however, you can have much influence by providing a work climate that promotes motivation and provides a reason to be motivated. If he is happy in his job, and the organization's future seems good, he then has been provided with the working climate. If he feels appreciated and is permitted to contribute in a participative manner toward achievement of well planned goals, he then has reason to be motivated. If to these ingredients you add appreciation for effort and accomplishment, you should have the complete package for continual and above average motivation.

"Contributing in a participative manner toward achievement of well chosen goals" is so important to the motivation process, that it deserves further discussion. If a person has participated in choosing the goal, it is more likely that he would be motivated to work for it than he would for a goal assigned to him to which he is not especially attracted. If you have a goal which you have chosen for the company after much careful thought and wish to assign it to a particular employee or to a team, use this participative approach. Suppose you have decided that a person named Robert would be ideal for the assignment. Call Robert in for a conference on the subject, and describe for him the goal of the project, as you see it, and why the project will benefit the company. Invite his comments and ideas about the goal, it's potential benefit, and what steps should be taken to reach that goal. After adequate discussion, he will begin to feel that, because you have consulted with him, he has participated in choosing the goal; he, too, will think it a good idea. If he finds room for criticism, his input may help you to better define the goal. By this time, you may have reached the same plan you originally had in mind, or perhaps even a better one. You will then have accomplished what you originally intended with the assignment having been given to an employee who feels *turned on* to the project. It will be done better, probably faster, and you will receive useful feedback during the process.

Even though the participative approach to assigning a task takes more time than merely assigning it, you will find that good results will soon make it a part of your normal procedure.

Many leaders have found that *hard-driving* inspirational talks or other types of pressure can produce short term positive effects in terms of the amount of work done and the extra effort given. Such effects usually are short lived and often produce an offsetting negative effect shortly thereafter. It has been found that people who are "motivated" by constant pressure from bosses, family, or peers often suffer job *burnout* — further evidence that **the motivation which counts comes from within.**

29 · Group competition

An early steel industry pioneer visited an open-hearth floor in his plant one day, shortly before a shift change. Because he made it a frequent practice to visit employees throughout the plant, this visit was not unusual. After greeting the crew, he calmly asked how many heats they had poured that day. A *heat* is a process in which a large ladle, containing many tons of iron and alloying elements, is heated until the metal reaches pouring temperature. The contents are then poured into large molds producing billets of steel. One of the crew replied that they had poured five heats. The executive expressed great pleasure with that level of performance and in the spirit of "flattery will get you everywhere", proceeded to draw a large 5 on the floor with a piece of chalk.

Soon the next shift showed up for work, noticed the 5 on the floor, and asked one of the previous shift employees what was its significance. The first shift employee told the story of their performance and that the "big boss" was so pleased that he drew the big 5 on the floor. One of the second shift employees commented, "Big Deal!" Not to be outdone, the second shift proceeded to pour six heats during their shift and changed the 5 to a 6. The third shift was able to change the 6 to a 7.

In 1980, after arriving at Vancouver by train, my wife and I took a taxi to the airport. We had about 3 hours until plane time and were talking to the driver about Vancouver. I soon observed that in terms of his ability to communicate, he seemed superior to any taxi driver I had encountered before. I told him so. He smiled, thanked me, and then indicated that in Vancouver a taxi permit cost $35,000 which accounted for a higher level of education among them. Learning that this was our first time in Vancouver, he asked for permission to turn off the meter and show us a couple of Vancouver's floral parks. We accepted and showed our appreciation at the end of our ride. The two parks we saw were magnificent, with absolutely beautiful gardens. We asked him how the park department could get its employees to put such apparent love and effort into their work. He indicated that the employees were broken up into teams, each team being responsible for a section of the park. The resulting competition, with each team wanting its section to be best, was the reason for the beauty we enjoyed.

After returning to work, I found we had a problem in a department where we assembled fairly complex electrical switching devices. The competition was under-selling us by an appreciable percentage. Our shop superintendent held a meeting of the foreman in charge and the 12 people involved in the process and presented our problem with the appropriate figures. He asked for ideas that could improve our efficiency, keeping in reserve a few of his own. Out of the meeting came a large number of suggestions that resulted in our having two teams that operated in an unstructured manner. That is, each person would do only a few of the 18 operations involved, but would be trained and able to do any of the others. Each team would work at a round table so the work could be easily passed to the next work station without the need for a conveyor belt, and there would be spare tooling to prevent slowdowns due to defective tools or unavailability. Assembly time was reduced from 16 minutes to 8.5 minutes. When, one day, one of these employees was observed at work with a bad cold and probable fever, she said she did not want to stay home and have her team get behind. Of course, we had her go home and take care of her health. Team competition again proved to be a great motivator.

It is significant that although the two teams each had an assigned goal, they were organized in an *unstructured* manner. Had they been totally organized, as industry in the United States is prone to be, there might have been little if any competition. Given trust and the freedom to innovate and make subtle improvements that cannot usually be prescribed by production engineers, competition produced surprising results. Over-structuring through job descriptions and operational procedures can have negative impact.

The reasons that team effort usually has such a positive influence on productivity include the following:

- A team is ideally motivated when the entire group is permitted to participate as partners in establishing a goal and a plan for achieving the goal. In the process each member enjoys elevated self esteem and experiences a type of euphoria that is frequently a part of the sense of participation that results.
- Being a member of a team affords a *sense of belonging.*
- When properly structured, the team profile tends to compensate for individual weaknesses.
- Interdependency obligates each member *not to let the team down.*

- A team is usually few in number. Hence, they get to know each other well, and the sense of obligation to the others on the team is strengthened.

Of course, many work situations are not adaptable to a team effort, and some individuals are inherently more comfortable working alone. The typical researcher in science, the inventor, and the truck driver are examples of people who often prefer the increased flexibility afforded by working alone. As a manager, you must be sensitive to when a team approach is appropriate. Care must be taken to prevent team competition from having a negative influence that can result from the *desire to win* exceeding commitment to the organization and its goals.

30 • Recognition

"Praise will get you everywhere!" "You can catch more flies with honey." These are quotations that have almost become trite with common usage. None-the-less, they are true when managing people, although it might be better to *say* that people desire and value *recognition* as much or more than *praise and honey* — recognition of them as individuals and recognition of their abilities. Recognition gives a person a sense of belonging that transcends merely being a paid hand; it is a basic ingredient of any formula for motivation.

I have two close friends referred to here as Dave and Martha (Mr. and Mrs.). On an early one of their voyages on the Queen Elizabeth II, from England to New York, they took their meals in the top dining room so that they could eat with business friends. In that dining room, if the sea was at all rough, the diners were subjected to a maximum of roll, making those who were susceptible to sea sickness very uncomfortable. They had one cocktail before arriving for dinner and had been seated but a short while when Martha began to feel queasy and soon asked Dave to take her back to their cabin. After seeing that she was comfortable, he found George, their steward, and asked him to summon the nurse because Martha was feeling ill. The nurse took care of Martha until, after a very unpleasant hour, she slept.

The next morning Dave asked the steward to get Martha some tea and toast and mentioned that she finally had been able to rest thanks to excellent care of the nurse. George responded to the effect that Martha's discomfort was typical for people who drank too much aboard ship, a remark that annoyed Martha so much she would not talk to George from then on.

On their next QE-2 trip from Los Angeles through the Panama Canal to New York, they invited Martha's Mother, sister, and brother-in-law aboard for tea and a tour of the ship before departure. When they went down to view their cabin, Martha was dismayed to observe posted in the cabin the name of their steward — George, of whom she had only bad memories. She was ready to leave the ship. Not knowing how he might salvage the situation, Dave prevailed on Martha and the family to go upstairs for tea. Inspired with a plan, he found George, shook his hand, reminded him that he and Martha had been on the ship twice before with George as their steward. He then told George how nice it was to renew acquaintances and how happy they were that George would again be their steward. George, who seldom smiled, suddenly became pleasant, friendly, and even solicitous of Dave and Martha's well-being. During their trip not only was George personable and friendly to them, but he saw to it that their favorite beverages, ice, and delicious candy were always in their stateroom.

On a later QE-2 trip, they arranged to have George as their steward and, received favored service from him. During that trip, Dave learned that George was on his last voyage before retirement. At the end of the trip, they thanked him and gave him two envelopes, one containing a gratuity and the other a retirement gift. They wished him long life and happiness and George was deeply moved.

Through simple recognition you can often can bring out the best in people. The story also points out that good communication can often correct serious misunderstanding. Even Martha realized that George had probably "jumped to conclusions" because he had been troubled by so many passengers who had over-imbibed, and she had come to respect George.

31 • Perspective

The effect of the past

The past has both positive and negative influence on the perspective of people. On the negative side, it often causes people to make improper decisions. I recall that my parents and all their many siblings had lived through the great depression which resulted in their being quite conservative with regard to money for the rest of their lives. An aunt, who was very intelligent and financially very comfortable, would not send an important letter via airmail (that was back when people wrote often as opposed to using the telephone) because it cost five cents, whereas a stamp that was not airmail cost but three cents. The value of early arrival seemed relatively unimportant. In management, you encounter people who do not make wise financial decisions because of warped perspective that is usually based on their past experience. It is good policy to understand people well enough to be aware that such lack of perspective can be a cause of errors. Proper decision-making tactics will virtually eliminate improper perspective and prejudice from influencing important decisions.

On the positive side, the experience that is gained over time will permit a person in a position of responsibility to make decisions that are more mature and are more likely to stand the inevitable tests of surprise and change. During the business climate of the early 1980's, many executives who had never experienced bad times caused their companies problems by not being prepared for an economic downturn. In petroleum related businesses this was particularly noticeable. Many, if not most, small companies were forced out of business because they were too highly leveraged to handle their excessive debt when business declined. Those who were conservative and expanded only as they could afford to, largely using internally generated capital, came through the bad times very well and will be stronger when the cycle repeats and good times return to the oil industry. Most of those who acted conservatively did so because of perspective gained from long experience.

The view of the future

In decision making, having a view of the future or, as is sometimes said, "seeing the big picture", is most important. But this foresight can remain undeveloped if you do not establish thinking habits that are conducive to such a management style. When to think short range and when to think long range calls for perspective — the perspective of where you are in relation to the business cycle, the weather cycle, the population trend, the impact of politics, and numerous other influences which must be kept in mind at all times. This seems so obvious, yet it is overlooked by most managers. Having the proper perspective with regard to the future requires that one be reasonably well read, be able to ask the right questions, and possess the ability to make intelligent assumptions.

Awareness of the potential for change and its impact on us as managers should be very humbling in its effect. History constantly reaffirms the validity of the saying, "The best laid plans of mice and men often go astray". Respond to this in *boy scout fashion*: be prepared.

Those who are small business managers tend to be more isolated and, with fewer people on the management team, are prone to be un-prepared for the future. They tend to expend most of their energy responding to emergencies that are ever-present.

Having perspective also involves the ability to envision things from an historic viewpoint — that is, imagining how your actions of today may be judged if reviewed ten years hence; or, what will be the future impact of your present decisions? I am reminded of the saying, "The future leaves footprints in the present".

Perspective is aided by cross fertilization

Perspective is improved in any organization when every participant has knowledge of the function and activities of all other departments. Some companies do this by transferring employees around to give them work experience in different areas and find that it has long term value even though it is an added expense. Many companies try to provide such experience with a training course for new employees, rotating them through all departments of the company during the first year or more of employment. This may help a great deal initially, but if it is not repeated, much of the benefit is lost after a few years because of inherent change within most areas of any organization.

During the later part of 1978 and early 1979 I had the very interesting experience of serving on an advisory committee on industrial innovation which was organized by the United States Department of Commerce at the request of President Carter. The committee was broken up into sub-committees, and each was assigned a different aspect of industrial innovation. Our sub-committee was charged with addressing the problems of innovation in federal procurement policy and direct federal support of research and development. The members of our committee, about twenty five in number, were mostly research directors or executive officers of large companies. By my definition, I was the only member from small business. We had sixteen to twenty in attendance customarily and our meetings would last all day. It became apparent during our first meeting that the discussion lacked perspective. That is, people were discussing the problem of enhancing innovation only in terms of government involvement without first having some common understanding of the problem from other vantage points, especially financial. Because ground rules were set that prevented us from discussing other aspects of the problem, I asked if could take but a few minutes of the committee's time to make a statement about the financing of research and development so that we might have better perspective for our discussion. I was firmly but politely turned down with a reminder from the chairman that he had to abide by the guidelines given him.

A few meetings later, our chairman had to leave for the rest of the day and an assistant chairman took over. After lunch, I decided to be bold and proceeded to speak on the subject that had been denied me before. Luckily, I was not interrupted. I pointed out that the average publicly owned company made less than 20% gross profit (before a then prevailing tax rate of up to 50% was applied). At that time, we were suffering double digit inflation that usually required retention of over half such profit just to pay for the cost of inventory replacement. Equipment replacement also required above normal funding, and if the company's stock was widely held, dividends took a sizable percentage of the dwindling unallocated profit. For many companies, research and development allocations had to be paid for by increasing indebtedness, especially during periods of high inflation. I apologized for the interruption but suggested such facts be considered even though we might not discuss them further. To prove the need for these comments, one of our members then advised me that his company had much higher profits than what I had indicated as typical. Because his company was one of the larger companies in our country and enjoyed considerable competition, I felt sure of my ground. I asked him if he could indicate for us what his company's profit might be in terms of percentage of sales. He indicated that they made 30% profit as a percentage of sales. It took the concurrence of others present to convince him that the 30% was before taxes and therefore my comments also applied to his company. From that point on, The committee's whole tenor seemed to change.

I am not sure that my effort to improve the perspective of the committee's work was beneficial in its end result, but it did indicate that by fragmentizing our work, the Dept. of Commerce limited our effectiveness. Cross fertilization, in which people are given knowledge of the function of other departments or divisions, considerably improves perspective, communications, and decision making. Judging from their response, it seemed to me that our committee members would have been better able to participate in the work assigned to them had their companies exposed them to a cross fertilization program. The need for adequate profits to fund research would then have been obvious.

To my knowledge, the reports and recommendations emanating from our committee in Washington have produced little benefit insofar as increasing industrial innovation in our country. Experts who were asked to give reports to us on their study of the status of research and innovation in the U.S. did reaffirm the previously established fact that small business was responsible for the majority of our innovation. There are, of course, some types of Research and Development that require huge financial and physical facilities available only at large companies. There is also a class of research of such magnitude that it requires government sponsorship.

32 · Remuneration

Wage scales

Establishing proper wage scales is a very difficult task. The result from being either too low or too high can negate many of the otherwise good management practices you have implemented. Perhaps the easiest approach for a small company is merely to be sure it is competitive in its geographic area and also within the industry. Current information of that sort is usually available from a local Chamber of Commerce, your trade society, and the Census Bureau. It is important, however, that you conduct your own survey, because all data that you solicit from data gathering groups is subject to marked distortion. As examples, in an area where there is a large aircraft industry, their potential for hiring and firing, as contracts expire or renew, requires that they have wage scales considerably above the norm; in the past, automobile manufacturers and steel mills would considerably distort a wage survey on the high side; often, apparel industries have very low wage scales in their attempt to compete with apparel manufactured abroad in countries having low wages.

Conducting a survey can be done by your own personnel or by employing an outside consultant to do it. It does not necessitate contacting every business or every competitor in the area. It is sufficient, usually, to make a list of a few local companies who are likely to have an employment profile similar to yours and canvas them by contacting their personnel departments. If your persuasion level is good, you should receive cooperation from most of them. Particular attention will be required with regard to specialties such as technical employees, tool and die makers, and computer programmers. Care must be taken, however, that your pursuit of such information is not viewed as *price fixing*.

After your survey, it should not be too difficult to establish low and high pay-ranges for each job classification. Where you should be within these ranges is a decision that you, with input from others in your organization, must make based on many factors such as the level of availability of applicants.

Assuming you have complied with all governmental regulations pertaining to minimum wage and discriminatory practices, you are now prepared to establish your own code of wages. They should provide entry level (trainee) scales and graduate up to top level for each category of employee. They must be monitored frequently enough to assure continued competitiveness. If your wage scales result from negotiating a union contract, however, this entire discussion will serve only to make you a better negotiator.

If yours is a mature organization with a variety of vocational disciplines, there is a service available from several consulting groups that analyzes each job and assigns a relative value to it. A job to which they would assign a value of 900 could be deserving of twice the pay of a job that had a value of 450. The process by which the values are determined is quite complex but is recognized as being soundly based. Further, it has been refined over several years of application. It involves listing all the skills, risks, and responsibilities of a job and assigning numerical values to each. With regard to personal danger, the job of erecting high rise steel might have a value of 100 whereas a secretarial job might have a value of 1. With regard to communicative skills, steel erection might have a value of 10 and secretarial work have a value of 500. Once completed, such a survey would serve your company for a long time since it only establishes relative values to jobs which typically change very slowly. These values can then be applied to any wage scale you use and adjusted for inflation. They would prevent a problem I once encountered when a person who was doing light assembly work complained he was not making as much as our maintenance man, referred to by the complainer as a "mere janitor".

Doing your best to establish fair pay scales will not prevent occasional complaints about them. If your company is reasonably profitable, however, employee sensitivity about pay can be very much reduced by heeding the recommendations which follow relative to sharing the spoils.

Sharing the Spoils

As part of the *stealth management* process, most employees are given an opportunity to contribute to the company's overall plan. As a result, they usually exert a greater effort towards achieving company goals. It then follows that if the company does reach a higher level of success, your employees would expect to share in that success along with the owners or stockholders. Management, in appreciation of the employee's part in that success, should have a policy that combines remuneration, fringe benefits, and bonuses in a manner that properly rewards employees at all levels before they have reason to think you are unappreciative. Employees who know they are appreciated will be anxious to contribute their ideas and their energy toward maximizing the organization's progress.

The entire area of employee reward varies so much from industry to industry and company to company, that it is impractical to make recommendations that would be universally applicable. In my former company, our management group decided we wanted to be in the top third of regional companies with regard to generous fringe benefits and entry-level pay-scales. That decision made our employment efforts easier, and with the application of good management practices, it afforded our company the reputation for being a *good place to work*. We particularly did not wish to be the highest paying company in the area, since we would find it difficult to reduce our pay-scales and/or benefits in the event of a serious downturn in our industry. We decided that, for above normal achievement, above normal reward would be made via a bonus system which could be tied to profits.

We first began addressing this problem by establishing a long-range plan and completing a wage survey of other businesses. We found that we were in the lower half of the wage scales revealed to us. We timed each wage improvement to associate with progress being made by the company and thanked our employees for their help in achieving that progress. Within two years we had raised our wage scales enough to put us above average. We were very forthright in communicating our financial progress or lack of progress to our employees. We did this through verbal communication as opposed to putting it in writing, and expressed it in percentages rather than dollars, although we were specific with regard to sales figures. We established a profit sharing plan that provided for sharing profits after a suitable return to shareholders. In that regard, investors in a business deserve a reasonable return on their investment before employees share in profits, and employees should be taught to understand this.

Profit sharing plans should not be established hastily or without proper legal counseling. It is strongly recommended that you adopt a philosophy toward profit sharing that encourages future progress, not only the current period's profit. To a lesser degree, it should also encourage long-term employment. Rewarding only short term achievement will have a bad influence on long range success.

Whether profit-sharing is in the form of cash bonuses or a contribution to an approved plan which invests the funds of the plan for the future benefit of the employee, is a difficult choice. Because of legal considerations and the potential psychological impact on the employee, much consideration should be given to these decisions with the help of experienced advisers as well as asking for input from employees.

33 · Reward systems

The relationship of salary to motivation is complex and important. An employee wants to know that he is being paid fairly in relation to others who perform similar work. He also wants to enjoy life now — not work all his life merely to enjoy retirement. Management must address both of these desires to prevent them from becoming a source of discontent.

In smaller organizations, the problem of relative worth is usually solved by making the pay relatively fair. When there are discrepancies, the underlying reasons should be discussed with the employee. As the company grows, or if there is frequent difficulty of this nature, it might be necessary to establish more formal evaluation standards. Performance standards, which also figure in this calculation will be discussed as a separate subject in a later topic. Evaluation standards consist of a set of guidelines used in evaluating the performance of an individual or a group. For example, individual performance might be rated on a scale of 1 to 5 in the following categories: attitude, production, creativity, motivation, improvement, versatility, quality, leadership ability or potential, and job skills. The list should be compiled for each type job, be job related, and be applied as part of employee reviews. Employees then become aware that many factors enter into their evaluations, not merely production rates. Discussion of the ratings gives employees a basis for improvement and an understanding of the relationship of earnings to job performance. The employee review process and how it relates to reward is covered in topic 46.

Some types of savings/retirement plans that accrue to employees only after retirement, though well intended, have drawbacks. As managers, we should be concerned not only for the well-being of our employees but also for the impact of various reward systems on their productivity. It has been proven repeatedly that if part of these benefits are paid to the employee on a current basis, thereby enhancing his sense of well being or his life-style, improved motivation results. Such current reward, beyond normal pay, should be associated with specific individual, group, or company-wide performance. A year-end cash bonus for over-all good performance is usually not so beneficial as giving the same total bonus in two or more parts for specific achievement during the year. Reward systems that are not well-received are ineffective and can be *personnel land mines*. Reward systems require careful planning!

If your employees are directly or indirectly involved in the establishment of a reward system, they are more apt to understand and appreciate it. In the process, they will learn to better understand the overall finances of the business, the company's obligation to its stockholders, and the importance of the many factors involved in the cost of doing business. Their perspective about business will have been improved and their attitude toward the company and its goals will be much better.

In the Harvard Business Review of November, 1990 there is an article about Ralph Stayer, C.E.O. of Johnsonville Sausage Co. entitled "How I Learned to Let My Workers Lead". His profit sharing plan is excellent for small to medium sized businesses.

Profits are shared on a basis of performance in which each employee rates himself on a scale of 1-9 in 17 specific areas which are grouped into 3 categories — performance, teamwork, and personal development. The 17 rated areas would vary for each company but could include such things as productivity, innovation, quality, adherence to schedule, attendance, and attitude. With each of these areas, both the employee and his supervisor, independently, would complete a rating form. If they were rating with regard to quality, for example, he would be rated from 1 to 9 in each of the categories of performance, teamwork, and personal development. With regard to performance, his rejection rate would easily be quantitatively rated. With regard to teamwork he would be rated on his effort to reduce quality flaws in a team spirit that put the company first. With regard to personal development, he would be rated as to what he was doing to improve his knowledge and abilities.

After the employee and the supervisor each have filled out the same forms, they meet to discuss all items therein which may result in agreed changes. A rule applies that after this meeting, the two totals must agree within 9 points. These totals are then averaged for a final score. If they cannot agree within 9 points, an elected arbitration group takes over. So far, they have not had to resort to arbitration, and often the supervisor rates the employee higher than the employee rates himself.

The total company bonus is determined based on a previously agreed-to formula and the plan provides 5 levels of performance which share the bonus as follows:

Superior performers	*top 5% of all employees*
Better than average	*next 20% of all employees*
Average	*50% of all employees*
Below average	*next lower 20% of all employees*
Poor performers	*lowest 5% of all employees*

(the lowest group must improve or be in
danger of losing their jobs)

The plan then provides that group no. 1 receives 125% of the average bonus, group no. 2 gets 110% of the average bonus, group no. 3 gets 100% of the average bonus, group no. 4 gets 90% of the average bonus, and group no. 5 gets 75 % of the average bonus.

Because in this example, an employee profit sharing team participated in establishing the formula upon which the total company bonus is based and each employee participates in determining his share, this bonus system has worked wonders in elevating both morale and productivity in Ralph Stayer's company. The best part of this system is that the employee rates himself, and there is not the need for the often-times demeaning process in which only a supervisor rates an employee.

STEALTH MANAGEMENT

Section V

BUILDING THE "TEAM"

34 · The Personnel Department

If this book were written as a hard-core management text intended primarily for large company managers, much of this section would be omitted. The typical manager of human resources might find it unsophisticated and even patronizing for me to include it. In the small business, however, often there is no designated personnel department or established personnel policies. If such is the case with your organization, you may find this section very helpful or at least a source of reinforcement for existing policies. It does concern management activities for which the personnel manager (or human resource manager) is usually responsible. Of course, all managers are involved constantly in human resource management.

It is unfortunate that we live in a litigious society, and because we do, you must be very protective in establishing your management policies. Try to do so without conveying distrust — sometimes, a difficult task.

Also, keep in mind that your policies and the manner in which you apply them can have appreciable effect on your cost for several types of insurance coverage. These would include fire, theft, medical, liability, and product liability.

In the field of management, people, as a factor, gradually are being thought of as increasingly important (relative to capital, for example). This trend is making personnel management a much more sophisticated specialty. Many organizations have found it appropriate to improve the stature of the person responsible for people management and now have created the title of *vice-president in charge of human resources.* Certainly such recognition is justified by the increasing administrative responsibilities that are associated with that position. No longer does a personnel manager merely supervise additions and deletions from the employee roster, wage and salary changes, and personnel policies. He now copes with a myriad of governmental regulations and legal defense conditions. His duties include arbitration and often-times acting as an ombudsman.

In most companies having fewer than one hundred employees, there is no personnel department, nor is there need for one — that is, there is no single person responsible for those duties normally handled by such a department. When your growth does suggest that you delegate personnel responsibilities, it is important to do so in such a manner that you, as manager, do not seem distant and aloof from those people who previously looked to you in that capacity.

In the company having between one hundred fifty and five hundred employees, where such a department might consist of but one or two people and perhaps a secretary, their responsibility requires an unusually high level of alertness to psychological considerations and communicative ability. Sometimes, in the absence of a public relations department, they must assume those duties as well. By way of contrast, in a larger organization the organization chart of such a department may look like this:

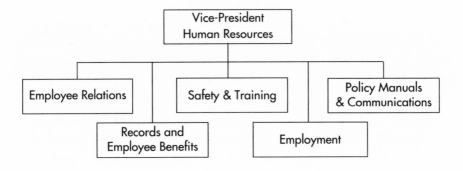

In addition to the duties shown above, someone must handle grievances (in accordance with an established grievance policy). This normally would be assigned to the person in charge of employee relations. Depending in the size of the organization, one or more of these responsibilities could be delegated to a manager who might, as necessary, utilize assistants plus secretarial help.

When an employee receives a message to report to the personnel department, he often senses some level of fear or apprehension. To prevent this from happening, it is recommended that those in personnel conduct their business with sensitivity and that they try to do so at the level of the employee. If, for example, you have an apparent discrepancy in your records that requires a discussion with him, it might be better to go to him at his work area and *ask for his help* in clarifying the record. If you choose to have the employee visit you in your department, it might be well to provide a small conference room rather than have an employee separated from you by an imposing desk.

In the small company, calling the one-person personnel manager "our manager of human resources" seems inappropriate, but the title of personnel manager has come to have less than friendly connotations to the average hourly worker. The only other name that comes to my mind is *Liaison Department* which may or may not work out well in actual usage. One dictionary definition of liaison is: communication for establishing and maintaining mutual understanding — an apt description for one of the major functions of the personnel department.

In personnel work, as in all areas of management, you will be more effective if you perform in a manner that establishes a feeling of *being on the same team* with employees as opposed to *conveying authority*. Your success as a manager will be influenced very much by the kind of personnel manager (or whatever title you assign) you have and by the manner in which he performs his duties. Certainly, you can influence such performance by the use of a job description and by conveying your personal value system and that of the company's to him. However, nothing will compensate for having the wrong person in the job.

35 • Training

Importance of management training to small business

Most of our innovation and job creation is derived from small business and the entrepreneur. At the same time, this large portion of American business also suffers the highest percentage of failure. Small business not only suffers failure early-on due to ill-conceived start-up plans but, more tragically, often suffers failure after having enjoyed initial success during the transition from the entrepreneurial stage to that of a maturing business . In the latter situation, not only is failure common, but often the business is then taken over in a predatory manner by more mature talent who successfully capitalize on the entrepreneur's creativity but leave him un-rewarded for all his effort.

A friend of mine has been active in a small business investment company (S.B.I.C.) and in a venture capital company, both of which make substantial loans to businesses, most of them small. In addition, he and his associates have been active in national societies of each of these organizations. While playing golf with him, I asked what would be typical for the failure rate of businesses that they aid financially. His response was somewhat lengthy because he did not feel a simple answer was sufficient. He told me they only loaned money to three types of business organizations — newly formed start-up companies,

companies that needed financing for expansion or turn-around after suffering temporary reverses, and take-over situations. In each category, failures were often due to such problems as illness (either mental or physical), drinking, divorce, and drugs. He agreed that the rate of failure exceeded twenty percent, but because of the unpredictable causes, he doubted that failure would be reduced through the use of training in professional management. I, of course, had in mind a different view: the exposure to a book such as this one followed by enrollment in a suitable formal training course.

There was not time to further pursue the subject, but good professional management training should elevate self esteem and make one much more goal oriented. These changes add to a manager's level of contentment and happiness. As a result, health is improved, divorce is less likely, and dependency on alcohol or drugs is usually reduced. This concept is discussed in the story of "the company town" at the end of topic 11. It should also be noted that there ought to be proper monitoring by the venture capital company. A person seeking support from such organizations surely should be investigated for these shortcomings before financial help is offered. With proper monitoring, subsequent personality changes would not progress far without warning. With proper management, even in a small company, the contingency of a key person not able to perform should be provided for in the planning process.

In my own small company, every manager had a back-up person to take over should that manager become unavailable for any reason. To avoid over-staffing, this was done by having someone who would be prepared to take over. That back-up person was chosen by consensus of the manager and all those who reported to him. For example, if the lead-man of the machine shop were ill, his temporary replacement would be someone who normally would report to that lead-man and who had been chosen previously by all the machinists in the group. If the lead-man felt strongly that the choice was a bad one, he had a veto right. I do not remember that veto right ever being applied, because employees always made their choice intelligently. Without such consensus, conflict and morale problems could result when the back-up had occasion to take over the vacated key position.

Implement a training policy

One of the most important obligations of a manager is to see that he and those who are in his sphere of responsibility are properly trained for their jobs. This not only requires continual reading, study, and (sometimes) membership in trade and technical organizations but also, in some instances, enrollment in formal training courses. With the increasing reliance on computers, it has been commonly necessary for businesses to send their accounting personnel back to school for computer training. When industry experienced the impact of electronics, it was necessary to seek training for electrical engineers who received their degrees before 1945. Two other areas that require frequent training update because of the rapidity of change are: the impact of business on our environment and safety programs.

As a person advances to a position in management, it is important that he or she be skillful in dealing with people. For this purpose, enrolling in a management training course can prove invaluable. Without a policy that encourages employee improvement and provides effective training, an organization unwittingly provides a breeding ground for under-achievement. If the organization grows and its people do not expand their knowledge and abilities to accommodate such growth, the organization will ultimately lack good leadership.

Cross fertilization of talent is a type of training that has been referred to in topic 31 for its value in improving communication. It also minimizes harmful competition within the organization, and enhances perspective. This is sometimes done by transferring people to other departments on a temporary basis. New employees can be put through a long training course involving exposure to many departments. It can also be done by sending a chief engineer to a training program in finance or a quality control manager to a course in marketing. The latter approach is usually effective and less disruptive, particularly in the small company.

Providing training at the right time requires appreciation by management of the value of that training. One company president with whom I discussed this subject told me that he had a rigid policy in his company requiring every manager or supervisor to attend a training course of some appropriate kind at least once every two years.

Before installing that policy, there were too many instances of people in jobs for which they had insufficient training. He indicated that since instituting the policy, his company had grown much more rapidly, which he attributed to his managers being better prepared for growth.

It is not uncommon for an employee who has just returned to work after attending a training program to be interviewed by his manager. After reporting on the course he attended and indicating appreciation of how much he learned, sometimes the employee might suggest changes the company should entertain. Many employees have gone through that scenario only to be told, "Come on Joe, we're doing great. Let's not rock any boats," which indicates that the manager has had inadequate training to properly respond. Training must start at sufficiently high level or the desired benefits will not be realized.

Just as a progressive company might budget a percentage of profits for research and development, so should they provide adequate funding for training at all levels. Further, training should not be applied merely to bring an employee's level of expertise up to a standard that would seem appropriate for his current job description; it should anticipate both potential growth in the job and any new responsibilities. Such an attitude toward training will enhance the potential for growth of your company considerably.

Most of the foregoing advice refers to training that would be acquired outside the organization. There also is in-house knowledge which may be used as a training resource. Such training includes new job orientation, the implementation of new procedures, the transfer of job knowledge from one employee to another who may be replacing him, or merely the review of on-going procedures from time to time.

Every manager must ascertain that those reporting to him have adequate training for the job to be done, and the need for such training must be anticipated so that its absence is never a deterrent to progress.

36 • Monitoring and Encouraging

During the travails of President Reagan with what has been called *Irangate*, he was called upon to defend his management style. He stated that he believed a good manager should pick the best people for the job and give them the freedom to perform well and that is what he had done. He still believed in such a management style and, hence, saw no reason to change. It should be apparent to any student of management that the President's management philosophy was fine as far as it went but was clearly incomplete if he expressed it accurately. As stated by him, it failed to provide for monitoring and failed to embrace adherence to a cohesive value system. In industry, a value system becomes inherent and reflects the values of the leader. In the political arena, because the leader has limited tenure of office, value systems that would serve to guide a leader's appointed staff need to be defined and agreed upon. Monitoring in an effective manner not only assures continual and in-depth knowledge of the activities of your staff but also virtually obligates them to be open with you about the potential gray areas of conduct that confront us all from time to time.

In a large organization, it sometimes is necessary to formalize a system for monitoring individual performance. In a small company, unless you are obligated to document activity to the extent required of a supplier to the military, it is relatively easy. One simple way is to have frequent meetings on a one-to-one basis with each manager reporting to you. Such meetings should have no ostensible purpose other than an exchange of thoughts and even *pleasantries*. The real purpose, of course, is to monitor and keep up-to-date with his job activities; it also permits you to offer any help and encouragement that may be needed. Such meetings should be held with some regularity. Then, should a staff member desire to communicate with you, barring unforeseen circumstances, an exchange of ideas can take place at regularly planned meetings. Of course, the need to see you sooner should also be provided for, if that is deemed necessary. Many is the time an employee wanted to communicate something to me in private, but found that my time was tightly scheduled for the next day or two. Except for the usual one-on-one meeting the employee can anticipate within a few days, his means for unburdening and communicating with you may be lost — either because of his timidity or insufficient time on your part.

While having breakfast with the president of a corporation that I was leading through the planning process, I asked him if he provided all those who reported to him with a means of easily communicating with him. He assured me he did and proceeded to cite examples of recent instances. In each case, his examples were of meetings triggered by some specific need and were not held with regularity. In one case, the meeting was other than private. At a subsequent planning meeting, he had to excuse himself to accept an emergency phone call. While he was gone, I decided to find out from those present, all of whom reported to the president, whether they found it easy to reach him on a one-to-one basis. Not only did they find it quite difficult, but most even felt frustration in that regard. My observation is that most executives fail in this area of communication, even though, as in the example, they do not think so. As always, "It is not what you think of yourself and your actions that is important — but how you and your conduct are perceived by others." That statement is meant to refer to employee relationships and does not refer to self-esteem.

Such meetings should be informal and relaxed, should have no structure, and ought to encourage open discussion. You, as the leader, should have an unwritten informal agenda that permits achieving the desired results; you should apply that agenda very subtly. Part of the meeting time, in fact, should dwell on current events, family, personal health, etc. Talking about these things deepens relationships, enhances communication, and frequently will introduce a topic that has important bearing on your business. You should encourage the employee to keep you up-to-date on his job activities including discussion of difficulties and suggestions. The question, "What can I do to be of help?" will often prove to be a good one. It would be well to make the employee aware of another benefit of these discussions: In the event he has to be away from his job due to illness, vacation, or travel, you will be better able to assure continued pursuit of his goals because of the information he has provided to you.

If you agree to meet with an employee at 9:30 A.M. every Thursday morning and on a given Thursday you find it inconvenient to do so, if possible you should personally contact the employee and set another time rather than sending him a message. These get-togethers should not take longer than thirty minutes and sometimes can be held in less time than that.

Section VI

HAS STEALTH MANAGEMENT THEORY BEEN PROVEN ?

---

37 • Theory Z

If you are considering the rebuilding of your management style and even changing many of your attitudes about and toward people, you can be assured that carrying out the suggested changes will be very beneficial to your business. William Ouchi's "Theory Z" cites excellent statistical research in the application of such behavioral precepts and how, when properly applied, they appreciably improve productivity.

A professor in the school of management at the University of California at Los Angeles at the time of this writing, William Ouchi has devised a philosophy of management he calls Theory Z. Theory Z is most interesting because it applies those management precepts typically used in Japan that are also applicable in the United States in a modified manner in order to make them more useful here. In doing so, he has formed a management style that, a few years ago, American industrial psychologists might have considered paternalistic in character. At the outset of his book, "Theory Z", he says the book is about trust, subtlety, and intimacy, without which no social being can be successful. He then says that all organizations are, in effect, social beings. Perhaps he means it would be better to regard them as social beings. Akio Morita, Chairman of the Sony Corporation, says that Theory Z combines the best of American and Japanese Business styles.

The Ministry of International Trade and Industry (MITI), in effect, regulates all business in Japan since such a large percentage of Japanese businesses have foreign suppliers and/or customers. MITI has been a trust organization having monopoly characteristics in every sense of the word. It is a government agency that influenced price and the parceling of big orders among those in a given industry through most of the 1980's. It even made decisions, in some cases, that resulted in production expansions to permit quoting on a large order. An example is the large steel tubing purchased from Japan for the oil pipe line that was built to the north slope of Alaska. If you were trying to purchase a large quantity of steel pipe from Japan during that period, it would be typical for your tender to be routed through MITI. They would dole out your specifications to those steel pipe manufacturers they thought were best able to fill your order at that time and then pass on to you what they considered was the best quotation. If you were a Japanese manufacturer of steel pipe and you were not permitted to bid on an order, you might be angry; but, under such circumstances, you would typically resign yourself to the probability that MITI made a wise long-range decision and some future order would be better suited to your facilities. Business is conducted there in a manner that makes implicit trust essential. Of course, such near monopolistic practices would not be legal in the United States. However, there are benefits that derive from trust that can certainly be enjoyed everywhere. Such trust is prevalent throughout Japanese business and is accompanied by a corporate memory.

While attending a meeting being addressed by the Japanese ambassador to the United States, he responded to my question about MITI by assuring me that although my perception of how it operated in the past is true, its operations have significantly changed since 1990. He said that it had become more of an advisor to industry and less of a manager of foreign sales. It does not have any authority granted by their government.

The corporate memory is that moral influence that justifies having trust in someone, even when doing so could, under some circumstances, come back to haunt you at a later date. Suppose you managed a manufacturing department that used a particular fastener and you determined that a recent shipment of such fasteners were all faulty. There also happened to be another department in the company that was using the same fasteners and circumstances were such that the other department was unlikely to find the flaw on its own. A potential promotion was soon to be offered to either you or the head of the other department, tempting you to keep knowledge of the bad fastener to yourself and thereby enhance your chances of promotion. If mutual trust prevailed in your organization, you would naturally advise the other department head of your discovery as soon as possible. At the same time, you would have the confidence to understand that the department head that you helped would remember and could be expected to react in a similar manner. Such behavior inadvertently provides that in the future those around you, recalling your actions, will react with the same decency and consideration. Your good deeds will be ingrained in corporate memory, not forgotten. Usually, in Japanese industry you do not find "game playing" where blame is wrongfully passed or credit is inappropriately assumed. Doing so would be a severe breach of trust and could result in disciplinary action.

This kind of subtlety in Japanese business, as described by Professor Ouchi, is most interesting not only for its marked positive influence, but also because it is absent in the typical United States business where rules or trade practices usually prevent it. A subtlety, in this context, is somewhat difficult to define and its meaning is best conveyed by citing an example. One common characteristic is that it is usually qualitative in nature as opposed to being quantitative. If you were asked to assemble a team of six employees for a specific job, an obvious approach would be to seek the six employees who had the experience best suited for the task. However, subtle attention to how well those personalities would blend in communicating and cooperating might suggest that a different combination of six people would be better.

Earlier, concluding my account of the two teams assembling electrical switching assemblies, I said, "Had they been totally organized, as industry in the United States is likely to be, there might have been little competition. Given trust and the freedom to innovate and make subtle improvements that cannot be prescribed by production engineers, competition produced surprising results." That experience occurred before I read Theory Z. Professor Ouchi's emphasis on subtlety reminded me of it and made the use of subtlety by the Japanese particularly interesting. Many reward systems so common in the United States, such as piece work, virtually eliminate the beneficial application of subtlety. The piece work system does not exist in Japan.

Intimacy is the third facet of Theory Z that is considered so vital. It describes intimacy, as applied in management, as "the caring, the support, and the disciplined unselfishness that come from close social relations." In the United States we observe intimacy traditionally fostered through family relationships, in religious and social organizations, and through other appropriate groups. However, it is usually frowned upon in business. If intimacy permits the expression of feelings, and we admit that human beings cannot leave their feelings at home when they go to work, it follows that it would be sensible to cater to this psychological aspect of people in the work-place.

In a later section, under the subject "roaming the ship", I speak of the benefits that are derived from having a "*happy ship*". Part of having a happy ship is the result of the intimacy that, in my experience, is encouraged by appropriate partying during which employees learn to know each other better.

Intimacy, as encouraged by the Japanese, permits easier communication, better cooperation, a ready base for the practice of subtlety, and a higher level of trust — all of which will add immeasurably to performance.

By no means have I given a comprehensive review of Professor Ouchi's book. You will find it excellent reading. Much of what I have said about MITI does not come from Mr. Ouchi's book but is derived from interviews with other people. Although MITI was operated as a trust by the Japanese government in the best interest of Japan, it did not seem to be operated for the direct personal gain of those in charge or for political benefit of those in political power. It should also be pointed out that, since Japan is relatively small and lacking many natural resources, without the influence of an organized international trading approach such as that provided by MITI, it is highly unlikely that Japan would have prospered as it has.

I once attended a one day seminar given by Professor Ouchi on Theory Z and Japanese management. Prior to that time, I had not been exposed to substantive data correlating *Stealth Management* with corporate performance. In his presentation, Professor Ouchi reported on an in-depth research project he led, with the help of several graduate students, in which they studied twenty-two fairly large electronically oriented manufacturing industries. Electronic manufacturing, by nature, is labor intensive as opposed to capital intensive and therefore was an ideal industry in which to study management systems. By previous agreement, they had almost free reign to study each of these companies in considerable depth and were able to come to the following conclusions:

- The group of companies they studied represented a broad variety of management styles.
- The closer a management style was to Theory Z, the higher the profitability, the lower the employee turnover, and the better the employee morale.
- The closer to Theory Z, the more innovative the company.

In conducting this study, care was taken to be impartial and statistically accurate. It included a vast amount of production data, financial data, and psychological data derived from company reports and interviews with a broad cross section of personnel. Professor Ouchi related that interviews with management at those companies most closely adhering to Theory Z, corroborated the fact that it took a long time to engender trust between employees and management. It was his opinion that it could take from 10 to 20 years depending on the combined personalities, style, and other characteristics of the company and its managers.

Because I was expecting to lecture in the near future on the subject of organization, I took the opportunity to talk with Professor Ouchi, during morning coffee break, to ask if the Japanese used an organization chart, and if so, how it differed from a typical American organizational chart. He said that they use organizational charts very little. Then he smiled, and turning to a blackboard, drew a brief sample of a Japanese organizational chart. Instead of the vertically organized chart used by American companies, he had drawn a horizontal chart. He explained that the Japanese preferred the horizontal presentation to prevent the image of those at the top being over or superior to those at the bottom.

Before leaving the subject, let me emphasize that *stealth management* embodies all the precepts of Theory Z. The conclusions of the study of twenty-two electronic manufacturing companies that associated adherence to the principles of Theory Z with a higher level of organizational achievement, confirm the effectiveness of *stealth management*.

Earlier, mention was made that Theory Z perhaps seems paternalistic. It is certainly all right to be somewhat paternalistic if you do not reduce standards of performance, do not show favoritism, conform to all legal obligations, and do not permit such an attitude to dilute your own performance. In fact, the more I study professional management, the more aware I am that **the same qualities used in good parenting are needed to be a good manager in the business climate of today.** Very often, when you have the occasion to observe that a manager is not a good parent, you will also be able to observe that he is not a good manager.

Indulgence certainly can be carried too far, however, and in some cases, has resulted in severe problems. Such apparently was the case for a time at Tandem Computers and at Apple Computers, where informality and excess partying reduced achievement and innovation. Fortunately both of these companies have corrected that situation by making changes in their management styles. Certainly, a manager should not include paternalism as a consistent part of his management style. It would portray a demeaning attitude toward employees and compromise his ability to lead.

38 · Who Is In "Power" With *Stealth Management?*

In accomplishing the goals set forth here, it is important to ingrain your management conscience with a profound appreciation of the truism, **"A manager has no power that has not been granted to him by those whose efforts he coordinates — and the spirit with which that power is granted greatly affects both the manager's and the organization's potential for success"**. This contrasts with the authority that is given to you from above (unless you are the sole owner of your business).

As we continue to change from an industrial/agricultural society to an informational/service oriented society, the spirit with which power is granted to a leader or business manager becomes increasingly important. The Japanese have taken this into account as their industrial prowess has grown, but unfortunately, in the United States and the rest of the world, we are just beginning to do so.

Being an effective leader in the twenty-first century will require that you be more of a facilitator and coordinator, and less of a director. You intuitively will be more subtle in your leadership technique through the use of the principles of *Stealth Management*. Goethe, a German poet/writer, is quoted as having said, "A good leader inspires his followers to have confidence in him. A great leader inspires his followers to have confidence in themselves."

A vital part of management is to influence beneficially the spirit with which your fellow-workers grant you the power to manage or lead. The words, influence beneficially, have complex and broad connotation. In the context of management expertise, they mean maximizing both self-motivation and the desire for achievement of well-chosen goals within those people you lead.

The difference between what an employee does to merely keep a job and what he might do if totally motivated is vast. It has been estimated that the average person uses less than twenty percent of his mental capabilities. This hypothesis is borne out to a large degree when a group of average achievers is placed in a think tank atmosphere and lead by a person trained in the application of the creative thinking process. In management, we call this brainstorming, which when well done, can be very productive. It usually results in achieving levels of creativity and decision making far beyond what might be realized normally.

As a manager, even if you have well chosen goals of your own that you assign to your organization and if you are regarded as a reasonable boss, the organization will be responding only to "your goals". Performance will be greatly enhanced if, through good management, you lead them where "they" want to go. They would then be striving for goals that were both yours and theirs. You can do that only if you both want to go to the same place, a management condition that results from proper organization, training, motivation, and goal setting. The *stealth management* style will permit you to reach and accomplish such common goals better than any other management approach.

The duties of management are often broken up into two categories, those that are perceived to have a more direct bearing on the hard numbers referred to as the bottom line, and those that are more oriented toward people and the psychological influences that affect them. To simplify, the first kind are referred to as hard duties, and the skills oriented to people are called soft duties. We must recognize that with our improved education and life style, today people generally are more independent and certainly less subservient than was the previous generation. More importantly, we have learned better ways to stimulate achievement. In the management climate of today, being a good manager requires much greater attention to the soft skills than ever before. For that reason, a large portion of this book is devoted to that aspect of professional management.

Suppose you had twenty-four new products each of which had been expertly designed and had been shown by market research to have great sales potential. You then offered a choice of one of these to each of twelve budding, well educated, highly motivated entrepreneurs. After adequate consideration, each was permitted to request a sum of money with which to start a new business based on his product of choice. The money requested would provide for establishing the business and taking it over the anticipated initial financial hurdles. If each of the twelve were given fifty percent more than requested (because it usually costs more than anticipated), what would you expect of the twelve new ventures if you checked on them a few years later? Experience shows that, using oil parlance, there might be as many as ten dry holes. However, if each of the twelve entrepreneurs had been trained to be professional managers before any of the foregoing procedures, it is more likely there would be ten gushers.

Occasionally, I have met a business owner/manager who is content with his status and is not motivated toward growth and larger profits for his business. He usually feels that it would be a waste of time for him to expose himself to management training. "Let others worry about big progress", he thinks. You might believe that person is the exception — the one type of manager who really is not a candidate for management training. Wrong! Even he would benefit if he could be persuaded to put it all in proper perspective. If he contemplates being in business very long, he may suffer from: (1) the effects of inflation (however modest they may be), (2) obsolescence because of the relative progress of competition, (3) greater vulnerability to unplanned contingencies than the competition, (4) difficulty in providing a motivating environment for his employees, and last, but not least, (5) insufficient asset value at the time of retirement. He may have difficulty selling his business, or otherwise transferring ownership, for what he would consider fair value. Even he has to grow and plan to an extent that permits overcoming each of these potential problems.

If you are now convinced of the potential of *stealth management*, and wish to implement this management style into your own organization, the procedures outlined in the next section are set forth in near recipe-like fashion. If you are not yet convinced, perhaps you owe it to yourself to study or read further on the subject.

Of course you could accept any portion of the implementation process which follows and realize some benefit, but to gain the most from it, you must believe in and be committed to it. If you are not committed, you will probably be inconsistent in applying it and thereby fail to generate trust and commitment from your employees. Well applied, this management philosophy will permeate the entire organization making each person aware of his importance to the overall team effort. Enhanced performance will make your effort very rewarding. You will sense "being a leader."

Section VII

IMPLEMENTING STEALTH MANAGEMENT

39 · Initial Steps

Introduction and Preparation

This section details the implementation of *stealth management* in a manner that permits flexibility with regard to your personal adaptability or your particular type of business.

If your company finds itself in need of crisis management skills, you should review that subject in topic 55 before trying to apply any changes to your management system.

It is not necessary that the techniques used in *stealth management* (described in sections I through VI) seem natural to you, but you must believe that your company will benefit from this management style. Long-range, they are more important than planning and if implemented first, will make the planning process more effective. Most changes require time before feeling "normal". It may take many re-readings, with your decision to try but one change after each, before you really become "turned on" to the process. The early changes will be mostly self-changes as you become less authoritarian and learn to be more sensitive to others. Before long, there should be solid evidence that will make you pleased with the transition, even before you have begun the implementation process that follows.

During the implementation process, try to compensate for areas in which you, personally, may need reinforcement. For example, if you would not feel comfortable leading a planning session, perhaps it would be better to delegate that to someone else. It could be someone in the organization or, someone you would employ from outside. In any event, the C.E.O. of the company should be active in the planning group and its work.

Top management team analysis

If you and those who report directly to you have a true team spirit, the performance of the entire organization will be enhanced. As has been pointed out, the perception others have of you may very well be different from your perception of yourself. That also applies to those who report directly to you. An excellent exercise your top management team can apply that will aid in this regard is Exercise #2 shown at the end of the book. Using it requires everyone in the group, including you, to fill out a questionnaire that permits each one to individually grade the others on several important areas of management. As in the case of the employee attitude survey (Exercise #1), it should be conducted so as to assure individual privacy. It will provide each participating manager with a set of personal evaluations that usually are considered invaluable because they answer the question "How am I perceived by my peers?".

I have participated in such an exercise and know others who have. We all found the results very worthwhile. It usually motivates subtle changes in management style and makes those participating closer as a group than they were before.

Preparing for the implementation process

The several parts of stealth management are: leading, communicating, establishing working climate (both physical and psychological), planning, organizing, and controlling. Each part can be broken down into several smaller parts. Sections I through VI of this text are concerned with leadership and the psychology of working climate.

Section VII covers the techniques used to implement needed changes in working climate, the planning process, and controlling. Leadership has a part to play in all of it, but do not neglect the premise that **every part of managing is something you should do *with* people not *to* people.**

First, those who report to you need to be taught stealth management and in the process, transformed into believers. If cost is not a deterrent and the time required is available, formal training is usually superior to in-house training. However, if after having done all you can to convince your people, some still remain unconvinced, you have a challenge — a predicament that is not uncommon. Some people are just not amenable to this change, perhaps because authoritarianism is too deeply ingrained in them. Some still believe that if you pay an employee a fair wage, he or she should perform as expected and, therefore, a change in management style is unnecessary. Such obstructionists must change or be removed in the interest of progress and for the long-term benefit of the organization. It is vital that everyone is committed to the same management style.

Another type of person who will be in the way of progress is "Good Ol' Charlie." Good Ol' Charlie is a euphemistic name for an employee who has not grown with the company. A classic example of a Good Ol' Charlie is the corporate vice-president who has been with the company for twenty years, belongs to the same country club as you, whose children are friends with your children, whose wife plays bridge with your wife, etc. and who really doesn't contribute much to the company. He is Good Ol' Charlie at this stage because he was not properly trained at earlier stages of his career, he should not have been hired to begin with, or he was promoted beyond his ability. Any of these reasons indicate bad management on the part of Charlie's superior.

If you have an obstructionist, or an Ol' Charlie, you must make a personnel change. It should be done with great care and sincere consideration for the person involved. When this problem became evident after deciding to apply *stealth management* in my company, of seven people reporting to me, three were obvious misfits. Our plant superintendent was liked by everyone — but his people were not

motivated and he was poorly organized. He constantly required rein-
forcing, and I finally determined that basically he was a task-oriented
person who never would make a good manager. We promoted him to
the new position of production engineer with a job description suitable for him. He soon was given much more respect and was happier
in his job.

Our purchasing agent was a highly intelligent person with im-
peccable character. Everyone liked him, including suppliers, but he
also was poorly organized. Further, because he did not set priorities or
plan, we sometimes had raw material shortages and resulting production problems. I regarded him as a friend (and still do). He was 64
years old and was planning retirement. I permitted him to retire, and
another problem was solved.

Our sales manager, also a long-time friend, had so many outside
activities that he did less than a good job. We were growing so fast I
had rationalized his bad performance. He was a strong authoritarian
who would be difficult to change. I let him go, as tactfully as possible,
and replaced him with a person strong in marketing skills and in
agreement with our new management philosophy.

If faced with such problems, be decisive in making the required
changes or you will be unable to implement *stealth management.* This
type of personnel problem is prevalent in smaller companies and very
often the process of making progressive change is virtually side-
tracked by the inability of a C.E.O. to cope with the "hard facts" that
require replacing people. Instead, it is too easy to put off that which is
difficult or to try to apply the rest of the process without making the
needed personnel changes first. Experience has proven that such
changes are vital.

When all those reporting to you are amenable to the contem-
plated management style, you are ready to start the job of implementation which can be, and usually is, along process. The benefits,
however, will become apparent sooner than you expect.

Announcement and first actions

Now that you have decided to apply *stealth management* in your
business, should you try to do it yourself or hire a consultant to

facilitate the process? This is not an easy question. The answer varies with the kind of person you are, the size and maturity of your organization, the flexibility of your time, and financial constraints. The right consultant could greatly facilitate the implementation process for you, and also help you accommodate to or compensate for areas where you need to change or improve personally.

If you decide to go ahead with the process on your own, there are many steps you can initiate that will shorten the time required to do the job. In the opinion of experienced management consultants, the complete implementation of this style of management in a medium sized company can take six years.

If you can arrange to do so, you will improve your chances of success by first enrolling in a management training course such as The Management Course for Presidents or Top Management Briefing, both offered by The American Management Association. These courses will take a week out of your schedule but will recover it for you many times over. Schedule this training first, even if it is your intention to employ consulting help.

In any event, whether or not you seek outside training, when you begin applying the process, the implementation procedure will be the same. Suppose the following hypothetical situation: You are the president of a manufacturing company employing 200 people and have been in business for 10 years. You are growing slowly but feel frustrated by the ever continuing problems concerning money, people, and constant change. There seems to be an annoying gap between where you are and where you would like to be. Such feelings are common among managers and CEO's. With the *Stealth Management* program, you will not suffer such feelings.

After taking a course such as those previously suggested, or to proceed without that advantage, the following steps should be taken:

1. Advise those who report to you of your intent to implement *stealth management* and that you will need their help and commitment to the process. Explain what *stealth management* is and why it will benefit the company and them individually. Invite discussion and even disagreement. In no event should you accept deterrence of your plan to change your style of management. This should be an authori-

tative decision, albeit one of the last decisions you will have to be authoritative about. However, you must evaluate each person's ability to accommodate to this change, and by whatever means required, replace anyone who cannot be trained to participate in this new approach. Precipitous action by you toward any individual must be accomplished as tactfully as possible with consideration for both the person and the company. Constant awareness that you are dealing with people and not things is important, especially in a small organization.

The previous discussion with your management group (those who report directly to you) can result in much disagreement and, in all probability, arouse criticism throughout the organization. Hence, early follow-up is important. You must spend as much time with each of those reporting to you as you consider necessary and productive, for the purpose of making them aware of and committed to the advantages of *stealth management* — or, at least, agreeing to give it an enthusiastic try.

2. Within the next several days, arrange for a meeting, preferably away from your company so as to eliminate distraction and also to emphasize its importance. The purpose of this meeting is to elicit from the group a list of steps that ought to be taken to eliminate any hierarchical image or attitudes in the company. Do not announce the purpose before the meeting. A hierarchical image is a condition within an organization in which management style has permitted those at the top to develop an apparent aura of superiority. Many employees may have developed resentment toward management as a result. Such an attitude by management often results in inane rules that provide, for example, an assigned square footage of office space and a specified amount of money to be used in furnishing of offices. Such rules often are tiered in value to create an increasing image of importance as you go up the organization levels, and usually are set without regard for the actual needs of the employee who uses the office. I have seen corporate management offices where the level of opulence might generate real antagonism, even from stockholders were they but aware. Under such circumstances, how can you prevent employees at lower levels from having a negative image of the hierarchy at the top?

If you sincerely desire the high motivational influence that results from encouraging everyone in the company to share in the decision making process, it is of prime importance that your company's managers refrain from *strutting* in performance of their jobs. It usually suggests they consider themselves superior to others who are lower on the organization chart. If you or your subordinate managers are perceived as having such an elitist attitude, there is little chance of your convincing lower level employees to adopt a team attitude toward shared goals.

In a March 23, 1987 review of Digital Equipment Corp. by Forbes Magazine, it was described as "a big company in small company clothes." The article noted that Digital Equipment doesn't believe in hierarchy, rule books, dress codes, company cars, executive dining rooms, lofty titles, or country club memberships. Its employee turnover rate is only five percent compared to a ten percent plus average for the rest of their industry. Further, their performance with regard to profit and growth is exemplary. These are the expected results of **stealth management**. Their example and that of numerous other companies are evidence of the value of eliminating hierarchy in your organization.

When arranging a meeting away from company premises, seek a meeting room that affords privacy. Provide flip charts, marker crayons, scratch pads, coffee, water, and soft drinks. The meeting might begin about mid-afternoon, end three hours later, and then break for a social period and dinner. It is not necessary to go to this expense, but it will add to the effectiveness of the meeting and give you a better atmosphere in which to sell the program.

Begin the meeting by listing on a flip-chart those things in your company that might cause employees to regard management as elitist. This is best done by asking the group to suggest items for such a list, and writing them on the chart. If, as sometimes happens, the meeting seems to stall, be prepared to ask questions such as, "How about reserved parking for executives?", or "How about our executives' vacation plan being different from others?" By having little input yourself and managing to get most of the list from the rest of the group, you will be encouraging the participative attitude necessary throughout this implementation process. Your preparation for this meeting also should include an agenda and as much thinking on the subject as you can put on a couple of sheets of paper. The agenda and notes are for your reference only should you need them. The meeting could result in a long list of items that will arouse worry, annoyance, and perhaps a little disgust — all of which may become evident, or they may subtly lie dormant. "After all, if we are to have no special privileges, why should we work so hard!", will be on the minds of most. It is your job to bring this thinking out and convince everyone that if these changes result in gradually improving company-wide performance by a large percentage, they as individuals will gain more than they give up. Further, when the process is completed, they may not have given up very much.

The list you compile of special top management privileges could include any or all of the following:

- Special parking location
- Special vacation and sick leave benefits
- Shorter work hours
- Better insurance or retirement benefits
- Benefits that include food, cars, and country clubs
- Miscellaneous time-off privileges

Eliminating these inequities will be hard to face. They need not all be changed at once. In fact, for your organization, spreading the process out over several months, and even timing portions of it with the start of a new fiscal year could be best. In my company, we made these changes concurrent with writing a new employee manual. It took us a few months to complete. Each section was written as a proposal and posted on the company bulletin board for all to see. A few days later, input was solicited from every employee — at the bottom level through personal contact by supervisors. This approach worked well because it fostered understanding of the new decision making process. Also, the input received from employees that might otherwise have been missed, helped us prevent mistakes.

In eliminating hierarchical influences, it is not necessary to eliminate all privileges, just those that are elitist in nature. For example, it is not elitist to have special parking areas near working sections of the business to minimize exposure to bad weather. Thus, you can provide a parking area near the office entrance for office personnel so long as it does not provide special places for key people. You should provide special convenient parking for the physically handicapped. It might be appropriate to provide a more convenient area for older employees. Such group privileges should be extended to personnel at all levels, not only office personnel. You may find it advisable to point this out to your planning group before their emotional responses take hold.

If your company owns country club memberships, they do not have to be discontinued. The company may still own the memberships and assign them to personnel who can use them to promote the company's goals. Those to whom a membership is assigned should be personally responsible for all membership fees and other charges. Those charges incurred in the direct interest of the company (defensible to I.R.S.) may be charged to expense accounts.

Initiate a management committee

If you do not already have a management group that meets with some regularity to exchange ideas and solve problems, it certainly would help to appoint such a group. If you are basically in manufacturing, for example, the group could include you, the production superintendent, the chief engineer, and the production engineer. In our company we held breakfast meetings at a nearby motel once a week. If you are a managing partner of an accounting firm, the group might consist of those who report directly to you plus any others who would be helpful discussing a particular account or a potential change in operations. An informal record of the discussion should be maintained to permit continuity and follow-up. Each meeting should be limited to a few problems and should end with assignments being made to insure completion of items un-finished by the end of the session.

As is true throughout the process of applying *Stealth Management*, when the management committee reaches consensus, its thinking and tentative conclusions should be communicated to the organization to invite further refinement and constructive input. This downward communication should have purpose and not occur inappropriately. For example, if it was decided to make changes in the shipping department, the plant superintendent should confer with the shipping foreman and discuss the changes being considered. After receiving the shipping room foreman's comments and suggestions, the foreman should confer with his shipping room employees and then return to the plant superintendent with any additional comment. In this way, by allowing communication on the subject or problem to filter up and down, it finally reaches back up to the management committee where it becomes a decision. It is not necessary that everyone agree — it is important to make everyone aware that their input is desired. Decision-making does not have to be subjected to such a time consuming process, nor is it necessary that all decisions be derived from a management committee or any other committee. An important purpose of this committee is to give you a communication and motivational tool that will engender a sense of progress and a participative company spirit.

In an article in the August 31, 1987 issue of Fortune magazine, Mr. Thomas J. Watson, Jr., former chief executive of I.B.M., was quoted as saying he had managed with the help of a council of eight to ten executives without whose opinions and decision making input his job would have been much more difficult. Whenever he found that some of this council were not growing in ability to keep up with the rapid growth of I.B.M., he would dissolve the committee and establish a new one with a different name. To the new committee he would appoint some new people and those of the former group who were still very valuable in the decision making process. His use of a management committee served him well during a period of amazing growth.

Orientation brochure

Establishing an orientation brochure for new employees is an excellent exercise to apply early in the process of implementing *stealth management* in your organization. Such a brochure will aid in establishing a good start for new employees, and by soliciting help from present employees in composing the brochure, you initiate the change in management style in a manner that is unlikely to be disturbing to anyone.

It is important for a new employee to feel wanted and become aware of what the company's business is, its value system, and the fringe benefits he may expect. Because all supervisors may not be able to do this consistently well, and also so that the employee will have something to show his or her family, a brochure specifically designed for this purpose should be provided. This brochure should be given some flair so as to convey the impression that you consider it important. An example of such an orientation brochure is the following:

"WELCOME TO COMPANY"

Your becoming an employee of _____ is the result of careful consideration by both you and the company. We will make every effort to see that you are pleased with your decision to accept this employment. We hope your job proves challenging and that you are motivated to help us achieve our company's goals.

Our business:

We started our business in and have enjoyed healthy growth ever since. You will discover that our company has respect for you as an employee and as a person. Your supervisor will be ready to help or counsel with you on problems you may have about your work.

Your value as an employee will be judged only by your perform-ance at your job and your participation as a member of our team. We hope you have a sense of obligation to your job and your fellow workers.

_____ (the company) strives to support many civic activi-ties, and in turn, depends on the community for many direct and indirect benefits. We encourage our employees to be good citizens and to contribute to our city and its institutions.

The following information should help acquaint you with our company. Please feel free to ask questions of your supervisor.

Hours and Pay

———

Overtime

———

Vacation and Holidays

———

Absence and Tardiness

———

Sick Leave

———

Performance Review

———

Profit Sharing

———

Medical and Life Insurance

———

Tools

———

Employee Manual

— — — — — — — — — — — — — — — —
— — — — — — — — — — — — — — — —

Most company policies referred to herein are subject to further explanation and possible revision. For this reason, the company employee manual governs all employment practices. Your supervisor will try to answer questions regarding the company's employee policies. Our plant manager and our personnel manager have copies of the employee manual which are available to you.

Work Environment

We believe that a pleasant work environment and a clean atmosphere in which to work is important to everyone. We all strive to reach this goal by keeping our work areas neat. Accidents can be prevented by your personally correcting safety hazards such as loose parts left on the floor that could cause someone to fall. Point out any hazards to your supervisor which cannot be so easily corrected.

Company Philosophy

We regard you as a thinking person who wants to do a good job — an employee who has or will have ideas to contribute to our mutual progress. You are invited to communicate your feelings about your job and your ideas for improving company performance to your supervisor.

We want to continue to grow and prosper for the benefit of our customers, our employees, and our stockholders. It is an undertaking that depends on all of us cooperating for success.

When our company went through the process of writing such a brochure, we posted copy of the proposed orientation brochure on the bulletin board and distributed copies to all lead-men and foremen who in turn personally solicited suggestions from all personnel. Many suggestions were adopted that contributed to the final version being more sensitive to the questions that new employees so commonly have. It provided a "hand-out" that all employees enjoyed taking home to their families.

Please note, in this example of an orientation brochure, there is no suggestion that the employee will be on trial for some extended period such as the typical 90 days. It is much better to promote a feeling of trust and optimism along with your expectation of good performance. Certainly your company policies should provide for supervisors to be inherently watchful of an employee during the early orientation period, but it should be a subtle part of the training process.

It will take longer for an employee to trust you if you start out not trusting him by suggesting that for the first several weeks he is on trial, and leave the impression that his job could be short lived. If a new employee for some reason does not fit in or does not perform satisfactorily, appropriate action should be taken. Such action is in no way precluded by starting the employee out with the more positive attitude suggested.

In spite of good intentions, some people may not properly read the employee orientation brochure. Therefore, supervisors should make it a policy to review it with all new employees to be sure it is understood and to respond to questions.

Orientation procedure

The time to provide a new employee with your orientation brochure, procedures, and information as to when and where to report to work is immediately upon hiring. A new employee should report to the personnel department or whoever has that responsibility, in the absence of such a department, when first reporting for work. The new employee should be escorted and introduced to his supervisor in a warm manner, assuming they had not met previously, and the supervisor should be made aware of any information about the employee that is related to the job. That might include experience, education or special training, and even interesting hobbies. The supervisor should see that the new arrival meets other employees in the department, and one other employee should agree to be close to the new employee during the first several days, acting as a trainer and/or mentor and thereby shorten the orientation period. The supervisor should, within the first couple days, see that the new employee has a tour of the facilities and is given an explanation of what is being done, insofar as such explanation may add some perspective to his job. Also, within the first several days, the supervisor's superior should be introduced to the new employee.

These procedures, which should be part of your company operations manual, are intended to give the employee a good start and see that he is welcomed into a friendly work environment. That should be followed up by attention from the supervisor during the first few weeks.

Housekeeping

It is certainly easier to motivate employees when they are proud of their work environment. If it is not neat, clean, and as attractive as practical, changes are in order. The following questions are simply illustrative and could be much different, depending on the type organization involved:

- Is there a pleasant place to enjoy coffee breaks and lunch?
- Are the rest rooms clean and well provisioned?
- Are all work areas properly lighted?
- Are air conditioning and heating adequate?
- Is the air kept clean and refreshed as necessary by filtering and change?
- Would a color scheme be helpful for the entire work area including desks, work benches, and equipment?
- Is janitorial service, or its equivalent, provided to keep things clean and reasonably neat throughout the work day?
- Are safety and noise levels given adequate attention?

These are the kinds of questions that should be asked. If practical, you might even seek decorator help, and whenever possible, ask for input from your employees as to what they would like. If they have no suggestions or they are less than practical, usually the desired participative effect can be gained by providing a choice. If employees are permitted to influence their work environment, they will inadvertently do a better job of keeping it neat. Neatness usually improves productivity.

The benefit of having a pleasant work environment extends far beyond improving employee morale. Industrial psychologists have written much on this subject, and such information is easily found. Your banker, customers, suppliers, and all visitors will have a better impression of your facility and a higher opinion of your ability to manage. When I went through the throes of selling our company, the initial appearance possibly added fifteen percent to the value of the company and, in one case, made the difference between interest or lack of it by the potential buyer. In some organizations, the executive offices are beautiful but at lower levels employees work in an atmosphere that suggests no one cares about them. Under such conditions, the worker is inadvertently encouraged to believe he does not rate.

"Roaming"

Roaming the ship is an expression used by Mr. Alex Katz, a frequent speaker for American Management, to describe the process of circulating among the employees of an organization. Perhaps you have also heard this referred to as *Management By Walking Around.* It is a rewarding activity for a manager of an organization so large that visiting with a majority of employees would not occur normally without making it a special activity.

If, for example, you have an organization of two hundred employees, it would be unlikely that in any given week you would visit with more than twenty-five of them. It is important that you visit most of them occasionally and that you be seen roaming the ship frequently — at least once or twice a week. Managers who have experienced the benefits of *roaming the ship* and have become committed to it often spend as much as one third of their time in this manner. It is not necessary that you visit everyone during each trip through the company, but over a period of several weeks it would be well to have visited with as many as possible.

Your visit with an individual should not seem perfunctory, but should focus on what the individual is doing. By showing interest in what a person is doing, you are showing interest in that person. The employee will feel good that you are interested and you will be amazed at what you can learn about your company. It affords an employee the opportunity to offer an opinion or a suggestion that might otherwise have been unshared.

When exercising this privilege, care must be taken not to leave the impression that you are by-passing other supervisors. Prevent this by first making your organization aware that it is an activity that you enjoy and one which you feel builds morale. You should never make a decision for another supervisor that would normally be his responsibility unless required to do so because of an emergency. You should communicate to an employee's supervisor any information or observations that might be helpful. This process will not cause discomfort at any level if done properly. After you have been doing it for some time, you should find each such individual visit a pleasant one, enjoyed by all. There is much less likelihood of creating impressions of hierarchy within your organization if you *roam the ship*.

To the activity of *Roaming the Ship* I like to add *Roaming the Ports*, by which is meant in-depth visiting by management with both customers and suppliers. This should be done not only by sales and purchasing personnel but also by top management. In an attempt to economize, sales people often are pressured to make a target number of sales calls per week and purchasing people too often are allowed insufficient time to visit a supplier's facilities. In most companies, management personnel never find time to visit suppliers and rarely visit customer facilities.

Roaming the Ports by managers should not be done in a manner that duplicates what is done by sales and purchasing departments. Your visits of this type usually would be infrequent and would be monitored to keep your time spent in this way within reasonable limits.

If you visit a major supplier and become acquainted with those in that company with whom your purchasing department does business and also visit with their management people, the mere fact that you show such consideration for them will reflect in improved regard for your purchasing agent thereafter. While there, you might bring up the subject of what your company could do to make their job easier, the results of which might astound you. One time, while visiting a foundry from whom we bought castings, such questioning resulted in our spending about $2,000 for new patterns from which we received better quality castings at a lower cost and, at the same time, improved the foundry's profits. We paid for the cost of this change in about seven months. Yes, our purchasing agent had previously discussed the possibility of such changes with them but had not received encouragement. The difference was my visiting the foundry personally and meeting with people within their company who chanced to have more imagination than those in contact with us previously.

Being participative with customers by discussing mutual problems with them is usually very productive. Failure to do so can sometimes be most harmful. In my former company, we had a customer who purchased nearly $1,000,000 per year of high-tech rubber parts which we custom molded for them. The customer had a high degree of faith in James, the supervisor we had in charge of their work. With our permission, they would occasionally visit our rubber department and knew James well enough to feel free to call him when they had problems having to do with quality or delivery. James was a very dedicated employee. It was not uncommon for him to forget to eat lunch. He also was very well liked by his employees for his knowledge and personality. On the negative side, he did not have a neat department and he was most reluctant to criticize an employee when necessary. Sometimes, rather than emphasize a deadline that had to be met, he would take over and do the job himself, during which period his other supervisory duties would be neglected. There were those in our company who wanted James to be fired because he had not changed as a result of criticism from his immediate superior. Fortunately, I was made aware of the situation and prevailed on our people to work around it by compensating for James' shortcomings and to try to change him over a longer period of time. Another factor was that he had only five years before reaching retirement age. Two days after the new owners removed me as president, James called me at home to inform me he had been fired, of which I had known nothing. Within a month, the large customer, who had been fond of James, decided to start their own rubber molding facility and hired him. Within six months, my former company completely lost the account. Had they gone to the customer and discussed the problem, a corrective program could have been worked out without having to lose that business. The customer would have preferred not having to do their own rubber molding and ceased doing so a few years later.

If your company is product oriented, visiting with customers by your managers is particularly important. It is said that overall, as much as one half of new products and/or product improvements stem from customer input. Without soliciting such participation from customers, much of this benefit could be lost to your company.

Inasmuch as this discussion is about metaphorically *roaming the ship* and it's ports, let's go a little further in thinking of the company as a ship. If it were a cruise ship and we wanted to ensure a happy voyage, typically we would want to encourage the passengers to become acquainted and have a good time together. Only good things will result from your people enjoying themselves while achieving at high levels. One of our production workers asked for permission to have an April birthday party for four employees who were having birthdays that month. We approved, and during a normal lunch period, a buffet table was set up supplied with dishes of food brought in by the employees. The party took some planning during which people got to know one another a little better, the company opened up the soft drink machines, and people had a good time. They were careful not to encroach on job time and did a good job of cleaning up.

Whenever there was a retirement, a transfer, or even on the occasion of an employee leaving our employ for good reason, we usually had a party, either at lunch or after work. At such occasions I would say a few words about the employee and present a gift from the group. My few words were always chosen not only to create a positive atmosphere but also to convey some information about the honoree that could make the others feel a little closer to that person. At our company, there seemed to be a party for some reason every few weeks. It made communication easier, and cooperation seemed better as a result.

Overview of first steps

The first steps in implementing **stealth management** may require considerable compromise and change in their application to your organization. It will make a difference whether your organization is "white collar" and service oriented or manufacturing with largely "blue collar" employees. It will certainly make a difference if your company employs a large percentage of scientists or engineers, as in the case of a research organization. The same principles apply, however, and a participative approach should still be used. The fact that change based on your new *stealth management* style is happening is the important thing. If applied in a gradual manner, there will be less potential for disturbed morale at the outset. In fact, instituting too much change at one time could prove difficult to manage and also create unrest and dissatisfaction. The end result will be greater participation at all levels of the organization, improved communications within the company, reduced labor turnover, and elevated levels of motivation. Coupled with the impact of proper planning, these changes will contribute to greater profitability and increased personal satisfaction at all levels.

40 · What Is Your Business

One of the most important questions to be addressed by the management team of a business is, "What *is* our business?"

The story is told of a business man who, when asked, "What business are you in?" replied, "We make bobby pins, the best bobby pins in the world!" Six months later hair sprays were introduced, and before long the man was out of business. Had he replied, instead, "We are in the business of making hair care products," and operated his business with that broader definition in mind, he might have adapted to change as required.

In our company, until we properly addressed the question of "What *is* our business?", most of our key personnel were suffering from very narrow vision which, in turn, inhibited growth. Our principal activity was the manufacture of cable assemblies used by the seismic industry in oil exploration. Because such cable was complex and "high-tech" in nature, we often would be offered jobs involving "high-tech" cabling for other industries. Each time we took such a job, I would receive severe criticism from subordinates (see topic 1) with comments such as, "We're too busy! We don't need it!" During the exercise of defining our business, we reflected on the fact that we were totally dependent on an ever-continuing search for oil, of which there was but a finite amount to be found. Further, the best estimates by geologists and geophysicists, at that time, indicated that the world might very well be nearly out of oil within thirty to forty years. Obviously our young employees could not look forward to a long career in such a company. As a result, the group decided that henceforth, in that division of our company, our business would be defined as, "The design and fabrication of high technology wire and cable products." Never again was there resistance to expanding into other fields, and within a year, over twenty-five percent of our wire and cable business was from outside the seismic industry.

Literally, a book could be written depicting a myriad of fascinating stories about companies that experienced great benefit, and (sometimes) rejuvenation from redefining their businesses. By all means, define your business! And, most importantly, have your employees participate in this exercise. The definition for each division of a larger company, or for the entire company in the case a smaller business, should be one sentence or phrase in which each word is carefully chosen.

The most effective way to address the question of what is your business is through use of the brain-storming technique as described in topic 51. If you are intimidated by such an activity or feel someone else is eminently more qualified, you might appoint another person to lead this session. You will, however, improve your leadership image by conducting it yourself. Also, because there will be so many occasions for group discussions and group decision-making, each such experience will make you more comfortable in that type of management role.

When you next have a family oriented decision to be made, such as the purchase of a new home or a new car, try using a group discussion to arrive at a consensus. Even though you and your mate, in

effect, make the decision, involving children of thinking age by re-
questing their opinions will have a very positive effect on them, and
they may even have some beneficial input. The practice will be good
for you. I know of one former chief executive officer of a sizable
business, with a large family, who used this conference technique in a
rather unusual manner. Once a week he would hold the equivalent
of a board of directors meeting at which each of his five children,
his wife, or himself could bring up any subject appropriate for
family discussion. The purpose of the meeting was to solve problems concerning the children, eliminate causes for dissension, promote the sharing of chores, and give everyone an opportunity to
"let off steam". The technique may not have eliminated all family
problems. But after many years and with the children all gone from
the nest, the family is a very close and caring one. They take every
opportunity to be together.

41 • Value System, Mission, and Philosophy

Creating a statement of mission, philosophy, or ethics is encouraged generally, but such statements need not be committed to a
written form for most small businesses, particularly in their early
years. This does not mean that your organization does not need a value
system or a mission — it most certainly does, although in small
companies, such important influences are established by the leader's
example. If your business has grown to the point at which you no
longer know everyone in it by name and do not get to talk with each
of them occasionally, perhaps you then need a mission statement and
a statement of your value system. When written statements of your
organization's values, mission, or philosophy are required, have them
completed and make all managers aware of them.

A mission statement must include an expression of what you
want to be, not merely what you now are or what you now do. Too
often a mission statement is a mere abstract and platitudinous statement of purpose that has not been framed with intent to provide
direction for the organization. Not only should a mission statement
provide direction, but it can also add zeal to the pursuit of well chosen

goals. It is more than mere purpose. For an organization that is involved with charity or considered socio-cultural in nature, defining its mission is very important. Examples of such organizations are the Y.M.C.A., a university, a chamber of commerce, or a museum. In such cases, a statement of mission might replace the answer to the question "what is our business?" Sometimes, particularly with larger companies, a statement of mission serves to improve a company's public image by including a claim of unusual service, superb quality, patriotism, or civic pride. A manufacturer of military equipment could include, as part of its mission, dedication to preserving the peace. In organizations that suffer frequent changes of leadership, a mission statement could serve to keep in better focus their purpose for being in business.

If your organization does have a statement of mission, philosophy, or ethics, it is important for management to approve it fully and consistently apply its precepts in their activities. To have a mission statement that belies or exaggerates what is actually practiced by your company will cause employees to be more cynical toward management rather than respond in a positive influence.

You may wonder what is meant by adding purpose and direction to your company's operation. For example, a writer of historical novels might define his business as the writing of historical novels for that portion of society who find such reading enjoyable. If he adds a mission as part of his vocational orientation, he might include as part of his mission the enhancement of historical knowledge for those who read his books. To include such a goal as part of his mission does add purpose and direction to his work. It then requires him to be careful to ascertain that his historical references are accurate, and doing so requires considerably more time for him to complete each of his works.

In the future, if you could look back at your organization and evaluate its performance and impact within your industry or on society at large, you might divide these considerations into two categories, those that are profit oriented and those that are other than financially oriented. Those achievements that are not so financially oriented would be furthered through adherence to a mission. Indirectly, even the bottom line performance is often benefited, albeit on a long term basis. If an automobile manufacturer defined his business as the manufacture of multi-wheeled vehicles, designed for highway travel, that use petroleum products for fuel, for both personal and commercial use, he could proceed to do this with his primary goal being the making of profit for the owners and with little attention given to his impact on society and its standard of living or to his customers.

Suppose he added to his mission: (1) To so conduct his business as to make his employees and community proud of his company; (2) through the application of good design, to improve safety, convenience of operation, and pride of ownership; and, (3) endeavor to have a positive long term influence on society by pricing his product reasonably and yet permitting a fair return on investment for the investor. With these changes the mission statement includes a bit of philosophy. You can readily see that such a mission statement would have a profound influence on the future of the company. We can also conjecture what a difference there would be in our automobile industry had they had a well defined mission to guide them through the past 50 years. As a company matures, having a proper mission statement becomes increasingly important.

A university is an especially suitable type organization with which to associate the application of a mission statement. A possible mission statement for a typical state university having a varied curriculum, in excess of 25,000 students, and offering degrees in most of the arts and sciences through that of a doctorate might be:

- With an admissions bias that will result in 90% of our student body being residents of our state, we will admit all applicants, without regard for race, creed, or color, who meet selection criteria that permit us to maintain average academic standards as determined by nationally recognized testing procedures
- We will offer degrees through that of doctorate in engineering, arts, sciences, law, and medicine

- We will endeavor, with the help of state and alumni support, to establish tuition fees not to exceed 35% of our gross expense per student and, further, to extend scholarship aid to at least thirty percent of our enrollment
- We will conform to all applicable state and federal laws and require that our student body deport themselves as good citizens while attending our university

Most universities have a statement of mission as part of their plan. Both the mission statement and plan are too detailed to indicate a complete sample. The foregoing mission statement, although much abbreviated, might not be too different in its broad context from that of many universities. But suppose in addition to the four items mentioned, the following were added:

- As a long range goal, it is our intent to contribute responsibly to a better society by exposing each of our students to secular training that will make them more apt to be happy and therefore potentially better parents.

With the above addition, a university's planning would be different, and perhaps their approach would become an extremely popular one. We can assume that if all people are brought up well, and in happy families, the world will have fewer problems. If true, then with the addition of the last long range goal, it would seem appropriate for the university to offer a course in parenting and social responsibility to every student.

A statement of mission can have great influence for all organizations. All the psychology that applies to being a good manager also applies to being a good parent. Therefore, references to parenting have their place in a management book. In fact, it would be difficult to find a good manager who does not have those characteristics that make for a good parent. There are many managers, however, who fail to make the connection and do not take home these selfsame skills.

A cautionary note about the hypothetical university mission statement: the long range goal associated with the need for a course in parenting and social responsibility would be the subject for considerable brainstorming. Only after much debate should a decision of such magnitude be reached. It is important to note in connection with a mission statement for your company that it can have a serious impact on your future.

As head of a business, if you consider it important for those in your organization to participate in civic affairs and be good citizens, this philosophy can be encouraged by the message in your mission statement. For example, if you manage a steel foundry that markets regionally, it would be beneficial if your people had such an attitude toward community service. Your mission statement could read (in part): "We will strive to be at the frontier of industrial modernization, as it may pertain to our business, so that we can offer our customers superior products and service. We will conduct our business in a manner that fosters excellent relations with our suppliers, our employees, our customers, and our community."

In all mission statements, whether you are providing a service or a product, those who receive the service or purchase the product should be kept in mind. Without them there is no need for the organization. The mission should not be directed principally at serving owners or stockholders. Those companies who are strongly customer oriented are usually most successful. You take care of your obligation to the stockholder in your planning process; after all, if you do not prosper financially, even your customer soon will be unable to depend on you. A non-profit organization or a publicly franchised organization such as a regional bank should consider the people they serve as their constituency and primarily direct their mission statement toward that group. In so doing, they engender maximum customer support. They should set financial goals for their business during the planning process and address them through the on-going operations that follow.

Any organization's leaders should, through their example, define the value system that they have chosen to prevail throughout the organization and its activities. As chief officer of the company, by consistently applying the golden rule (do unto others as you would have them do unto you) and otherwise conducting yourself ethically, those who report to you will know intuitively that the same standard of ethics is expected of them. It should not be necessary, for example, for a purchasing agent to refer to a written code of ethics in order to know that accepting a bribe in the course of performing his job would result in censure or dismissal. Therefore, a written code of ethics is not necessary in many small companies. The value system of a small business is the value system of the founder, owner, or top manager. However, with proper legal advice, appropriate claimers and disclaimers should be included in your operations manual and associated writings. It is important, for example, to indicate that the company's employment practices follow the federal guidelines for equal opportunity.

If your organization's stock is publicly traded or about to be listed on any exchange, a written statement of your company value system would be desirable in addressing values that concern overall corporate behavior. In the small company, a value system is directed more toward individual behavior; the chief executive officer of the company is responsible for corporate behavior. With larger companies, the importance of a written statement of values cannot be over-emphasized. Thomas Peters and Robert Waterman in their book, "In Search of Excellence", assert, "Every excellent company we studied is clear on what it stands for, and takes the process of value shaping seriously. In fact, we wonder whether it is possible to be an excellent company without clarity on values and without having the right sorts of values."

Regardless of how you establish your value system, it is vital that your employees know what their organization stands for. Such knowledge will permit easier decision making and help them realize they are associated with a company of character.

Some companies have a written code of conduct that differs from a value system in that it more specifically concerns the attitude employees are expected to have toward their job. Such a code might include the following:

- Be receptive to change and the ideas of others
- Strive to achieve your potential
- Be honest in all communications and attitudes
- Be a good team member

- Do whatever is appropriate to help the organization achieve its goals

The greatest benefit that you will derive from exercises that define your business, establish a mission statement, or state your values is the unifying effect on your employees. This effect can be very marked if the exercise is done in a manner that involves everyone and uses language that is understood by all. Little benefit will result from establishing a mission statement as a result of deliberation by only those managers at the top, without others in the organization having had an opportunity for input. An employee who likes what your organization does, what it stands for, and what its long range goals are will obviously be a more dedicated member of the team.

42 • Planning

Introduction

This topic addresses the process of operational and strategic planning as it might be implemented by a small to medium sized business. There is no set planning process that would be ideal for all organizations, but there are some basic steps that are almost always applicable.

Business planning improves the likelihood that an organization will progress and grow to become what it wants to be; it tends to make the future happen on purpose; and, it increases management effectiveness. It can be likened to planning a trip. You know where you are and to where you want to travel. You next, or simultaneously, decide when you will begin the trip, when you will arrive at your destination, what it will cost, and how much time the trip will take. Finally, you decide what will be your means of travel, what financial arrangements you have to make, and what clothing and luggage you will need. The last group of decisions and preparing for possible contingencies are the strategic portions of the plan, because they have options, they require assumptions, and there often are contingencies beyond your control. For example, health considerations for you or a close relative could make it necessary to cancel your travel plans at the last minute. You would be wise, if such circumstances exist, to purchase travel insurance that would prevent financial loss of prepayments toward the trip.

Very few people would take a vacation without going through such thinking, so it is difficult to understand why, in the world of business, so many leaders fail to use a similar planning process. It certainly is true that success can be achieved without it, but most often long range achievement would be enhanced greatly by good strategic planning. Perhaps too many business leaders confuse budgeting with planning, whereas budgeting is but a small part of planning.

Never in history has mankind been subject to change that occurs so rapidly as now. In the field of manufacturing, competition is causing product life cycles to shrink, while at the same time technological considerations and the need for better quality is lengthening new product development time. If you are involved in selling a service, the service you sell and the marketing procedures you use are probably in a constant state of flux. More than ever, risk and change are inherent in business, and therefore good planning is necessary to minimize failure. The tangible result is a written guideline for the development and control of the organization.

The question has been asked, "Can an organization over-plan?" There is no positive answer, but the question does deserve discussion. A more appropriate question might be, "Can too much attention and importance be given to planning?" Just as an investor should provide for financial flexibility to permit taking advantage of unforeseen opportunities and being able to cope with unexpected contingencies, so must an organization provide for and be prepared to modify its plan. Such change could be necessitated by the contingencies provided for in the plan or by unforeseen problems. An unexpected opportunity could also be the trigger for a substantial change. Success often is the result of being able to take advantage of opportunity with good timing and decisiveness, and planning permits such action when the best interests of the organization are well served.

Planning is never perfect and goals often are not met. The effectiveness of a plan is best measured by the degree to which it helped optimize performance, not merely by goal achievement.

Planning overview

Planning is either strategic or operational in nature. Strategic planning has to do with the future and sometimes is thought of as answering the question, "What businesses do we want to be in the future?" As indicated in the introduction to this section, strategic planning also involves those influences and contingencies over which you have little control. Operational planning sometimes is thought of as answering the question, "How can we do the best job of running the business or businesses we are in?" Operational and strategic planning overlap considerably, to be sure.

The plan for a project or a campaign is usually for a relatively short period of time compared to the length of a strategic plan for a business enterprise. That was not true of the United States plan for putting a man on the moon, however. Called for originally by President Kennedy, it was a ten year plan and is considered by many professional management consultants to be an example of virtually perfect planning and plan implementation. It culminated with man landing on the moon and returning to earth successfully in accordance with a seemingly perfect schedule that required great creativity and the coordination of several teams of very diverse talents. However, in the business arena, as in other organizations, a plan for a given project would rarely be so long — usually not more than 24 months. Examples would be a United Way campaign, the opening of a new store, building a new office building, or the design of a new consumer product. Planning, applied to such projects will be discussed in topic 44.

The planning that directly addresses the future of an organization, or of your business, normally extends into the future at least five years and sometimes much further. Referred to as strategic planning, it usually is a time consuming and difficult task. It involves a greater range of influences that must be considered, is much more apt to require revision and, in reality, is never completed. The lack of completion is not negative — it usually means a five year plan becomes a revised five year plan a year or two later.

If your organization has not been involved with this kind of planning previously, be aware that becoming involved with and appreciating its importance is much more important than developing a perfect plan. In lieu of completeness, it is better to arrive at an abbreviated plan that gives the company direction accompanied by a sense of improved performance, and leave completion of the planning process until later. In fact, planning can be frustrating, annoying, intimidating, and sometimes even disruptive to an organization involved with it for the first time. In order to ensure long term acceptance and optimize the probability of initial success, it sometimes is better to apply planning in its simplest form the first time and apply it with more sophistication after proving it is of benefit.

The process of planning, properly activated, will involve most people in your organization and should give them a sense of participation in your goal setting, a deeper understanding of their personal importance, and commitment to the plan. It is these attitudinal influences that usually improve performance, communication, and team effort. To reiterate, the plan is important, but the process of planning is more important. It has been said that planning is learning and that its main thrust is to further the development of professional managerial ability within your organization.

Your planning group should include all those who are key decision makers in your organization. The group should not be too large, preferably not more than seven or eight people. You should call on other personnel to participate at such times as their particular area of knowledge would aid the group. Before you begin, it is important to appoint a planning coordinator whose responsibilities to the planning group include:

- Saving written records for subsequent meetings
- Keeping records secret from people not in the planning group to prevent information from being taken out of context prior to becoming part of the final plan (secrecy can be abandoned after the planning process nears completion)
- Writing up a review of each session for reference at the start of the next session
- Assembling the proposed overall plan as parts of it are decided upon

- Coordinating the garnering of comments and suggested changes from people outside the planning group when such input is called for
- Providing the chief executive officer with sufficient copies of the completed plan for him to distribute

Because the person you select as coordinator needs to have communication skills and be impartial in the keeping of these records, a trusted secretary could be a good choice. In a small company the choice may be limited, in which case a member of the planning committee could be the coordinator. In my company, because our treasurer had the proper skills and could perform these duties without interfering with his participation in the planning process, he handled them except for the typing.

Before the planning process formally begins, it would be wise for you to appoint someone, or assume the duty yourself, to become knowledgeable of predictions about your business environment for the future. That does not mean, for example, that you should be prepared to advise the group that interest rates will follow any particular path over the next five years; that could be too subjective. Instead, you would inform them that the average of information obtained from the trust department of your bank, publications from the federal government, and other reputable sources suggest that interest rates will vary between certain extremes and with some likely pattern of change. Any factors to which your business is sensitive should be studied in this manner. These might include the business cycle, weather patterns, inflation trends, commodity shortages, tax changes, population trends, political influences, and such influences as dress styles and product life cycles. How to factor such information into planning will be discussed later.

Although smaller companies often cannot justify such expense, employing an objective outsider as a facilitator is a very wise step if you are going into a planning operation for the first time. He should be familiar with the planning process and be given adequate knowledge about your organization beforehand, so that he can help your planning group stay on course with all participants contributing freely.

Where have you been

An organization that has not utilized group planning in the past should begin by reviewing the history of the company or organization in order to provide good perspective about the company's origins, trends, and past response to change. In a company that has been planning, in this manner, for some time, it is only necessary that those who are new members of the planning group be given this background.

As previously suggested, the planning group of a small company should be composed of the top person in the company (who would usually have the title of owner, chairman, or president), and all managers who directly report to him. The group should not number more than 10 people and should include the person in charge of each major area of responsibility. In a manufacturing company, that would include those in charge of marketing, sales, engineering, research, finance, production, and purchasing. Of course, some organizations do not have each of those titles and yours may have some I have not mentioned. At times, during the planning process, it may be desirable to invite others whose presence would not be needed at all such meetings. For example, when discussing manpower requirements or other facets of human resource management, it would be appropriate for the personnel or human resource manager to be present, and he should be invited if he was not already included in the group.

Because premature communication of their activities can permit such knowledge to be taken out of context, often to the detriment of the company, the planning group should be advised and convinced of the need to be secretive about their discussions until the time comes to seek input to the plan from personnel at other levels of the organization.

The discussion of where you have been is not normally a very time consuming activity. It should consist of a verbal history of the company, reviewed by the employee having the longest affiliation, and an ensuing question-answer period. The purpose of this review is to assure that those responsible for the company planning activity have a thorough understanding of the history of the company. It can help in a variety of ways not the least of which would be knowledge of the mistakes and successes of the past. During the same session, it would be profitable to continue on into a review of where you are now.

Where are you now

Reviewing where your company is now should consist of a detailed analysis of your financial condition, marketing effectiveness, potential for growth, personnel, employee relations, trends, and new developments. Much of this portion of the planning process consists of reports to the planning group given by the personnel manager, the chief financial officer, the CEO and others as necessary. These reports should be presented in a manner that permits easy reference during the process to follow. For example, they might include graphs, slides, or written data tacked on the wall or available as individual copies. Such data adds perspective and permits the group to more intelligently contribute to planning. You will not have to put up with outlandish suggestions in terms of financial requirements if every one has up-to-date financial information about the company. Your review might highlight a key person who plans to retire within a short time for whom there is not a suitable replacement. Since this portion of your planning does not encourage participation to the degree that other aspects of planning do, these reports should be given in a manner that promotes discussion. The background provided will help the group to participate more effectively.

After the foregoing review, a discussion should follow that produces a list of weaknesses, opportunities, threats, and strengths associated with the organization as perceived by the planning group. Such a list is often referred to as a "WOTS" list. It is important that there be general consensus for the conclusions of this discussion and that the results be listed on a flip chart and revised as necessary. The group needs to realize that your company possesses much creativity and design ability but is weak in marketing skills, if such is the case. It would be important to know that a small but potentially strong competitor could be purchased at a reasonable price. This discussion usually produces much information that is not generally known and serves to stimulate group thinking. Because it also encourages criticism, those present must feel they are trusted and will not suffer recrimination of any type as a result of their candor. Even though some suggestions for the "WOTS" list seem trivial, because each person believes his ideas have merit, it encourages participation to include them all whenever it is practical.

The "WOTS" list is intended to bring out changes needed by the company to correct weaknesses, minimize the effect of potential threats, or take advantage of a strength that had not previously been realized. This is a good time to discuss the need for such changes, but unless there is urgency, postpone them until you are further along with your planning. A change made at this time may need to be refined, revised, or reversed as a result of subsequent steps.

Where does the present path lead you ?

This is a significant question for the company. A more challenging question is, "are you progressing as well as you can, and if not, what should you do about it?" To begin this discussion, it is helpful to have a chart, half of which shows pertinent data about your business for the preceding five years, the other half to forecast the ensuing five years. There is nothing magic in a ten year period, but it is wise to use a sufficiently long period to provide perspective. The data that is reviewed should include sales volume, profit before tax, and net worth. Charts for each division, product line, or service offered should also be prepared, but these would show only trend lines for sales and profit before tax.

As the process continues, it may be desirable to add more data to these charts, such as return on capital, overhead detail, borrowing, and inventory. It is impractical to study all the factors that influence the well being of an organization in this manner. An example of such a chart follows:

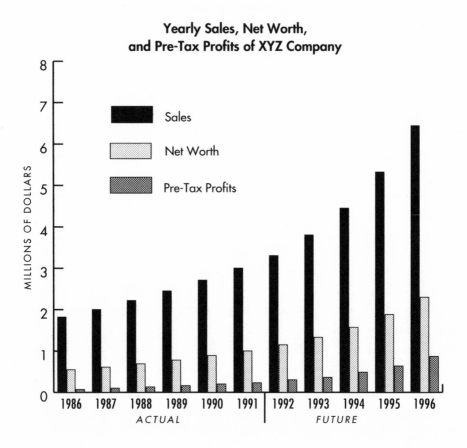

Yearly Sales, Net Worth, and Pre-Tax Profits of XYZ Company

In the foregoing chart, it has been assumed that the company will continue to progress about as it has in the past, without any major trend changes. It indicates sales, net worth, and profit before tax in solid lines for the five year prior period and in dotted lines for the five years you project. In projecting five years ahead, it is necessary to make many assumptions. These should be given careful consideration and be noted for subsequent reference. Typical assumptions would have to do with such factors as inflation rate, interest cost, market trends, tax rates, new competition, and new products or services to be offered.

After this exercise, if discussion is encouraged, the group will have a good idea where present policies and trends will take the organization over the following five years.

Where would you like to go

Ask the group to consider where they would like the Company to be five years out; are they happy with the projected gains and present trends, or should changes be considered that would produce greater achievement? If changes are needed, what changes would be desirable and how can they be implemented?

Perhaps the group favors necessary change to accelerate growth but cannot think of specific improvements that are practical. In such case, you would be wise to stimulate them with an appropriate comment such as, "Referring back to our review of company strengths and weaknesses, there seemed to be a consensus that we were strong in innovation but weak in marketing and sales. Let's address our weakness in marketing and sales. What can we do to improve in those areas?" You might ask the group to suggest a list of actions or changes that would enhance performance. Such a list could include nearly every aspect of business, but usually one or two would stand out as worthy of focus by the group. The discussion should be nudged toward providing some specific steps for the company to take. After a consensus has been reached in that regard, it should be made part of your planning and evaluated for impact on sales, profit, personnel and any other facet of the company that might be affected. A company probably does not exist for whom a planning group could not compile a list of improvements of this kind.

Many planning groups conclude their study of "Where would you like to Go?" with a vision of what they desire for the company five years hence.

After the above analysis has produced a consensus, or decision by you, of the changes that will be made to provide the desired progress and growth, go back to the chart prepared in your study of "Where does the present path lead you" and factor in the expected impact from these changes. You now have new goals to plan for. Now time out must be taken for financial analysis. What will be the effect on capital requirements, banking relationships, manpower, new equipment, available floor space, and any budgeted factors that must be considered.

To properly put all this into perspective, a chart such as the following should be prepared for the period you are planning:

XYZ Company – Projected Five Year Plan
Dollars in Thousands

	actual –1991	1992	1993	1994	1995	1996
Starting Net Worth	$1,000	$1,150	$1,331	$1,566	$1,882	$2,297
Total Capital incl. borrowings	1,500	1,675	1,930	2,220	2,820	3,540
Sales	3,000	3,300	3,800	4,446	5,313	6,440
Costs of products sold	1,980	2,178	2,508	2,890	3,453	4,150
Indirect expenses	790	825	930	1,070	1,222	1,420
Earnings before tax	230	297	362	486	638	870
Earnings after tax	150	193	235	316	415	565
Ending Net Worth	1,150	1,343	1,566	1,882	2,297	2,862
Additional Personnel (production)	–	20	23	26	30	34
Additional Personnel (non-production)	–	4	4	5	6	7
New Equip. needed	–	100m	0	25m	0	40m
Inventory	–	560m	624m	698m	840m	935m

Assumptions:

(1) No new floor space will be required if a second shift is added in 1992.

(2) With improved inventory control, growth of inventory can be kept to 75% of increase in sales.

(3) Interest rates will not change appreciably.

(4) No emergencies such as flood, fire, strike, etc. will be encountered.

(5) Inflation rates will remain under 5%

(6) Wage rates will not increase faster than 7% per year.

(7) Neither international events nor labor unrest will have impact upon our operations.

(8) Our competition will not perform in a manner appreciably different from our appraisal of them.

(9) We will not experience any major deterioration in the national economy.

(10) A tax rate of 35% will apply.

Many other assumptions could be added to this list. Your planning group must decide which ones are significant. Further, the example, which analyzes several important facets of the XYZ Company, will be much different if applied to your organization. After leading the planning operation and arriving at the foregoing plan, it would be well to consider it only as a proposed plan. That will afford you an opportunity to have it constructively reviewed by all those in your organization who have not yet been given the opportunity for input. This should be done by breaking the plan up into portions that can be identified with a given department. If you had three production areas, each responsible for a particular product, for example, the person in charge of each area should be provided with sufficient pertinent data to enable him to review the planning for his department. He should be encouraged to offer comment and suggestions. He in turn should see to it that every person who reports to him has an opportunity for constructive review. This process should reach as far through the organization as possible, not only to gain from the numerous suggestions that can result but also to make everyone aware that their thinking is important. This review process should be company-wide. Those who have suggestions or criticisms should be heard and thanked for their help. Suggestions not adopted should be acknowledged with reasons for them not having been used.

You need a timetable

You now know where you are going and when you want to arrive, but you also need a timetable that sets benchmarks for interim progress. Only with such a planned schedule of progress can you control adherence to the plan. The group must now decide how much change can be accomplished during each six months period of the plan (for example), and this projected rate of progress must be reviewed and approved by all department heads to establish commitment to the plan. Sometimes, this review can result in last minute change to the plan.

In the five year chart you have prepared (see XYZ Co. — Projected Five Year Plan), you have carefully estimated year end values for many measures of progress in attaining your goals. You should not wait until year end, however, to see if you are progressing as planned. Instead, break the plan down into smaller segments, perhaps three or six month intervals, and set targets for each such period. Necessary variance from projections and revisions will be easier to manage.

The trip is planned

You now have completed the group processes of defining your business, establishing a mission for it, setting long term goals for your organization, reviewing the necessary assumptions, and approving a scenario that can be monitored from time to time to assure adherence to the plan. You also have made sure that the tools (typically money and people) are all available as needed in applying the plan.

It now is necessary to take all steps practical to avoid hazards and accommodate to adverse influences that could make your planning program ineffective. Yes, you have already addressed, as part of a WOTS list, what threats you may encounter and in your planning have made many assumptions that relate to potential future problems; but, probably, your considerations in this area are still incomplete.

Suppose your organization has a large inventory of engineering drawings or a large data-base about your customers that could be lost in the event of fire, and such a catastrophe might severely test your ability to continue in business. Consideration of such eventualities may suggest that you have a fireproof storage facility for such data and permit dissemination from therein of copies only; or, alternatively, the establishment of duplicate microfilmed copies of all such data at a separate location.

In the event of fire, flood, or other disruptions that might prevent your operating at full activity, how could you provide for retaining your organization? "Use and occupancy" or "business interruption" insurance might be the answer for such a contingency. The possible contingencies of such severity are numerous, but experience and forethought should make you aware of them. Most require little more than an awareness of their potential and a plan for reacting to them. However, just as occasional fire drills improve reaction to a fire in a school or large office building, so does pre-planning improve reaction to emergencies of all kinds.

Problem prevention

Eliminating all problems is really an impossibility. Many can be prevented and, more often than not, you can minimize their negative impact by identifying them in their early stages. Preventing or minimizing problems requires close adherence to your plan, verifying the continuing validity of assumptions, and constant awareness of external influences. The upward flow of communications that occurs so effectively under the *stealth management* system is of vital importance. Your subordinates can be of tremendous help in preventing or minimizing problems if they have the ideal team spirit; they are aware of them first.

As the plan is being implemented, it is important to assess whether or not you have been too optimistic or too pessimistic with regard to goal setting or speed of implementation. If you determine such is the case, revise the plan to ensure achievability. If team spirit and free communication are encouraged, your potential for minimizing and eliminating problems is greatly improved. These characteristics are vital, particularly in the small organization, where controls usually are looser. The planning group should ask, "What can adversely affect success over which we have no control?" Such potential pitfalls should be listed and constantly monitored. The typical item on such a list is external, as opposed to originating within the organization, and might include such things as changes in the tax law, new competition, interest rates, international events, or any of the items covered in the following discussion of contingencies.

Contingencies

If a contingency occurs in your organization, will those who report to you know how to respond? Has a plan of action been reviewed and agreed upon? On such an occasion, time may not permit group consultation; prompt action may be required. As a first step in this area, a list of contingency categories should be made. These should include the following:

- Employee health and welfare
- Quality of service or product
- Physical damage to plant or equipment
- Supplier problems
- Catastrophic act of nature
- Economic downturn
- Changes in the competition

A proposed response to a typical problem in each category ought to be reviewed and established. Even if individual problems of this type are unlikely, preparation will make your people more able to cope quickly and effectively. For example, you might suffer a sudden high rejection rate due to a quality problem. Should you shut down production, should you notify salesmen and customers, or should you curtail deliveries from suppliers? These are but a few of the questions that could be applicable. If your shop superintendent operated merely on instinct, his response could be wrong and unnecessarily costly. It also might have a negative impact upon employees, customers, and suppliers that could take a long time to repair. An established checklist would permit rapid response with a high probability of being correct.

The following actions under such a contingency might prevent the mistakes that could be made as a result of instinctive reaction:

- Cease shipments of defective material
- Quickly determine if repairing defects would be less costly than a shutdown of production
- Make a fast estimate of changes needed to eliminate the cause of a problem and the time required to implement them
- Stop production if previous considerations determine that such action is wise
- If conditions permit, and with as little disruptive influence as possible, implement corrective changes without ceasing production
- Provide for corrective action on previous production on hand and resume shipment of approved product as soon as possible
- Notify management, purchasing, and sales as the situation requires

With the foregoing steps, corrective action can be accomplished rapidly. In most cases, this type of decision making would be natural and would not require prior thinking, but the world of management is replete with examples of bad decisions made under duress that could have been prevented.

In the event of a problem that could expose employees to harm, and if even short term exposure would be dangerous, prompt corrective action is mandatory. All personnel might have to be evacuated from the premises regardless of the cost. If short term exposure would have no dangerous impact, then corrective action as soon as practical with as little disruptive influence on personnel is reasonable. In our company, we became aware at one time that exposure to toluene could be very harmful. We did use toluene to clean rubber jacketed cable. In conformance with what then was considered acceptable safety practice, we began to use an O.S.H.A. approved type of safety dispenser for toluene. The change was not considered as having short term urgency, so we made the change within a few days — as rapidly as possible — without being alarming about the long range effect of excessive exposure. Since then, it has been determined that even the safety dispensers, under certain conditions, could be unsafe.

Another Approach to Planning

Another approach to planning could start with a conclusion that you would work toward. Suppose that, although your capacity for growth is higher, you would like to plan for only seven percent growth per annum over the next five years. Since such an approach usually would shorten the planning process, it might be the approach of choice. You should realize, however, that the more aggressive approach outlined previously can provide more rapid growth even though it may also be accompanied by greater risk.

Should you chose to plan with a more conservative growth target, you can use the steps outlined in the early portion of this topic and reduce the planning time required by only considering those changes needed to gain a desired percentage of growth. Also, since these changes would presumably be but a portion of the suggestions that your planning group developed, they could chose those that would be easier to implement and achieve. Otherwise the planning process should be the same.

Implementing the plan

Now that your planning group has formulated a plan, and all those who might possibly be involved, either directly or indirectly, have had an opportunity to review it and provide their input, it is your responsibility to see that it is promptly implemented. It should be written up in a logical and presentable format and complete copies provided to all who were members of the planning group. The plan should then be divided into sections for all managers, with a segment prepared for each that includes all parts of the plan which directly involve that manager or supervisor. Each segment should highlight the pertinent assumptions, the goals, and the performance schedule agreed to as they apply to that individual manager.

A note of thanks for their participation in the planning process should be attached to each copy of the plan or segment. Include in the note an expression of pride in the fine job that was done and the anticipated benefits to the organization. You should personally present each member of the planning group, plus anyone else who reports to you who may not have been a recognized member of that group, with a copy. When doing this, try to engage each person in a short discussion about the plan for the purpose of promoting commitment. Supervisors at lower levels should also receive segments of the plan from their managers and be similarly engaged in discussion to develop commitment to the goals of the plan. Each person should be prepared to give an initial progress report within a few weeks. Subsequent progress reports may be less frequent, but to assure that the plan has no inherent problems, initial reporting should be at fairly short intervals.

You, as the organization's leader, should *roam the ship* often to gain insight into how well implementation of the plan is progressing. At every opportunity, without being a nuisance, encourage prompt communication about problems, delays, or doubts in the interest of keeping the team on target.

When the plan seems to be progressing well, the planning group should meet to review its progress at suitable intervals. Certainly, once you have been involved with the planning process for a few years or longer, re-doing the plan is easier and participation by those involved should be more constructive because of their prior experience. For this reason, subsequent planning can be more sophisticated if increased sophistication would enhance the quality of the plan.

My suggestions under this topic have been detailed — even reminding you to thank everyone. Appreciation is so important but frequently it is neglected by managers who are "too busy".

Planning is a non-ending process

Once a planning group has completed a long-range plan, you might think they could go back to their usual activities, relaxed in the belief that they now know where they are going and how they are going to get there. Nothing could be farther from the truth. The plan required that assumptions be made that could prove erroneous. For this reason, the chief executive officer must keep a list of the assumptions and monitor them carefully. Whenever an assumption seems in error, he must assemble those responsible for the plan, and see that the plan is modified.

Plans often require revision because of changes that occur outside the business. Examples: an interest sensitive business must respond to a change in interest rates; a foundry must react to a change in the price of scrap metal; a hospital must respond to a change in insurance coverage by Medicare; a fuel marketer is faced with a sudden change in the price of crude oil; a boutique observes a marked trend toward less formality in ladies clothes. The potential for change is without limit.

In evaluating the tremendous benefit that can result from proper planning, an important facet frequently overlooked is the effect that this process can have on the employee. Through participation, he gains perspective of what is happening in the organization and the importance of his job in helping the company reach its goals. He finds it easier to communicate with other employees, because they also participated in the planning process. He is motivated at a higher level. Being involved in the planning process can be as beneficial to the organization as the plan itself — especially for a small company.

Thus far, topic 42 has extolled the advantages of planning. Suppose, however, that "from out of the blue" a new opportunity presents itself but capitalizing on it would totally upset your previous planning. You must be alert for new opportunities and be willing to totally revamp or even abandon a plan that was the result of much hard work if doing so would be of long-term benefit. Such opportunities can originate from within or from outside the organization and your people must be encouraged to be free thinkers in evaluating them. In large organizations, such opportunities usually have relatively minor impact compared to the major impact they often have on a small company.

In the process of planning, too often the planning team thinks of planning only as a way of stimulating growth. Often, growth is the natural result of good management and teamwork. For that reason, the planning team should also think of planning as a process of removing the factors that are limiting growth.

43 • Gap Analysis

Gap analysis is a unique approach to strategic planning that establishes an ideal scenario for progress. It assumes the company will be blessed with peak levels of success in all its endeavors; it supposes near-perfect performance by its people and an ideal business environment. It also theorizes that there will be no financial restraints or marketing impediments. With this utopian set of conditions as a basis, the projection charts referred to in topic 42 (planning) can be extended out five years to indicate virtually optimum achievement. If the area between this projection and that of any previous plan are compared on the same chart, a large area should exist between the two lines. Cross-hatch that area and label it "gap". It represents the difference between what was expected and the best performance you can imagine. A chart depicting such conditions follows:

Gap Analysis Chart 1

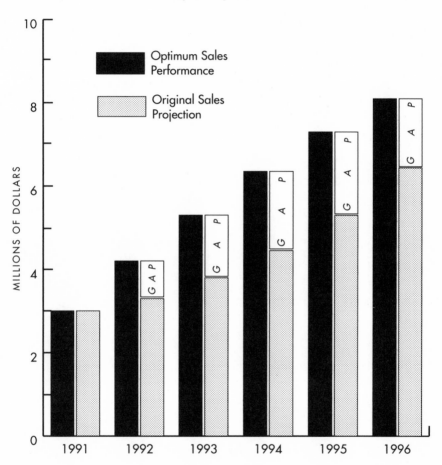

Now that your planning group has gone through the foregoing gap analysis exercise, and possibly had a good laugh at such far-out projections, ask those in the group to further use their imaginations by listing actions that might be taken to achieve any portion of the indicated gap. For example, suppose in your previous planning there was an assumed bank borrowing limit. If you could convince your banker that if he increased your line of credit by twenty-five percent, you would be able to reduce your indebtedness faster, starting one year hence, because it would allow increases of 30% in business volume and 35% in profit. Revise the lower portion of the chart to reflect this change, and note that the "gap" would be reduced as shown in the graph that follows:

Gap Analysis Chart 2

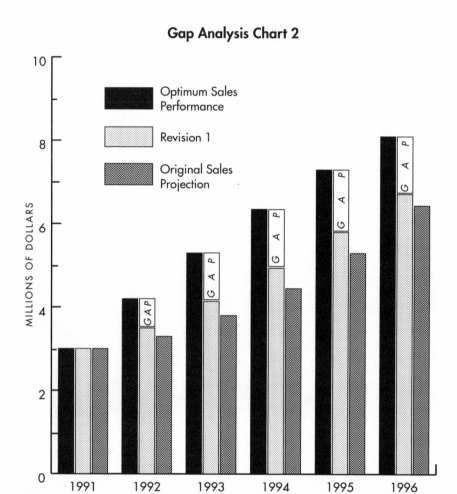

As a manufacturer, suppose you have a new product that will be ready for test marketing in about twelve months, and you project that full production and marketing will be "on stream" within 18 months. Ask the group to suggest ways of reducing that time. They may feel that it is possible to reduce the twelve months to eight months before test marketing and that you can be on stream in 12 months. Then you would be able to project sales of the new product during the following year of $1,000,000. That will be about the time you have projected improved cash flow to permit faster reduction of your bank borrowing. Now, further change the graph to add the influence of the earlier marketing of the new product and you may have a graph that looks like the following:

Gap Analysis Chart 3

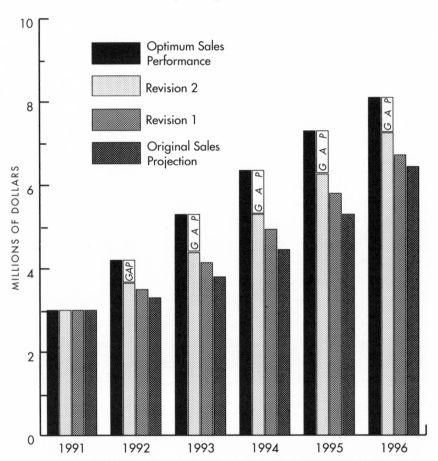

In the foregoing manner, you can lead the group to suggest many changes in operations that can reduce the "gap". As a leader, you may have to do some prodding to stimulate thinking, and you should be prepared to do it. The exercise in which you defined your business could suggest ways of increasing sales or you could pose questions such as: "Can we expand our market geographically?" "Would additional advertising stimulate sales profitably?" "Is our marketing and/or advertising as effective as they might be?" "Would improved quality benefit sales?" These are typical questions that might stimulate the group. Before long the "gap" begins to look relatively small and you have many challenging changes to investigate. Gap analysis, as you can see, is a method of stimulating a planning group to realize a potential for achievement beyond what they might otherwise imagine.

All changes that are made to your strategic plan as a result of gap analysis must then be put back into a revised plan in a manner that realistically fits the assumptions and permits implementation in a practical manner. It is not unusual, with a gap analysis planning approach, to project five year growth that is very much greater than otherwise envisioned.

After a plan has been decided upon by the planning group, using a gap analysis approach, completion and implementation should be like that previously described for more conventional planning. Because the organizational performance and growth assumptions are so optimistic, however, everyone involved must be attentive and dedicated to the plan at the every level and prepared for prompt adjustment of the plan if necessary.

44 • Project Planning

Project planning is done by most organizations and is a process that is fairly well known, but often it is not well executed. Therefore, it is appropriate that it be covered here. Unlike strategic planning, in project planning usually you know where you want to go, and you usually know when you must get there. A project plan is often an outgrowth of the strategic planning process. Examples might be a new building expansion, a new product, a new computer installation, or an advertising program.

If the project is relatively small, planning can be simple — that is, it can be coordinated and virtually completed by one person. Certainly that would be true if there had been a prior project of similar nature. If the project is large, in terms of its impact on either people or cost, a planning group is required. In either case, the need for the project should be established in a participative manner so that the plan will evoke a cooperation spirit from the rest of the organization.

As in other types of planning, a planning coordinator is needed to determine such matters as the following:

- Precise definition of the project
- Reason for and benefit to be derived from the project
- The time frame for completion
- How it will be organized and what tools or equipment will be required
- What data is necessary and who will supply it
- What are the goals to be completed or met
- What people will be responsible for completion
- What will be the cost
- Who should have the privilege of contributing to and approving of the plan
- What impediments to the plan exist that could require contingency planning

Answers to the first two items, (definition, reasons for, and benefits to be derived) would seem to be and often are obvious. Unless adequate thought is given to these considerations, however, it is quite easy to overlook such obvious obstacles to success. For example, I know of a manufacturing plant expansion that was completed only to find out afterwards that most of the company's employees felt the new location would be inconvenient for them. Another example, involved the acquisition of a computer, in which the people in charge did not properly encourage participation by others in the planning, and many who felt the wrong computer was being leased did not voice their opinions. As a result, the new computer never did get fully on line and eventually it was returned after considerable expense. It cannot be stressed too strongly that although project planning is part of *stealth management*, particular attention must be give to "people concerns" to ensure success of the project.

Determination of the time required for completion of the project is usually the result of integrating the time required for each of the many parts of the project, such as time to acquire data or equipment, installation or construction time, break-in or learning curve time, and many other variables that can be readily projected. If the estimated time does not permit completion by some important target date, it sometimes is necessary to apply expensive expediting techniques to complete the project on time.

Organizing the project with regard to people, tools and equipment, and the proper sequence of actions can also be a challenge that will frequently benefit from being creative. Suppose you were planning a new office building and construction time was estimated to be nine months. When you got into the phase of the project involving furnishing the building, it was found that the custom carpeting required eight months for delivery. Failure to place an order for the carpeting within the first month of the project's start could delay the occupancy of the building at the end or require a compromise in the desired carpeting. This might seem obvious, but too often it is assumed that furnishing such a building can be taken care of later. The result is that the overall plan suffers.

There is an approach called PERT (program evaluation review technique) which is very helpful in reducing the time and cost needed to complete sizable projects. It does so by a meticulous analysis of the ideal sequence of all actions, such as purchasing, funding, or construction. It also analyzes which actions can overlap. PERT has permitted a reduction of the time required for large building projects by as much as 25% with an accompanying cost savings of substantial proportion.

Assembling the data required to plan a project is the responsibility of the project leader. He should assemble the talent needed and seek input from those who will be involved with the use of the completed results. Such broad participation will make enthusiastic acceptance more likely.

STEALTH MANAGEMENT

If actual project costs are variable, it is necessary that they be monitored throughout the project so that deviations can be noted and provision for a change in funding be made if needed. When the plan is near completion, make a list of the possible pitfalls. Such contingencies should then be analyzed, and a response should be planned for each.

When a project of appreciable magnitude has been completed, plan a celebration, complement those involved, and emphasize the value of the results to the company.

45 • Organizational Structure

Introduction

The more successfully you implement **stealth management** in your business, the less important organization and structure becomes. The Japanese rarely use organization charts, and when they do, they draw them horizontally so as not to present anyone as being on top of or beneath someone else. In the United States and most of the Western World it is customary and important to have an organization chart. However, as your organization becomes more adept at Stealth Management, it will become possible to apply structure less rigidly. That does not mean an organization chart becomes unnecessary; but, the organization chart should become less restrictive upon managers. Through cross-fertilization, managers in multi-layered management organizations are sometimes able to improve productivity by by-passing another manager when it would be counter-productive not to do so. It is important, however, to communicate promptly with the by-passed manager to prevent embarrassment and preserve morale.

As an engineer in an aircraft factory, I once happened to be in the fuselage manufacturing area and noticed a worker drilling a series of rivet holes that were too large for the short hole spacing. Stopping to talk to him, I asked his opinion. He agreed the condition seemed wrong and could cause a severe safety problem. After suggesting that his foreman would appreciate being alerted to the problem, he informed me that the foreman was in a meeting and would be unavailable for some time. I asked was there any other work he could do in the meantime, and he agreed to delay the questionable procedure. I promised to back him up if he needed my support. The foreman called me and thanked me for my active concern. Such organization chart jumping might be frowned upon in a rigidly managed organization in which every one was jealously protecting his own turf.

Organizational structure, formal or informal, permits people to function more effectively as a group than working alone. Although it becomes less important as the implementation of stealth management progresses, doing without formal structure would be counter-productive. The following discussion of organization and the examples given are incomplete but typical for small businesses. As your business grows beyond two to three hundred employees, organizational structure becomes more important.

How to organize

There are several types of organizational structure, and the relative popularity of each has changed considerably through the years. Generally, they vary with regard to the degree of centralization and the degree of authoritarianism within the organization. Organizational structure and the accompanying organizational chart are meant to define areas of responsibility, provide for easier communication, prevent duplication of effort, highlight gaps in responsibility, and otherwise improve the effectiveness of the organization. They achieve these objectives by establishing the paths through which energy flows throughout the organization.

When a business is organized and in its entrepreneurial stage, the manager has little concern with organization or an organization chart. There are few employees and very few with managerial responsibilities. Many business grow rather slowly in the early years and do not require much structure for some time, although there are exceptions. When the need for structure becomes apparent, it is evidenced by duplication of effort, inefficiency, and lack of communication, and management typically realizes the existence of the problem much too late. To realize the need for formal organization or structure, in this after-the-fact manner, can be costly and have a negative impact on productivity. On the other hand, having a pre-established organizational structure that provides for anticipated growth can help to avoid many pitfalls.

In most organizations, there is the formal structure as depicted on the organizational chart; but, there also is an informal system of organization which sometimes is referred to as the social organizational system. The latter system is the way things work in reality and takes into account the strengths, weaknesses, and length of experience of all personnel. It is important to be aware of the many subtleties of the informal structure and their influence on the typical organization. An example could be knowing when to seek the advice of an old timer who has been employed for many years and whose experience could prevent you from making a bad decision. Some particular individual who is held in high regard because of his communicative ability might be the one to most effectively convey an idea you wanted to promote.

The social organizational structure functions best in a work environment that embodies good "esprit de corps". Without such spirit, the social organization can be an irritant to management. Most management books do not refer to social organizational structure. After all, although it usually exists, it is somewhat clandestine in character, and a surprising percentage of managers are unaware of it. It is unimportant and often nonexistent in new or very small organizations but invariably present in older organizations. However, in these days of mergers, acquisitions, and leveraged buyouts, new managers and C.E.O.'s can suffer severe operational problems by being unaware of the social structure within their organization. Many otherwise capable managers, new to an organization, fail because of insufficient or insensitive attention to the social structure.

As a business grows, there are both line and staff functions that evolve within the organization. Generally, line personnel are directly involved with sales, customer service, necessary record keeping, or production of the product or service being marketed; they are the decision makers. Staff personnel are not directly involved with the end product nor do they have line personnel reporting to them; usually they are not decision makers. Staff personnel would include such job titles as director of planning, comptroller, assistant to the president, or a personal secretary.

An important basic rule of organization is to keep the number of layers of management to a minimum. Obviously, that serves to keep overhead costs low, and managers are increasingly aware that reducing the number of layers of responsibility generally improves performance. Frequently, they are not aware of the subtleties that permit applying such efficiency most effectively. In a manufacturing company, it has been traditional that a manager has no more than seven people reporting to him except at the foreman level. Suppose, however, your people enjoy high morale, are well trained, through cross fertilization training are well aware of each others jobs and responsibilities, and that they have participated in an agreement as to who should take over your emergency responsibilities in the event you are temporarily unavailable. Under such conditions, there is no limit to how many people could report to you other than what your experience suggests. Using this management style, many department stores have eliminated an entire management level who functioned as assistant store managers.

The organizational structure of an enterprise must provide for performance of every function needed to conduct its intended activities and achieve its mission. At the top is the owner in the case of the individual proprietorship, or the chief executive officer in the case of a publicly held corporation. Below the top management level, the structure reflects various forms of divisionalization. In the event of multiple geographic areas of employment, there might be a division for each area of major activity; a wire and cable manufacturer with plants in Chicago, Little Rock, Birmingham, Buffalo, and Phoenix could refer to each plant as a division. Alternatively, the same company could divisionalize based on product similarity; in that case, the Chicago plant might manufacture telephone wire and cable, the Phoenix plant military oriented cable, the Little Rock plant automotive wire, etc.

It is readily accepted that if an organization at one location becomes too large, the benefits of professional management are more difficult to achieve because there is too much organizational distance from the top to the bottom. This fact, in itself, is a reason for large companies to decentralize and become a group of smaller organizations. Defining what is too large is difficult since it would vary broadly, depending on the type organization you have. When you are no longer able to roam the ship as you once could and the faces at the bottom seem like strangers, the organization is larger than desirable for the optimum use of *stealth management.* Of course, some types of business organizations do not permit decentralizing; you cannot have a small automobile manufacturing plant with a competitive assembly line operation; nor can you have a small manufacturer of 747 type jet airplanes.

There are other reasons for decentralization. The more decentralized you are, the less susceptible is your organization to natural catastrophes, fire, or labor unrest. Closer proximity to markets usually reduces freight expense, particularly in the case of heavy products. If you are offering a service, it may be desirable to have widely dispersed sales offices to permit ready access to clients. Sometimes, presence in a given geographic area permits closer understanding and accommodation to an unusual market. If you catered to senior citizens, there might be an advantage being located near a large senior citizen population such as there is in Florida, for example.

If authoritarianism is part of your management style, the degree of decentralization within your company will seem less important. Your organization would largely be controlled by rules and strong leadership authority with disciplinary responses provided for disobedience or infractions. However, since this book is principally directed toward the smaller organization the following samples of organization charts are applicable:

1. The following chart is for a small manufacturing company with but one location and one product line:

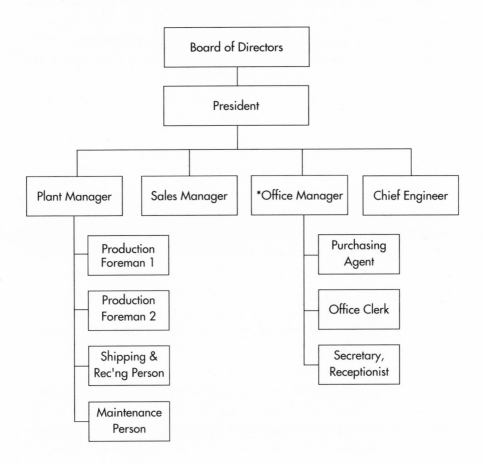

*In the foregoing organization chart, there is an asterisk adjacent to the office manager because it had been agreed by all those reporting to the president that in his absence certain authority will be assumed by the office manager. Such authority would include decision-making situations requiring action that could not wait for the return of the president. Note that the purchasing agent, all secretarial help, and all clerical help report to the office manager. The office manager, in addition to his managerial duties, would be responsible for personnel related duties and maintenance of all accounting records. Most small companies generate their sales from a small number of customers or utilize commissioned sales representatives. Hence, the forgoing organization does not indicate any salesmen other than the sales manager. Such an organization chart could serve a company until it grew well beyond one hundred employees.

An organization chart usually will show only personnel who are in management roles plus some who are in staff positions. However, in an organization having few employees categorized as secretaries or clerical help, such help become deeply entrenched in the organization and the need for replacing one of them can be upsetting for some time. Including such personnel on the organizational chart is another way of telling them they are valued. In my experience, this gesture seemed to be positive in its psychological effect.

2. The following organization chart is for a larger manufacturing organization that has three product lines, each requiring different product engineering and different sales approaches. In order to keep the organization's non-productive employee roster as small and efficient as possible, there still is little divisionalization. In this company, still small — but with over two hundred employees, it would be important for every supervisor to be intimately acquainted with each of the three product lines.

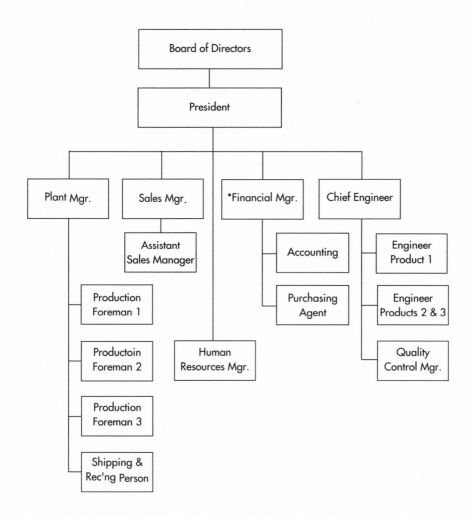

This organization, similar to example number 1, reflects its larger size in the need for an additional foreman, a human resources manager, a quality assurance manager, and an additional engineer. The human resource manager's position on the organization chart should be at the same level as other managers who report to the president and is reflected as shown due to limited space. Now that the chart is for a larger organization, staff positions such as secretarial help are not shown. There is much argument as to whom a quality assurance manager should report to minimize conflict of responsibility. In smaller organizations, such considerations often have to be rationalized in the interest of functionalism.

3. The following organization chart is for a company that manufactures customized equipment for the petroleum industry. It has three locations which are necessary for market penetration because their highly technical product requires follow-up service that often must be provided on an emergency basis. The home office is in Dallas, with other locations in Houston and Denver.

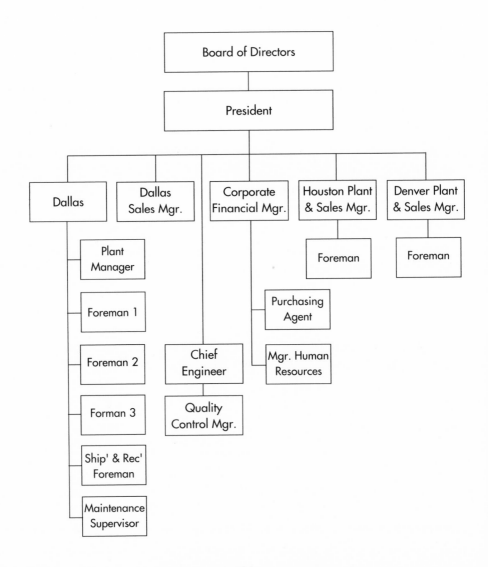

In the company represented in this chart, the home office (Dallas) produces many of the components needed by the other plants so that the other plants are only involved in assembly and sales. Hence, the Dallas plant has many more employees, does much more shipping and receiving, and does the engineering and purchasing for all. The Houston and Denver plants each have fewer than fifty employees and do not have designated maintenance, shipping, receiving, or quality control personnel. As in example 2, the financial manager has been selected to assume other duties in the event the president is unavailable and need arises.

When we consider larger organizations, the organization chart would look much different. Should your company grow to five hundred or more employees, or should you feel need for help in updating your organization chart before reaching that level, it probably would be wise to seek consulting help.

The organization and the chart representing it are further defined by proper use of job descriptions which are covered in a subsequent topic. It is important that assigned work loads be reasonably balanced. It would be inappropriate for one employee or one department to have such a heavy workload as to require excessive overtime compared to others or, conversely, to provide for insufficient challenge. Change makes it necessary to review workload balance periodically. Organization and structure should follow planning and strategy and always should be reviewed after planning has been completed. You must tailor your organization's structure to fit its needs; do not merely copy someone else.

On-going committees, such as a management committee, are really a part of organizational structure and are often indicated on an organization chart. Teams that are formed to deal with a particular project can be very important but because they are considered temporary, they are not usually shown on the chart.

There are many organizations whose operations require people to report to more than one manager. That could be true, for example, when you have several project managers, each in charge of a different project and each intermittently in need of engineering talent. In such an organization, you could have an engineering department headed by a chief engineer, but that department would assign one or more engineers to a project manager to temporarily serve the engineering requirements of that project. While on that temporary assignment, the engineers would actually have two managers, the project manager and the chief engineer. Such organizational structure is referred to as a matrix organization and is prevalent in medium to large sized organizations. It does require careful monitoring to assure that job performance and inter-personal relationships remain on a high level, and special training is often required. This form of structure is mentioned only because it magnifies the importance of tailoring structure to fit the organization.

46 · Job Descriptions

If you have been implementing *stealth management* in the suggested sequence, you are now ready to write job descriptions for your managers or supervisory personnel. If your company is large enough to apply the following recommendations, the process can be highly rewarding.

Written job descriptions are uncommon in smaller companies. Whether written or not, however, everyone in the organization must have an understanding of his job and the relationship it has to the entire organization. I have known of situations in which new employees are encouraged to "design their own jobs" and a job description would presumably follow. Such a situation is unhealthy and most often will be a source of trouble. A manager who does not provide for every person reporting to him having a clear job description indicates weak leadership.

For medium to large companies, job descriptions should be given much thought and perhaps coupled with an employment contract. It is difficult to say how large an organization needs to be before written job descriptions should be used. Certainly, the less paperwork we have, without detracting from performance as a result, the better off we are. The tendency, however, is to go without job descriptions long past the point where they would be helpful. The more layers of management you have, the more important it is to have job descriptions. In most organizations, when three or more layers of management exist, job descriptions are necessary. If the financial level of responsibility is relatively large, a job description could be important regardless of how few layers of management there are. Job descriptions are not usually written (but are established verbally) for the "line" production worker or for most direct labor employees because they would change so often; they are used primarily for supervisory personnel.

If a supervisor, new on the job, is given a job description, it is usually unlike one written for the same person after several months on the job. After a person has been on board for a sufficient length of time to become well known to those with whom he works, the job description can be re-written to take cognizance of his strengths, weaknesses, personal goals, and personal attributes; it should be tailored to the uniqueness of that individual. Having a job description that dovetails with a manager's personal goals serves as a great motivator, and recognition of his unique ability enhances his self esteem. For example, suppose you had hired a new manufacturing superintendent and found out after hiring him that he had considerable experience and expertise in programming computer controlled machines. Previously that programming was done by your engineering department, who were overloaded with work. Because of the unique ability of your new manufacturing superintendent, you could now alleviate the work load in engineering by transferring that duty to him, and along with it, the observation that with that activity he would have better control of his department. Very often, a person's job description can advantageously reflect his aptitudes and personality.

Since a beginning job description is but temporary, let us be concerned with the more permanent one at this time, and when applying it to a new employee, modify it as necessary.

The purposes for having a job description are:

- To communicate understanding of a person's job, and its responsibilities, to all concerned

- To provide perspective of the job in terms of its overall relationship to the planning, the goals, and the operations of the organization
- To enhance a sense of belonging
- To define duties and responsibilities and provide priority levels
- To define limits of authority and responsibility
- To establish standards by which job performance can be measured
- To establish a method of performance review and bonus determination (if appropriate)
- To establish a job philosophy that provides for extending the limits of responsibility and prevents limiting either motivation or creativity

Too often, managers are prone to write the job description for a subordinate and have it delivered — a way of saying "Here is a description of your job, now go do it!" This is a practice that occurs frequently, and it happened to me. In my case, after having sold my company, my new boss sent me a rather lengthy job description (through the mail) with performance numbers assigned to each of my various duties and obligations, with the funniest of all, "honesty", being assigned a potential award of 3 points, out of a maximum total of nearly 200. The points were toward a yearly bonus, and all points were to be awarded on a discretionary basis. As far as possible, bonuses should be awarded on a non-discretionary basis. Bonuses should be based on measurable performance.

This brings up the question, "Who should write a person's job description?" The foregoing list of purposes for a job description are all improved by good communication, both downward and upward. If you pass on to your subordinate (see topic 1) a copy of your own job description with a comment such as, "This is for your information", he would probably scan it and then bury it somewhere. If, instead, you informed him that you have been asked to prepare a job description for your own position and would appreciate his giving you his written understanding of your duties and obligations, an entirely different response would result. In responding to the request, he would have to give thought to you as a person, to your relationship with the organization, to your obligations to him, the limits of authority you have, and the duties you perform. After providing you with his best effort on this subject, you and he could then discuss it further and refine it in the process. You would then take the result and submit it to your superior. Discussion with him would result in further refinement.

Your final written job description should then be made available to those reporting to you in addition to the usual distribution. Their knowledge of a manager's job, the duties involved, the limits of authority, and any standards of performance that apply should provide deeper understanding and better communication between you and your fellow workers.

There are many forms used in writing a job description and numerous sources of detailed instructions. The following example is one type of written job description. It is for a plant manager who also is responsible for regional marketing. His facility has 45 employees. He reports to the company president who operates a home office and manufacturing facility in another city.

JOB DESCRIPTION

John Doe, Manager — Dallas, Texas

A. Job Objectives
   1. Manage Dallas manufacturing facility
   2. Coordinate and supervise marketing throughout Louisiana and Texas
   3. Provide direction to all subordinates to assure high productivity
   4. Maintain good working climate and employee morale
   5. Maximize company progress through effective team effort and good communications with other locations

	Priority level
B. Duties and Responsibilities	
1. Participate in setting company-wide goals and policies	2
2. Implement company goals and policies in Dallas plant	3
3. Supervise and participate in marketing to all Dallas area customers	3
4. Provide direction for all activities at Dallas plant	1
5. Provide timely flow of specified data systems to home office and be responsible for accuracy of such data	2
6. Participate in establishing wage and salary levels for all subordinate personnel	2
7. Participate in establishing company-wide quality standards and implement them in Dallas plant	3
8. Establish influences needed to ensure high productivity in Dallas operations	3
9. Review and advise on activities of competition	4
10. Make suggestions for product improvement and new products	4
11. Implement company personnel policies in Dallas plant	1
12. Participate as member of company management committee, preferably once per month — or more often if practical	2

Priority Levels Applied to Duties and Responsibilities

1. Must be done on a continuing basis, leaving no gaps
2. Must be done in coordination with home office in a prescribed manner and/or at prescribed intervals
3. May be done in an unscheduled manner, but are necessary for maximum job effectiveness
4. Necessary or desirable actions that should be completed when practical, but usually can be subordinated to categories 1, 2, and 3

C. Levels of Authority/Responsibility

1. Capital funds	May approve expenditures up to $2,500. Approval by company president required for larger amounts
2. Leases, contracts, and agreements	Advice of legal counsel and approval by company president required
3. Employee relations	May hire or fire using established company guidelines. Actions affecting key employees require approval of President
4. Emergencies	Expected to act in an expeditious manner, without regard to level of authority applicable

There are many more categories of job related duties and activities that sometimes are used in job descriptions. They all fall into four authority levels: (a) do it, (b) do it and tell, (c) do it after consultation, and (d) do it when told.

D. Key Attitudes and Performance Criteria

1. Should set high personal standards in all job oriented activities
2. Should effectively contribute to the process of planning and goal setting
3. Should display positive attitude toward all company goals and convey such attitude to other personnel
4. Should encourage creativity and high productivity among Dallas employees
5. Should delegate responsibility to subordinates to maximize achievement of company goals and objectives
6. Should provide proper training for all Dallas personnel
7. Should maintain close working relationships with key personnel throughout organization

Having outlined a job description writing procedure that is so long and detailed, you could well wonder if it is not too much trouble.

If you have not used job descriptions previously, you might also wonder whether they could inadvertently serve to stifle a person by restricting his initiative or creativity. The answer to these questions is "yes". Like the planning process, however, the document is not as valuable as is the process involved in producing it. That it is so much trouble is offset by the need for such a document to minimize a future chance for some types of litigation in addition to the other aforementioned benefits. As for it being too confining, all restrictions should provide for exception under emergency conditions and the suggestion that, with proper authority, the limitations can be changed. Further, every person, after having adequate experience in his job should be encouraged to perform in the best interest of the organization without undue restrictive limitations being imposed by a job description. This does not mean, of course, that an employee has the right to reach out and, without good reason, assume responsibility that infringes on the authority of others. It does mean that, with good reason, he may reach out and act beyond the sphere of activity normally ascribed to him — providing he does so in a spirit of cooperation and advises others on the team who should be informed. After receiving a copy of his job description, the person for whom it is written should file it away and only refer to it from time to time for the purpose of assuring accurate recall.

As people change or the organization changes, job descriptions often require revision. This should be attended to as necessary. Note, that in the previous example no mention is made of performance standards, salary, or bonuses; such subjects are usually of a sensitive nature and are more appropriately addressed in another manner. There are, however, some companies who practice complete disclosure in which there is even group consensus about individual salaries. I do not reject such a management style, but feel it approaches a near utopian situation that would be impractical for the average manager.

47 • Performance Standards and Reviews

Most management training programs and most books on the subject deal with performance standards primarily as they relate to managers. Standards of performance that apply directly to labor or non-management functions seem to be neglected. The latter type standards may be referred to by many other descriptions, such as production standards, and are the subject of a myriad of training courses offered for non-managerial employees.

In a small business, the number of managers is relatively small, but performance standards (or production standards) are still important at all levels of the organization. The chief executive of the organization usually is involved in establishing all such standards. Therefore, it seems unnecessary to differentiate between establishing standards for direct labor employees and the process as it applies to managers.

Performance standards should be beneficial in their influence on productivity; when improperly drawn they can be overly optimistic or restrictive. Too frequently, they cause people to figure out what the standard sets as good or acceptable and perform at that level but no better. Performance standards only have a positive effect if they are designed well, for the proper reason, and by the correct people.

Performance standards are important, for they permit defining how well work is to be done. A standard of performance is a statement of observable conditions that will exist when job functions are satisfactorily performed. It should not tell how work is to be done; it should not be a statement of wishes or good intentions; it should not create more paperwork than is justified; it should never be judgmental.

Not too many years ago it was quite common for more progressive manufacturing companies to have on-going time and motion studies which were used as a basis for establishing production standards of performance. Imagine yourself doing any type of manufacturing job, operating a lathe for example, while a young engineer with a record book and a stop watch is timing each portion of your work and making detailed notes of your specific movements and actions. After he has finished observing you, he then does the same for the lathe operator next to you. You could not help but wonder, "Am I doing as good a job as my competition? If not, what will happen as a result?" You could easily find yourself worried, resentful toward the company (and the young engineer), and lacking in concentration. If within the next few months there were any company actions that did not meet your approval, it would be natural for you to associate them with that young engineer and his time and motion study of your work. Time and motion studies are not always bad, but they should be used infrequently — especially in small organizations. They should be used only when the worker, whose work is being observed and measured, feels that they will help him in his job.

When performance standards are used, they should be applied to everyone in the organization. To be sure, a performance standard for a maintenance person will be styled differently from that of a production welder. For a plant manager it would be different from that of a purchasing agent. Each individual or group should have considerable input in establishing such standards for themselves. If you establish or greatly influence the standard by which your performance will be judged, does it not follow that you will be more concerned about reaching or surpassing it? Also there will be little probability of your considering the standard as unfair or unrealistic. If you have helped set the performance goal and each day, after work, you leave the job with the awareness that you are reaching or surpassing the standard, you will have a sense of accomplishment and greater self-esteem. That awareness can make you a happier employee and have a beneficial impact on your performance; in fact, it may be the most important good that can come from establishing performance standards.

Another purpose for performance standards, especially as they pertain to direct labor, is to establish production costs upon which selling prices are based, at least in part. That also can be done by having pay scales for piece-work which provide a fixed remuneration for each part completed. Providing the resulting pay exceeds the legal minimum wage scale, piece-work is legal and still used by some companies. Because it is considered demeaning and psychologically affects employees adversely, it is becoming less common; it is never used in Japan for these reasons.

In summary, the desired results to be obtained by establishing performance standards for production employees include the following:

• Establish labor costs needed to determine selling price

- Establish a base for evaluating employee performance
- Permit an employee, when leaving the job after a days work, to be able to say to himself, "I did a good job today" — assuming he reached or exceeded the established performance standard
- Make for common understanding through participation in establishing the standards
- Convey to the employee the fairness with which he will be judged by his performance rather than on an arbitrary basis

All standards of performance should begin with a statement similar to this: "Satisfactory performance has been attained by _____(the manager of sales, for example) when _____." Each manager or supervisor should have his own standards of performance; every employee to whom performance standards apply should participate in establishing those applicable to him. Before such standards are established in final form, they should be subject to review and constructive input; there should be agreement between an employee and his manager, and the standards should be revised when necessary. All performance standards should be in concert with the overall plan and goals of the organization. A manager should have his own performance standards established before asking any employee to help in establishing theirs. Such management commitment along with an explanation of why performance standards are beneficial to the individual as well as the company will result in ready acceptance by all concerned.

Well-drawn performance standards are:

- Reasonably achievable and clearly understood
- Primarily established using data and the thinking of the person for whom the standard are being drawn
- Committed to by the employee and accepted by the superior
- Quantitatively expressed without the use of vague language (e.g., do not use such words as promptly, efficiently, profitable, aggressively, timely, or such expressions as "as soon as possible", "early in the month", etc.)

197

An operations sheet depicting a description of operations performed and a suggested sequence for doing them can be helpful for jobs that are repetitive in nature. When military quality control guidelines must be applied, operation sheets are usually required, and workers must initial the sheet as they complete each operation so that a continuing trail of responsibility is established. When operation sheets are utilized, they should be referred to in the preparation of standards of performance. Because most small businesses would not be using operations sheets, examples or detail relative to their application is being omitted; each application would be different.

Standards should establish performance goals that are readily achievable. The effect of having them so high that they are difficult to attain is very negative. They should be easier for a trainee than for an experienced performer. They should become more challenging, as the employee becomes more adept at his work, through discussion between the employee and his manager. The goal should be to establish an achievement range for that person above which is excellence and below which are degrees of failure. A performance standard should set performance levels that are measurable in terms of time, quantity, or cost. Individual performance standards should be kept confidential between an employee and his manager — although this cannot be the case when referring to group standards.

The following example indicates a performance standard that might be drawn for the president of a manufacturing company having 125 employees, a board of directors, fifteen stockholders, and seven managers reporting to him:

Performance Standards
for John Jones
President — RXQ Manufacturing Co.

1. Satisfactory performance has been achieved with respect to stockholders and the board of directors when:

- Stockholders and directors meetings have been held in accordance with an agreed-to schedule (usually specified in the company policy manual)
- Stockholders and directors have been fully informed of company performance prior to meetings to permit them to prepare for discussion
- All actions have been adhered to that require approval by the board of directors and are specified in the president's job description
- All inquiries or suggestions advanced by board members or stock holders have been satisfactorily answered and followed up

2. Satisfactory performance has been attained with respect to strategic planning when:
   - A planning group has been appointed, trained in the planning process, and has begun to meet for the purpose of establishing an accepted long and short term company plan
   - A proposed plan has received appropriate company-wide participation, has been put in presentation form and been approved by the board of directors
   - All assumptions used in the planning process have been listed and are being monitored
   - The finalized plan (typically for 3 to 5 years) has been passed down through the organization and is being implemented
   - Every manager involved with implementing the plan has benchmarks by which progress toward goals set forth by the plan is being monitored

3. Satisfactory performance has been attained with respect to organization when:
   - An organization chart exists, with copies distributed to all managers, that shows their lines of authority (This is unnecessary where there is less than three levels of supervision)

- Written job descriptions exist for all supervisory positions that are acceptable to both the individual and his supervisor, have been reviewed jointly by both within the past year, and have been revised as necessary
- Satisfactory provisions have been made to provide temporary back-up managers when needed and plans for replacement of key personnel who may need to be replaced within the near future (6 to 18 months)
- A training program is in place assuring growth and development for all managers

4. Satisfactory performance with respect to employee morale has been attained when:

- There is no evidence indicating attitude problems or job dissatisfaction among those reporting directly you
- Each second level employee has been reviewed with regard to performance within the past year
- All employees are provided with a continuing avenue for communication with management
- All company policies are known to and understood by employees
- Company wage scales, benefits, and reward systems have been reviewed within the past year
- Not more than one supervisor or manager has resigned except due to retirement within the past year

5. Satisfactory performance has been attained with respect to growth and profitability when:

- The sales volume called for in the yearly company plan has been attained for at least two out of the previous three years
- The net profit called for in the yearly company plan has been attained for at least two out of the previous three years and that the average return on investment (R.O.I.) for those three years has equaled or exceeded the average R.O.I. called for by the plan
- For the preceding year, the dependency on any single product line or single customer has not exceeded guidelines set by the company plan

- For the preceding year, each product line has contributed to the company's financial well-being within the guidelines set by the company plan
- Growth and profitability are keeping up with the competition and evidence no trends that are negative relative to your industry

6. Satisfactory performance has been attained relative to financial condition when:
   - Satisfactory banking relationships exist that provide lines of credit needed to achieve company goals
   - Financial records are current and financial ratios considered to be important are being met
   - Potential financial contingencies have been planned for with insurance and/or appropriate action plans

Depending on the size and nature of an organization's operations, there could be other standards of performance that might apply. If an organization performs in such manner as to permit the chief executive officer to pass this review with a good evaluation, the organization at-large also will have performed well. Usually, the C.E.O. is better able to perform well if he also applies performance standards to those who report to him and, in turn, they apply such standards to their subordinates (see topic 1).

In most organizations the question exists, "Who should appraise the performance of the president?" It should be the board of directors, if there is one. But, often in a small company the board of directors is ill prepared to perform this task. If there is no other means of having his performance reviewed, a company president should go through a self-appraisal, applying the same diagnostic techniques he would use in appraising a subordinate, endeavoring to be as objective as possible. Experience indicates that most managers are more severe in appraising themselves than when appraising others, so self-appraisal can be a productive exercise.

After performance standards have been established for an individual, his performance must be monitored at appropriate intervals — 6 months for supervisors, 12 months for others is suggested. The monitoring procedure is vital to the control process; if it is poorly implemented or neglected, performance standards will be of little help. Because a performance review necessarily must refer to the written performance standards which were jointly agreed to previously, many companies find it convenient to use a combination of performance standards and an evaluation form. This also minimizes paper work. In the case of the C.E.O., performance is typically reviewed by the board of directors; results usually ought not be committed to written record to be viewed by others. The review should be candid and constructive, resulting in revised standards for the following year and should serve to influence salary and bonus determination at a later date. To discuss salary or bonus during a performance review adds an element of tension that usually prevents maximum benefit from the review.

Although confidentiality should be kept with regard to all performance reviews, managers should retain a written record of reviews of those in his department. With this in mind, using a combination of performance standards and an evaluation form would be appropriate in smaller organizations. Such a form for the sales manager of RXQ Manufacturing Co. might be the following:

Performance Standards & Performance Review
Fred Brown – *Sales Manager, RXQ Manufacturing Co.*

	Performance	Appraisal
Sales	Above $X00	Superior
	Between $X00 & $X00	Above standard
	Between $X00 & $X00	Standard
	Between $X00 & $X00	Below standard
	Between $X00 & $X00	Unsatisfactory
Sales forecasts	Correct within 2%	Superior
	Correct within 2–5%	Above Standard
	Correct within 5–10%	Standard
	Correct within 10–15%	Below standard
	Not correct within 15%	Unsatisfactory
Sales expenses as percent of sales	Less than 6%	Superior
	Between 6% and 7%	Above standard
	Between 7% and 9%	Above standard
	Between 9% and 10%	Below standard
	Over 10%	Unsatisfactory
New accounts opened	Over 100	Superior
	Between 80 and 99	Above standard
	Between 60 and 79	Standard
	Between 40 and 59	Below standard
	Fewer than 40	Unsatisfactory

There probably are standards of performance that would be unique to your company in addition to those shown in the examples. Whenever possible, however, it is well to quantify all standards to permit appraising performance, not the personality. An appraisal of this type can even be of legal help in some circumstances.

When evaluating performance with regard to the use of soft skills, it is difficult to be quantitative. For example, you cannot apply numbers to a supervisor's skill at enhancing team spirit or a salesman's ability to leave a sense of satisfaction with a customer beyond merely being a purchaser. Such things can be measured with reasonable accuracy through the use of surveys, but it is not practical to conduct a survey every time you want to evaluate performance. A person can be his own severest critic. When evaluating an employee, ask him to give you an evaluation of his own performance with regard to a soft skill that is difficult to quantify and then ask for reasons and/or background for that self-evaluation. Subsequent discussion on the topic should soon result in an agreed-to appraisal that is complimentary and/or produces a plan for improvement.

In a small organization, the president and those who report to him usually become very close in terms of personal and team relationships. Mutual trust and high regard for each other are paramount for measures of performance to be well accepted. Without such rapport, appraisals would be of questionable value, and unless such rapport prevails, a personnel change may be in order.

The preceding examples of performance standards are for managers. The following is a combined performance standard and appraisal form applicable to a machinist who operates a lathe:

Performance Standards & Performance Review
Joe Jones – *Machinist, Lathe Operator*

	Performance	Appraisal
Production quantity	Over sched. by 25%+	Superior
	Over sched. 5–25%	Above standard
	On sched. -5–5%	Standard
	Under sched. 5–10%	Below standard
	Under sched. 10%+	Unsatisfactory
Quality	Under .5% rejects	Superior
	.5%–.8% rejects	Above Standard
	.8%–1.2% rejects	Standard
	1.2%–1.5% rejects	Below standard
	Over 1.5% rejects	Unsatisfactory

Again, this is a partial list of performance standards that might be applied to a machinist. Such things as attendance, creativity (suggestions), neatness, and attitude are each very important to the organization but are difficult to quantify. It takes a great deal of tact and sensitivity to reach common understanding between an employee and his supervisor in appraising such skills with objectivity. You can justifiably claim that if an employee rates high in these soft skills, he generally would perform admirably in those skills which are easy to quantify. Much objectivity is provided by the adherence to a policy of making notations of lateness, absence, examples of unusual team effort, etc. in the employee's personnel file.

Quantifying lateness or inexcusable absence would certainly seem easy but might cause resentment. If you quantify such behavior, it must not be done so rigidly that it rules out consideration of cause. In the organization that possesses good esprit de corps, such problems are minimized, and they can be a subject for discussion during review without reference to a performance standard. Therefore, they should not be included among established standards.

Of the many types of jobs that come to mind when considering the application of performance standards, one of those most adaptable is that of a maintenance worker. In our company, there was a maintenance person whose attendance was below standard, who sometimes exhibited laziness, and too often was forgetful. On the plus side, he had a delightful personality, was very proud of the company, was inherently appreciative of cleanliness, exhibited creativity in his job, and the mood of our workers was generally uplifted by his presence. Quantifying all these facets of his performance would be nearly impossible. Although formal appraisal systems are of great value, you must put them in proper perspective by evaluating the person's soft skills as well as those skills that are easier to measure — especially in the small organization.

All standards of performance, whether applied formally or informally, must take into account long term goals as well as short term goals. If you reward achievement excessively based on this years sales, profits, new accounts, or production, any one of them can be accented for short term results in a way that will harm future performance.

With inadequate maintenance or lack of timely replacement of worn-out machinery, a manufacturing company can easily increase short term profit but find themselves uncompetitive a few years later. This is done sometimes by companies who desire to "sell out". By manipulating short term profit in this manner, they hope to justify a higher selling price. Some managers use such ploys to smooth out their performance curve in the belief that by doing so they will look better to their lending institution. Certainly such effects are desirable, but usually they are very short lived. It is a good guideline to design your performance standards to maximize contribution to the long range goals established by your planning process.

48 • Control

In management, control is the system by which: (1) all employees, especially those on the organization chart, are held accountable for performing their assigned duties in a manner that properly contributes to achievement of the organization's goals; and, (2) benchmarks are established indicating whether or not progress toward those goals is being realized as planned. Small organizations are often without controls, and by the time management discovers the resulting poor performance, the time and cost of correction is excessive.

The control process consists of establishing goals with target dates, standards of performance, and responses to deviations. Change can occur with little warning, and management is constantly pressured to respond to problems of the moment leaving little time for control. It is important that controls be established in a manner that automatically triggers the need for attention from management. You must also find time to monitor controls so that problems can be detected as early as possible.

It is important that controls be in place for the purpose of helping employees do a better job — not as a threatening policing influence, never as part of a witch hunt. Yes, they can and sometimes do detect poor performance resulting from bad attitude, negligence, or even intentional sabotage-like activity, but the large majority of employees will have an attitude as good as is your management style.

Your controls should, therefore, be directed toward good employees. They also should be given the opportunity to help design and improve the controls. Only in the area of monitoring cashflow should controls be directed, at least in part, toward detecting dishonesty — and minimizing temptation.

In addition to augmenting the precision with which an enterprise is managed, controls usually provide data that aids in decision making. It is important that controls do not make it difficult for employees to perform their duties. Only if easy to use and understand will controls work well for the organization.

In a manufacturing company, controls should apply to human resource management, production, marketing, and finance. In production, you monitor quality and several aspects of cost. In the area of human resources, you should monitor job satisfaction, labor turnover, absenteeism, wage and salary competitiveness, frequency of accidents, and training. Marketing should be monitored with regard to sales trends, advertising and sales costs, competitiveness, perception of company by customers, and need for product change. Your finance and accounting procedures should be continually monitored to ensure financial liquidity, timeliness and accuracy of accounting data, manufacturing cost control, and adherence to established practices with regard to cashflow. The reference to cashflow practices concerns inventory, purchasing, collections, credit policies, and banking procedures.

Large companies not only have sophisticated control systems, but usually have an internal auditing staff who are constantly reviewing operations. In spite of such effort, most companies suffer from mistakes that could be prevented or minimized by proper controls. Having the right kind of controls is as important as the controls themselves. Because each organization is unique, there is no system of control that can be set forth as ideal. Since you are responsible for seeing that your controls are proper for your operation, you should seek help and advice from your public accounting and legal professionals, your own key personnel, and your board of directors. Much of the control system necessarily will originate from your own thinking, because controls should reflect the strengths and weaknesses of your key people. In applying your knowledge of their strengths and weaknesses, you establish the controls before they are needed; applying them after-the-fact not only can be costly but also may trigger a negative response from those through whom the controls are applied. For example, if you have a manager who usually performs well but often is late in reporting important performance data, it is important to influence the timeliness of his reports long before his lateness in reporting becomes an established bad habit.

For the small businessman, the following examples should indicate the importance of controls:

Malfeasance: The company had been in business over forty years when due to a change in help, a new hiree in accounting reconciled their checkbook and found that the cash account seemed rather low for a company of their size and relative success. Checking with the president and principle stockholder confirmed that an investigation should be made quickly to see why that situation existed. They soon discovered an unfamiliar company to whom checks had been written repeatedly over a period of many years. Further checking revealed that each of those checks had been altered to change the name of the payee. This could be done without the knowledge of the person who had previously signed the checks and would not arouse suspicion at the bank. The total amount thus diverted exceeded $750,000 and was traced to a former employee. Less than 10% was recovered from the employee, an additional 13% from an insurance company, and a probable 20% more might have been recovered ultimately from reduced taxes.

This story is a true case, one that is repeated everyday in the voluminous files of large indemnity insurance carriers. Imagine the impact on a small company. Each case is different and management's excuses for not having proper controls are legend. In small companies, where managers are closer to their employees and tend to be more trusting, it often is more difficult to apply controls that would prevent problems of this type. There are at least four things which should be done by every business to prevent or at least minimize such catastrophic malfeasance.

First, assuming your business is not so small that such chores are handled by you and/or members of your immediate family, the person who reconciles the checking account should not be the same person who processes checks. If practical, neither should be responsible for signing, sealing, or mailing checks. You may think your people are above suspicion, and in fact that may now be true. Next year, a trusted employee may suffer personal financial problems that can pressure him to behave in an untypical manner — especially if his personal value system is below standard. A person who normally does a particular job may be on vacation and the substitute be in position to require controls. Bank statements should be reconciled as soon after they have been received as is practical. Having a separate payroll bank account into which you transfer funds in time for the issuance of payroll checks helps substantially in reducing your exposure to malfeasance. This is particularly so if your operating and payroll accounts are reconciled by different people.

Second, even if your business is so small that the cost of a true accounting audit each year cannot be justified, request your public accountant to completely audit one month's transactions during the year. This should be done at random, not necessarily choosing the last month of the fiscal year, and should vary from year to year. Auditing one type of transaction such as a purchase, for example, would consist of reviewing the original purchase order, the receiving documentation, the invoice, and the payment check. Such a review would ascertain that the material received and signed for agreed with what was ordered as to type, quantity, and price.

Third, you should be receiving timely financial data from your office staff that would indicate negative financial trends or conditions. Such data should be prepared for you by the 15th of the month following the month being reported even if portions of it must be assumed. Assumptions, such as a bank balance, must be estimated as closely as possible and be corrected as needed when final data is available. It would make sense for your public accountant to help design the form on which this report is prepared.

Fourth, inventory records must be kept, primarily to advise when to order new material, thus preventing shortages or excesses. When such records indicate excessive use of inventory, prompt investigation must be made to analyze the cause for shortage. If an errant shipping/receiving foreman was converting inventory for his personal gain or a production foreman concealed a serious quality problem, inventory records would help in determining and correcting the problem as early as possible.

Production controls: In our company there was a problem involving a custom molded rubber part that we produced in substantial quantities. The part weighed over two pounds when removed from the mold and material was over 50% of the cost of the part. Our cost control sheet provided for normal material waste and quality problems, but only after hundreds of parts had been made did our inventory control records indicate that we were consuming 30% more material than was priced into the job. Investigation revealed that because the production equipment was not ideal for that job, excessive scrap was being developed. The production foreman believed that the problem would be temporary and therefore the cost control data did not have to indicate this waste of raw material. Such behavior bordered on malfeasance although mal-intent toward the company was not evident.

In many companies, this would have been prevented by a job material allocation process in which only the planned usage of raw material would be allocated to the production department. Any additional material needed would require explanation and approval before it would be made available. In our small company, we were not so highly structured, nor would I recommend having that much structure in most small manufacturing operations. Instead, the personnel involved were educated as to how costly the oversight was, which prevented such an error in the future. Subsequent application of proper job-costing forms also kept us from that type of problem. Without the inventory records we kept, the waste might have continued much longer. In many small companies, such profit leaks often remain undetected — especially if overall profit is good.

Every production run or job should accumulate data that is summarized on forms that have been designed for that function and show everything you wish to know about the job. You should be able to determine whether labor costs are proper, whether there were any quality control problems, whether the job was completed on schedule, and if those who worked on the job have any suggestions for change. This same kind of report would be important for a company selling a service. Although these job performance reports would ordinarily be summarized in a monthly analysis, management should provide for their review as soon as each individual job or production run is completed. If the data requires change or suggests a few pats on the back, timely action will be well received by all concerned. Just as in applying discipline to a child, correction must occur at the time of the infraction to have any meaning. However, it frequently is difficult to have such production data analyzed within a day or two after the job has been completed. Under these circumstances, rather than wait until the complete report is available, it is better for management to review the partially completed report and promptly take whatever actions may be necessary to have maximum effectiveness. Many managers fail to follow such a procedure. I confess to having made this mistake repeatedly, early in my career, due to lack of training.

The following form used by a job shop operation, in this case a rubber molding company, is an example of a job cost/report that provides necessary production control data for a small business. It also is used in preparing a job quotation.

Job Cost – Rubber Molding

Date ....Quotation # .............................P.O.#............................

Customer ....Co. contact......................................

Address..

Part description..

Material ....Weight ....Quanity...........................

Special instructions or tolerances ....

Tooling

...............cust. supplied, used

...............Cust. supplied, new

...............New tooling req'd

...............Tooling to be quoted

Tooling description:

Press size required:

12x12 ....12x18 ....18x18.........

24x24 ....36x36 ....48x48.........

Shut height.......................................

Platen travel req'd..............................

Inserts used? yes ....no...............

cavities per mold ....

Engineering cost...............................

Tooling quotation $ ....

Tooling Cost $ ....

Notes:

Production Data

Set-up chg.@ $20/hr/pc. ....

Mill, extrusion, & prep.
  chgs. @ $26.50/hr........................

Material per part:

wt: ....@ $ ....per/#

........................$ ....per pc.

Insert $ ....ea. x 1.25 $................

Paint & sand blast time
  @ $22.00/hr. $ ....

Cycles per hr. ....

Press Time:

12x12 @ $21.25/hr. $ ....

12x18 @ $22.00/hr. $ ....

18x18 @ $25.00/hr. $ ....

24x24 @ $30.00/hr. $ ....

36x36 @ $36.00/hr. $ ....

46x48 @ $42.00/hr. $ ....

Scrap (rejects @ flash)
  est. cost per part $...........................

Technology factor $.............................

QUOTE $ ....

Total # rejects:.................................... Average act. flash/part ....#

Note that the preceding form provides complete data relative to the order involved, makes it easy to review from a production efficiency viewpoint, and provides data for revisions necessary on any reorder received. It provides for easy control of that department when introduced over its entire production and summarized into a reporting form at the end of each month (if you couple it with payroll analysis and inventory control). Payroll analysis makes sure that all the man-hours expensed are accounted for and ensures that all time that should be charged to a job is charged to it. Inventory control assures that all the material used is accounted for by the job cost sheets. In smaller companies these last steps are frequently neglected and leave controlling too inexact. The inventory leakage revealed when such controls are first applied frequently shocks management by its magnitude.

After a job or production run has been completed and data provided by this form is received by your accounting personnel, it should be promptly summarized so that an accurate per part cost is determined. Resulting data should be provided to department heads who in turn advise all others who are involved in the job.

Personnel and human resources management: The controls needed for a small organization in this area are very few compared to those required in a large organization. This is true because management is in contact with every one in the organization on a continuing basis. Reports that would be required much more frequently in a large manufacturing company might suffice if provided once a year in a small company. For example, indications that labor turnover this year was twenty percent higher than last year would require investigation. Absenteeism or the prevalence of work related accidents might justify reports every calendar quarter. An area-wide study to determine prevailing wage rates and trends would serve as a good control influence and ought to be conducted every few years or more often if conditions such as marked inflation are prevalent.

Much of a company's control is executed through job descriptions, performance standards, and the job review process. The need for controls sometimes results from experience. No matter how small your company, if controls can be applied without great cost or difficulty, do apply them. Usually, the cost will be more than offset by

improved performance and achievement. Further, unpleasant sur-
prises are less apt to sneak up on you.

Section VIII

SPECIAL TOPICS

This section addresses many subjects that represent special areas of management which deserve further discussion. Looking at the index might lead you to think they are a potpourri of topics included without logic. Untrue. They are areas of management each of which was a problem for me in my experience. For that reason I believe most business managers will also find themselves involved with them at some time.

Properly dealing with them sometimes requires employment of outside talent. Most would be handled by you or delegated to people within your organization. In each case, your awareness and understanding of the subject should enable you to manage them more effectively.

Some subjects that are important to management have been omitted from this book on purpose. Like marketing, they represent areas that are best applied with specific customizing for your business.

If you successfully apply **stealth management,** these special areas of management will prove surprisingly easy to handle, because with a **stealth management** approach you will be tapping into the vast storehouse of energy, creativity, and inherent ability of your employees. They will know that the organization's goals and their personal goals are compatible and interdependent. You might say that your managing in such a manner will act as a beneficial catalyst and an elixir in the process of achieving goals.

49 · The Employment Process

The Interview

Because, as a manager, you will delegate most of the employment process and be involved in interviewing only those who report to you, we will discuss only that type of interview. When you are hiring a person who is leaving other employment to accept a position with your company, you have a double responsibility. Not only do you have an obligation to fit the right person into the job but, if because of a misfit you subsequently find it necessary to discharge him, that person's career may have been severely upset. The things you must try to determine about an applicant during one or more interviews are:

- Does he have desirable education and training
- Is his work experience good
- Does he communicate well
- Will he be a good team member, liked by others in your organization
- What are his personal goals and do they conflict with your company's goals
- Can you depend on his value system — especially significant if he will have considerable financial responsibility
- Was he well regarded in his previous job
- Does he have any problems that may affect his being a good employee — health, financial, family, etc.
- Is his salary expectation compatible
- Is your company's management style compatible with his
- What have been his major accomplishments and failures in the past
- Does he have significant outside interests

It is important for you to be aware of the law — especially the Americans with Disabilities Act — as it applies to the employment process and that you do not give a rejected applicant the perception that you have evaluated him from any vantage point other than his ability to do the job. Although you are in the position of orchestrating the interview, the applicant should be made to feel as comfortable and communicative as possible. The setting, the level of formality, and a relaxed attitude toward time are important. Sometimes an imposing office or being separated from the applicant by a large desk can be intimidating during an interview. You must be prepared to lead the conversation with questions that are friendly, as opposed to being provocative. Encourage the applicant to talk about himself in relation to his career. Balance the interview by contributing information about your company and even discuss current events if doing so encourages a relaxed and friendly attitude.

It is vital that your other key people meet the applicant and participate in the process of hiring him. If they help in the selection of a key employee, they are much more apt to help him become oriented to his new job in addition to aiding in the evaluation process. This policy also gives the applicant an opportunity of getting to know the organization and better evaluate any offer you extend to him.

It is difficult to verify how well a person did in any previous employment because of how the courts have viewed such information with regard to privacy. However, it usually is easier if the previous employer is a small rather than a large business. If the previous employer is in your locale, there are many approaches you can use to circumvent the personnel department or the applicant's previous supervisor in seeking information. A third party, an employee of your company, or contact with any former fellow-employee can each provide useful information. If the applicant was in purchasing or sales, contact with a supplier or customer may be helpful. Sometimes an often used question such as, "Would you rehire the person if an opening for his talent existed?", will evoke a useful response. Sometimes a question that would not be a likely source of embarrassment will trigger an answer and useful information. For example, information about length of employment, initial responsibility and terminating job title may be revealing. If the applicant is being considered for a job of considerable responsibility, it could be worthwhile to hire an investigative agency or a professional reference organization to check out his background. In a small company, a mistake in hiring a manager or supervisor can be much more serious than in a large organization.

It is important to verify past employment and education and obtain all possible input. I once was involved in hiring a person to become an executive vice-president of my company. It was an important step, because of my approaching retirement age. Of the few applicants we had interviewed, one seemed to be outstanding. Checking with past employers was difficult because he was still employed by the company he had been with for many years. His previous employer had been the victim of a merger and the normal path for such inquiry was lost. Contact with the junior college and the university he attended indicated that although he had attended them both and had been a good student, he had not graduated. This was in conflict with his application and I confronted him with it. He finally admitted lying about his degree saying he did so because he felt I probably was very *degree* conscious. Because his attendance at college was over twenty years earlier, and the dates of attendance he had given us were slightly off, this took some persistence to dig out. Of course, he was eliminated from contention for the job — his value system was badly flawed. Although having a degree might have been a requirement at most large organizations, it would not have been a deterrent for us. One of the best engineers I have known did not finish college, and our organization had more than one manager who had not finished college but who were performing excellently.

As the number of applicants for a position is reduced, it is important that those being seriously considered are made aware of the job description, the probable performance standards that will apply, and the company policies and fringe benefits. These items should be discussed in detail. This entire process of hiring a key man should be conducted so that it will leave a positive impression on those who are not chosen. It should also serve to generate an enthusiastic attitude toward the new position within the chosen applicant.

When interviewing a potential applicant for a key position in a company using **stealth management** philosophy, it is important to focus on character, the ability to get along with people, education, experience, and other typically desirable traits. If you have a personnel manager or personnel department, even though it is intended that the perspective employee report to you, you must not go around them. You should permit them to do all the conventional things for which they are responsible and involve you only in the interview process.

Psychological Profiles and Aptitude Testing

I am not a strong believer in the use of psychological profiles and aptitude testing as they apply to managers except prior to employment. Repeated attempts by psychologists to establish a meaningful relationship between actual job performance and assessment of performance potential have been disappointing. New tests for the aptitude of good judgment, while improved, are still less than satisfactory.

There are many valid uses for aptitude testing, however, and as a manager you should know how and when to use them and be able to put such information into proper perspective. A taxicab company in Philadelphia, experiencing a high accident rate, hired a firm of psychologists to develop a test they could use during the interview process to minimize the chances of hiring accident prone drivers. Because the psychologists they employed were unaware of any such test having been developed before, they decided a research project was in order. They perused many types of test results, comparing them with driver accident records, and found no meaningful correlation. Starting afresh, they designed a new test with an unusually long list of questions that did not necessarily relate to driving and administered that test to an appreciable number of taxicab drivers. The only question on the test that seemed to relate to the problem was a question having to do with how long the person had lived at his present address. If the home address had been the same for six years or more, the driver seemed to be less accident prone. They then designed a new test with many meaningless questions plus the one having to do with length of stay at the present living address and applied it to all new driver applicants. With this test, utilizing the answer to but one question, they agreed to test all applicants for their client (the taxicab company) for fifty dollars per person and were successful over a period of time in effecting a very substantial reduction in accident expense.

Let us put the above experience in perspective. It is true that people who move infrequently may very well be a more stable group than those who move more frequently, but is it fair to refuse to hire a person who had just moved for the first time in fifteen years because his family had grown and he needed a larger home? Could such refusal result in a law suit? To all this might be added the possibility that people can experience temporary psychological pressure as a result of changing residences. There are many such variables which make the application of testing and the use of test results far from simple.

There are some aptitude tests that are very helpful — those having to do with our use of the physical senses. If a person suffers less than normal hearing, eyesight, finger dexterity, spacial perception, or any other problem relating to the physical senses, you as a manager must be particularly careful in utilizing that person's talent, not only for the good of the company but also in the best interest of the employee. I recall our hiring a teenage boy for a summer job and finding out through testing that he had extremely low finger dexterity. While interviewing him, he indicated his intent to become a dentist. I made it a point to indicate his poor finger dexterity and also said that I would not want to use him as a dentist for that reason. Fortunately, the boy did change his vocational interest.

Psychological profiles applied to managers already in your employ, in my experience, are of little value for several reasons. The resulting reports usually are so vague that they are impractical. The apparent reason for vagueness is the ever-present possibility of a law suit from conclusions that might be difficult to prove. Such profiles are also subject to considerable misinterpretation not only by the psychologist writing the report but also by the client who may discern unintended meanings in it. The psychologist, being less than intimately familiar with your company and the particular jobs involved may not have the proper perspective in applying his interpretation of the test results. For these reasons, the several psychological test reports I have experienced, failed in every case to make me aware of anything about the people tested that was not known to me before.

I have spoken with others in business management and with one rather prominent industrial psychologist. They all agree that, in most instances, there is little likelihood of obtaining meaningful results from psychological profiles of your existing personnel. Further, these same people have all observed the resentment of personnel when they are forced to submit to such testing. It is considered a demeaning experience. However, where safety is extremely important, where rapid reflexes are required, where national security is involved, and probably in other appropriate situations, there are valid and important applications for psychological profiles.

In spite of all the foregoing negative attitude toward psychological profiles and testing, I want to point out that we as managers should be aware that such testing is changing and is improving. Also, the application of computer software in the field of psychological testing is improving its effectiveness. Even though it can be without benefit when applied to present personnel, it can be very useful when properly applied to applicants. In utilizing such data, it is important to realize that, in a large percentage of cases where testing might indicate a lower than normal measure relative to some aptitude, merely being made aware of the condition often permits a person to compensate for the deficiency. Ascribing too much importance to a negative psychological test could cause you to erroneously cast aside a potential talent, one that could have been very valuable to you.

One other area of psychological testing to be aware of is handwriting analysis, a testing technique that repeatedly has been proven to have value. In using it, my experience has been good. Unfortunately, it is not an exact science and is very dependent of the interpretive ability of the graphoanalyst. It can be used sometimes without the knowledge of the employee, but legal opinions in this regard are changing and caution is advised. It can give you insight into an employee's personality that you were not aware of, or reinforce your existing knowledge. On two occasions it helped me make a wise decision regarding key employees. Handwriting analysis is increasingly being used as a personnel tool and is becoming a highly accepted analysis technique in England.

Using a consulting psychologist to aid in implementing major changes in personnel policy or in the conduct of employee surveys often can be very wise. In such instances, an industrial psychologist can extend the benefit of his knowledge and experience to maximize achievement of a desired result.

50 • Use of Consultants and Professional Services

I strongly favor the use of outside consultants to help introduce professional management into your organization. However, you must be highly selective in choosing a consultant or a consulting firm for this purpose. Certainly there are occasions for psychological testing of your personnel, but while you are instituting a major change in management style is not one of them — particularly in a small company. Such testing of personnel *already on board* too frequently causes resentment among workers and results in very little benefit. The risk/reward ratio is too high. Therefore, when you interview possible consultants, be sure to determine their attitude toward such testing. Also, become acquainted with the details of their plans to help you, how long the process will take, and how much it will cost. Even consultants can lack soft skills and be less effective in their work as a result. The most important soft skills for a consultant, at the outset, are those that assure that his employment by your organization does not affect the prevailing working climate. For example, if there is the potential for a cutback in employment as a result of a consultant's analysis, and your employees are aware of this, performance could suffer badly during the process. Such harm is minimized when personnel are aware of and in sympathy with the decision to hire a consultant.

Be sure that your hired consultant does not, as part of his style, merely lecture or direct. In order to improve your organization, he must involve those who will be managing the changes for which you have hired him. This involvement must be participative — at least up to the point where the C.E.O. decides that enough time has been taken for consensus building.

In reaching an agreement with a consultant, be sure to include an option for termination at any time without penalty. Also, try to obtain written assurances that the consultant, or his firm, will refrain from accepting employment from any competitor within a specified time period. Doing so will minimize the potential for proprietary information about your company being inadvertently shared. Establish benchmarks by which the consultants progress can be measured. After the process has begun, at appropriate intervals request feedback from employees to evaluate the progress being made and the value of the consultant's help. If you have the agreement of your management group on the employment of a consulting firm before such action is taken, you will reduce the likelihood of it becoming a problem and facilitate cooperation with the consultant.

After you feel satisfied that you have successfully instituted the desired management change, there may still be other reasons for outside consultants from time to time such as: revamping your wage and salary scales, changes in any aspect of your paperwork systems, raising of capital for expansion, or redesign of your facilities. When hiring a consultant to do a special job for your organization, try to find one with experience in your industry, and do not overlook the professional services you ordinarily use, such as your attorneys and accountants. Utilizing consultants unnecessarily can reflect on your self-confidence. It can also waste money, for such help is expensive. In addition to consulting fees, the cost of a consulting team's demands on the time of your personnel becomes appreciable.

51 • Decision-making and Brainstorming

Decision-making

Decisions can be made in many different ways. As a manager, you can make a decision unilaterally and announce it to those reporting to you afterward. This type of decision making is suitable for what are normally considered minor decisions and sometimes is justified in a crisis or emergency situation. There are also decisions that have to be made quickly to take advantage of an opportunity that may pass you by if a decision is delayed. Minor decisions could be those which will not have appreciable impact on people in the performance of their jobs such as: what trash handling service to use, should we be members of the local Chamber of Commerce, or what accounting firm should we employ.

When practical, decision-making can be effectively done with a combined bottom-up and top-down approach. For instance, suppose a product you manufactured required painting and your company was experiencing too many rejects due to paint blemishes. You could go to your shop superintendent and say, "Harry, I'm tired of the paint problems we've been having. I think we ought to try a new brand of paint. What do you think?" Having heard that you propose such a change, Harry could be intimidated and refrain from suggesting any course of action contrary to your thinking. Therefore, he might reply, "Yeah, it probably would be a good idea." Suppose, instead, you say to him, "Harry, we need to do something to eliminate the paint problems we are having. Study the situation and give me your recommendations." Harry can then go to the people actually doing the painting and investigate the problem. He might get an observation from the person doing the actual spray-painting that the problem exists only late in the work day. Further discussion could determine that the air compressor is drained of collected condensate first thing in the morning but by afternoon is causing the paint to have excess moisture. The cure is easy (draining the condensate every two hours), but it might never have been communicated in a manner that could result in proper change had you not originally asked *the right question in the right way*.

In all decision making, it is important that sufficient attention be given to each of the following:

- Do you have all the facts upon which a decision can be based
- Have you prioritized the facts so as not to be influenced excessively by data of little importance
- Have you considered both long-term and short-term results, if such consideration is in order
- Have you considered all the alternatives

- Whose cooperation will you need after the decision is made
- Who will be affected by the decision

Even if you find it appropriate to make a decision unilaterally, all six items in the foregoing list deserve your consideration. You can gain most of the benefit of participative decision making by at least involving those whose cooperation would be helpful and those who may be affected by the decision. This involvement can vary in degree. However, you are responsible for advising those people of the decision, the reasons for it, and any important facts such as timing and expected benefits.

Often, group decision making is necessary, and it can be a very rewarding process in that it more frequently results in a wise decision based on the best thinking of several people. The process usually improves morale because the group has participated. Usually, it works more effectively when the group is kept to seven or less, although there is certainly nothing magic about the number seven.

To improve group decision making, a leader should refrain from giving opinions until everyone else has had an opportunity to contribute. In fact, if you concur with the consensus prevalent within the group, it is unnecessary for you to voice an opinion — you merely agree. Encourage individual participation and thinking by asking questions. Discourage positive statements. They inhibit subsequent creative thinking. On a blackboard or a flip-chart, list pertinent factual data. If the decision seems complex, evaluate the data and assign relative numerical importance to each item. This process helps the group properly focus on the problem and minimizes prejudiced thinking. When you finally call for a vote, or use your own prerogative to decide based on the group's thinking, you are more apt to make a wise decision.

When individuals in the group are not thinking clearly, do not learn from others, are intimidated by the opposition, or use flawed data, poor group decisions will result. If adequate discussion has taken place but a good decision does not yet appear likely, it is usually wise to adjourn and reconvene at a later time after further study.

225

Too frequently, when the process is not well managed, a decision could be reached on a Friday that would be entirely different from one that would be reached on the following Monday even though the same data and the same people were involved. Such group ineffectiveness is not uncommon and prompted Peter Senge in his book, *The Fifth Discipline*, to pose the question, "How can a team of committed managers with individual IQ's above 120 have a collective IQ of 63?"

After a decision has been reached, if it requires monitoring or follow-up, it is your duty as manager to assign such responsibility. Further, if the decision can have appreciable impact on others in the organization, it would be wise to consider it as a proposal until they have had an opportunity to review and comment upon it. Then, finalize the decision.

Brainstorming

Brainstorming is an approach to group thinking and/or decision making that can be very creative and productive. If well directed, the process will have a highly stimulating effect on the group. If, as is frequently claimed, we ordinarily use but a small percentage of our potential mental capacity, brainstorming can expand this percentage appreciably. If we apply it well, brainstorming is a synergistic process that produces a result which exceeds the sum of creative thinking that individuals in the group might do on their own. In his book, *Managing Group Creativity*, Arthur Van Gundy cites several psychological study sources showing that ideational fluency (generating ideas in larger numbers and at faster speed) is very much improved through group interaction.

To lead a group in this process, the leader must be able to communicate well on the subject under consideration and pre-plan a *bag full* of stimulating questions that can be used when the thinking processes seem to be dragging. The solution sought, or several related solutions, may require considerable time and the experience can be unlike any prior group thinking exercise. The leader should have an agenda designed to aid the group in getting to the core of the problem or assignment. He also must create a feeling of mutual trust and a free thinking atmosphere within the group — a difficult task unless they have previously participated successfully in such a process.

You must make the individuals in the group feel comfortable letting their minds roam freely on the subject being considered without fear of making fools of themselves. In fact, they should realize that a silly or foolish statement sometimes can be the catalyst that permits the group to finally focus on a solution. Early judgment should not be applied to anyone's suggestions, ideas, or thinking. Rather, ideas should either survive, be replaced, or be added to as a subtle process of survival for that thinking which becomes dominant through group evaluation.

A brainstorming session should have four to seven participants, chosen because they are good thinkers and have knowledge of the subject. They should trust one another and each should be of a temperament that would be unlikely to produce serious friction. The group should not include any person who you know would prefer to work alone. If there is a previously established relationship involving the kind of intimacy referred to by William Ouchi (see topic 37) in his reference to Japanese management, a much greater spirit of participation will result. It is usually helpful to establish an aura of humor soon after the session begins — perhaps a mood bordering on facetiousness would be a good description. People feel freer to make an inane comment or suggestion in a spirit of jocularity than in a serious vein. Of course, too much of the type of humor which is primarily intended to draw attention to the would-be humorist can have a negative effect.

It is important that people participate in a manner that encourages further creative discussion, which would not be the case when a participant applies absolute statements. As leader, you should ask that all ideas and thinking be presented as questions or thoughts for discussion. "Should we begin marketing *that* product next March?" is much better than, "We should introduce that product next March." As ideas begin to crystallize, visibly recording them on a flip-chart is helpful. As overall conclusions or new directions become apparent, it is usually constructive to have a break to permit time for evaluation. There is no typical format for creativity or brainstorming.

At the start of a brainstorming process, as in any problem-solving activity, properly defining the problem is extremely important. After you feel the group has reached a definition, it is often helpful to challenge them to try defining it in other ways. Addressing the question "why should we solve the problem?" can add perspective to the discussion. Data gathering, research assignments, listing and evaluating solutions and all the usual problem-solving techniques should be used. The real difference between brainstorming and ordinary problem-solving is that in brainstorming, through good team selection and climate setting, you achieve a higher level of individual motivation and synergism. It usually is relatively expensive because of the man-hours involved, and should be resorted to only when ordinary problem solving approaches seem inadequate.

When the leader believes a consensus is forming, he should encourage the group to draw conclusions, formulate a plan, or otherwise finalize the process; before being finalized, all conclusions should be subjected to a complete *potential for failure* analysis.

Attempting to form a brainstorming group, unless you have participated in one, based on this somewhat sketchy description, could prove frustrating. It is a very unstructured procedure and difficult to describe definitively. Perhaps it will be constructive to relate actual applications of the process in my experience:

We were manufacturing a rather sophisticated cable used by the seismic industry in their search for oil. In one application, a segmented cable having a length of up to two miles and containing seismic recording instruments at rather close intervals is towed in the ocean as part of a seismic recording process. The towed cable does not stay at constant depth which results in compromised data being received. The cable depth varies over the two mile length to an appreciable degree. We decided to attack this problem with a brainstorming approach. During the session, one of our engineers facetiously suggested that we put a gremlin in each section who would blow up a balloon or let air out to cause that section to assume a proper depth. That humorous suggestion resulted in a patent being issued to us for an oceanographic cable design having a flexible air tube extended the length of each section; that air tube could be expanded or contracted in response to pressure sensing devices from an adjacent air supply tube connected to an air source from the supply boat.

In another similar experience in which humor played a part, we were trying to develop an electrical connector to be used in a deep-sea military defense application. The extreme pressures to be tolerated were at the outer safety limits using conventional sealing techniques to prevent incursion of sea water. Rather than depend on a nearly perfect performance of such a design, we chose to apply brainstorming to the problem. During the discussion, someone again facetiously suggested that we put a gremlin in the connector who would blow air into the connector to balance the pressure of the sea. That humor suggested two solutions, both of which proved valuable to us in the future.

Sometime later we were negotiating with the oceanographic products division of Lockheed Corp. about a cable application of a highly experimental nature. During the discussion, I was asked whether our small company had any understanding of pressure compensated oceanographic connector design. At the time, such technology was very new and not apt to be known — especially by a small company such as ours. I recalled solution number two from our prior brainstorming and could respond that we had knowledge in that area.

Brainstorming can often be more important to the small company than to the large company. In the small company, the depth of experience is often less than in a large organization and the cost of acquiring costly ideas or knowledge can be a stumbling block. Brainstorming can act as the equalizer by providing answers not otherwise available. *Stealth management,* by its very nature establishes the cooperative atmosphere needed to best reap the benefits of brainstorming.

52 · The Suggestion Box

In topic 24 reference was made to the use of a suggestion box. This practice has become so commonplace that there now is a trade organization made up of managers of suggestion systems. A common practice in most suggestion systems is to provide recognition and rewards that take many forms. Do not endorse such behavioral mal-practice!

In the well managed organization the psychological climate is inherently one of shared goals and motivation levels are high. Suggestions should flow freely as a normal activity. Motivation should be the normal desire to maximize company performance. The reward should be the good feeling that results from one's contribution to performance — the knowledge that "my company will benefit".

Psychologists have long ago determined that children, if properly taught, do not benefit from being rewarded for good behavior or scholastic achievement. Yes, compliments are very much recommended. They are good for self-esteem, which certainly is very important. Rewarding a child or an employee for doing that which is expected, however, only encourages attention to seeking reward rather than experiencing the pleasure of good performance.

Valuable suggestions should be noted on an employee's record and given due value when the employee is given a performance review or being considered for advancement.

A suggestion box is of value to the rare employee who is reticent or has difficulty communicating verbally. If used for those reasons, rewards should not be made, but response to suggestions is mandatory.

53 • Policy Manuals

There are numerous types of policy manuals used in management. They include corporate manual, operations manual, quality control manual, personnel policies manual, office procedures manual, and many others. As your organization grows, certainly there will be need for manuals, but in each case be sure of the need and the long range value to those who will most likely use them. Manuals can be helpful, and they can be harmful. Some of the helpful aspects of manuals are:

- If given appropriate manuals to study, new personnel can learn company procedures more rapidly.

- A manual helps in the defense of the organization's policies in the event of litigation.
- A manual by minimizing inconsistency of policy, improves overall employee behavior.
- An approved quality control manual is usually required for a company to be considered as a bidder for military and other types of contract work.
- It can serve as a checklist in preventing mistakes. All of us, at some time, have made a mistake that would have been easy to prevent. Airline pilots reduce this type occurrence to very low levels by using a checklist before takeoff.

Formalized manuals that define policies and/or operational procedures can cause people to have a stilted attitude toward their jobs, and can inadvertently serve to reduce creativity and initiative. A creative person or the type person we often refer to as "a doer", suffers loss of motivation if his job is excessively prescribed — a condition that can result from over-dependence on manuals. Therefore, be sure that manuals used in your organization are written in a manner that does not limit productivity or creativity. To ensure that this is understood the following admonitions, or their equivalent, are important:

- The mission statement, should be considered a very influential part of all job descriptions. Your employees should be strongly directed toward achievement of the individual goals set for them — in concert with the overall plan established for the organization.
- There is no portion of any manual used by the company that should be considered as cast in concrete. Departure from previously established practices, however, should be permitted only if done within certain guidelines. No departure should be permitted that would legally compromise the company. No departure should be permitted that does not conform to the established value system of the company. No departure should be permitted that in spirit, or in fact, breaks any agreement to which the company is a part; that includes employee practices as established by the employee manual.

- In the event of emergency that does not permit time to follow usual procedures or contact one's supervisor, a manager is expected to take action in the best interest of the organization and report the situation as soon as possible thereafter.

As your business grows and you develop many repetitive management actions which need to become established procedures, prescribing them in a manual is recommended. A second kind of manual that can be beneficial is a policy manual which is a series of statements of intent that cover each level and division of the organization. The policy manual, if properly established by management, can be very helpful in legally establishing the company's intent in liability cases.

54 • Advertising

In the small company, sometimes it is difficult to fund much advertising. Never-the-less, advertising all too often is a very important part of selling. Therefore, the various types of advertising available to your business must be evaluated and assigned priorities to ensure the most effective utilization of the allocated budget. Unless you have considerable advertising experience and can think objectively with regard to applying such experience to your organization, it is usually wise to seek professional guidance.

If you were introducing a product to an original equipment manufacturing market, at the outset you might depend entirely on personal sales by either your company's personnel or commission salesmen. Probably the only advertising you might need would be product brochures and pricing data sheets. Try to obtain suggestions from "close" customers about your proposed brochure. If your product or products have been marketed for some time, perhaps through manufacturers representatives, it might be necessary to back them up with some advertising at the national level. Soliciting advice from your representatives would be wise, since they should be familiar with the advertising effort of other manufacturers and might better be able to predict what approach would be most effective. Your advertising agency should be consulted and appraised of any advice you receive from your representatives. You must decide how to spend the budget your organization has allocated for an advertising program. Your advertising should be evaluated for effectiveness and appropriate changes made as necessary.

If you are involved with consumer goods, selling through wholesalers or directly to retailers, your advertising would be entirely different in character than if you were selling non-consumer goods. Your advertising agency should be sensitive to this and advise you accordingly. Usually, an advertising account executive who is familiar with one type of market is less than expert in another. You must be sure that you are working with the advertising firm and account executive who can be most helpful to you. At the retail level, even the small business usually depends on newspaper, radio, and/or television advertising. Changing advertising agencies is both time consuming and costly. Therefore, choose your advertising agency carefully. Your advertising should have a theme, perhaps a logo, and appear with optimum repetition. Appealing to the senses, as discussed in topic 20, will produce the best results.

In most small businesses, you cannot take averages of other businesses with regard to advertising budgets and apply them to your own. Instead, you must determine the potential value of advertising to your business and establish a budget for the purpose. As your business grows, you may be able to control your advertising budget as a percentage of sales, or by some other standard. When your business is small, very often it is necessary to apply a much larger than typical budget to gain a sufficient initial result from your advertising. When such is the case, you have to think in terms of what you can afford to spend, knowing that the desired impact may not be felt soon.

To be cost effective, advertising requires considerable planning. Above all, you must think in terms of the customer. What does he need to know about your product and does the brochure or advertisement provide that knowledge in a manner that is easy to read and easy to understand? Is it free of questionable claims? Is it tasteful? If the brochure is meant to provide useful data, is it in a form that encourages saving for ready reference? There is great disparity of printing quality and you must be careful not to waste money on poor quality.

Your customer will know the difference, and it can reflect on your image.

The foregoing discussion of advertising is abbreviated, because to be comprehensive about so complex a subject in a short span is impractical. The subject is included with the prime objective of making you aware of the importance of the following:

- Advertising is important to virtually all businesses
- Advertising will be ineffective if not done well
- Most of us tend to over-value our personal opinions of advertising
- When involved with advertising, employ professionals
- The effectiveness of advertising is largely the result of its appeal to the senses. Try to look at your advertising from the consumer's viewpoint
- Although it is difficult, particularly for the smaller organization, to evaluate the effectiveness of their advertising, it is important to set some standard by which it may be judged. Quantifying sales inquiries or actual sales against preset goals is one way

55 • Crisis Management

What constitutes a "crisis"? The worst aspect of crisis management is failure to recognize when you are involved with crisis. Too many managers think of crisis only in the context of imminent business failure or bankruptcy.

It would be much more realistic, perhaps even constructive, to consider your organization in a crisis condition when: (1) its performance has been in a decline compared to the overall economy for longer than three calendar quarters; (2) its cash-flow plus available credit are inadequate to permit the planning of necessary corrective action; (3) its management is without a viable plan for recovering from poor performance or, (4) A new definition of "what is our business" is needed because of changed market trends or conditions, and management has not re-addressed the question soon enough. Number (4) has been the cause of many companies falling prey to the smoke stack industry syndrome in which the company or industry has not "changed with the times".

If your company is in a crisis condition but there is no threat of bankruptcy, several steps need to be taken promptly. Often there is not time to implement them in a normal *stealth management* manner. Given that situation, consult with those who report to you if time permits but then decisively take those steps which are required. Each company is different and the following recommendations need to be modified as necessary, but they are nearly universal in their practicality:

- Be certain that your financial data is accurate and current, even if a special audit and a mid-year physical inventory is required.
- Initiate as severe a cost cutting program as possible without jeopardizing your long term potential. This effort will be most effective if you do consult with and get suggestions from your employees.
- Address the question, "What is your business?", as covered in topic 40. If, after this exercise, your definition does not provide for sufficient growth potential, your business definition is still inadequate. You also must have sufficient profit potential to attain acceptable goals, or your business has a bleak future.
- Convert any idle asset values that can be sold, which will not be needed in the near future, to cash. This would include inventory reduction and sale of unneeded fixed assets.
- Improve efficiency and reduce employment wherever possible. The management committee is an excellent resource to use for this purpose. Care should be taken when reducing labor costs that personnel are not dismissed who will be needed soon after your crisis is over. If practical, reduction of the work week helps, while lessening the need for laying off people. Any reduction in employment should be accomplished without affecting key employees, insofar as you can do so.

- Establish a planning group and, as outlined in topic 42, lead this group through the process of developing a plan to carry you through your crisis period. It involves establishing goals and the required strategies for attaining them. During these strategy sessions, a desirable change may become apparent to you that escapes the group. Examples might be the advisability of terminating an entire department, eliminating a whole layer of management, or replacing a less than effective person. Such changes will require prompt but decisive action. In a crisis situation, actions need not necessarily originate from the plan. When you find it appropriate to take action on your own initiative, communicate with the planning group as soon as you can to give them the benefit of your thinking.

- As soon as corrective change has been initiated and the future looks brighter, your sources of financial credit should be apprised of your situation. This should be done in a partnership spirit and with candor. How would you wish a borrower to behave toward you if you were a banker? The answer to that question may help you. When selling (in this case, to your banker), your actions should provide the buyer with information that will make him look good to his superior as a result of his becoming your customer — or in this case, your lender.

- Having determined where you want to go and how you are going to get there by the foregoing actions, you must now make sure that the plan progresses on schedule and that each person is accomplishing his part of the plan properly.

- If after the above steps, you do not sense progress, it could prove beneficial to call in a consultant to help you. A certified public accountant with experience in your type of business should be able to determine the cause of your problems.

If you have waited too long to take action, and your creditors will not give you the time to take successful remedial steps, it may be necessary to seek chapter 11 bankruptcy protection. Legal counsel would certainly be needed in such a case.

Assuming you have managed your organization's crisis experience successfully and the future is beginning to look better, you should soon resort to the normal strategic planning process. By doing so, you will have a better perspective toward the future and be more apt to make wise long-range decisions. Also, the normal actions associated with good planning usually are positive in their motivating effect on an organization, and at this time morale building could be especially valuable.

56 · The Board of Directors

A board of directors normally is required if you are incorporated. Often, however, management uses a board of directors in a perfunctory manner merely to fulfill this legal obligation. If a *board* is properly chosen, it can serve very constructively by adding the experience of those on the *board* to that of top management. In my own experience, many mistakes were prevented, and frequently our planning and goal direction was aided by advice from our board of directors. Such benefits can be anticipated if you have the right attitude toward your *board*, select able people, and give them sufficient data to enable them to be constructive

The duties of a board of directors include the following:
1. Establish policies for the organization. They should not involve themselves in operational activities unless the president so requests or doing so is necessitated by abnormal or emergency conditions.
2. Appraise the president's performance — should be done on an annual basis.
3. Review all sales and financial results — at least quarterly.
4. Review a financial audit of the organization — at least once a year.

5. Make decisions that could have major impact on the company, especially those which involve actions that exceed the authority granted to the president by his job description.
6. Act as a council for the president by reviewing and advising him on subjects brought to the attention of the board.
7. Where stockholders are involved, assure that the company observes its obligations to them.

For the small or medium sized company, a board of directors should be relatively small to permit rapid decision making and to control the cost of having a *board*. Seven to ten members is usually adequate. Ideally, the following expertise and people should be included:

- Legal counsel
- Financial expertise — usually a person with strong accounting perspective, not necessarily an accountant
- The top person in your organization
- A second person from your organization, preferably the person you regard as your potential successor
- A person with in-depth experience in a similar field. If, for example, you are a manufacturer of valves, a person with manufacturing experience that includes problems similar to yours
- A person with marketing expertise in any field similar to yours
- One or more key investors in your company whose business acumen you respect

At least one, preferably more, of the *outside* members should have a background in professional management. All of the members of your *board* should be able to contribute constructively without being either oriented to single issues or strongly authoritarian. All members should be sufficiently interested to want to participate actively without prejudice; that is, they should not have personal agendas that interfere with their sharing in the organization's long term interests and goals. If a board member, for example, was also a supplier to the company, he must never be guided in his board participation by what is best for his own company (the supplier).

Board members should be paid for attending meetings and for any out-of-pocket expenses incurred because of such attendance. The fee you pay for attendance should be approved by the board but must be reasonable in terms of the organization's ability to absorb such expense. It should be sufficient to obligate participation and should be large enough to reasonably compensate for the member's time. Small companies might pay as little as a few hundred dollars per meeting, whereas large companies often pay as much as a thousand dollars or more per meeting.

Small companies might have meetings every calendar quarter, but if you have a large number of stockholders and you have a high level of fiduciary responsibility because your stock is publicly traded, having meetings more often is advisable. Sometimes, conditions require that you call a special meeting. There also are times when actions requiring board approval do not justify convening a meeting, but written approval is needed from the board members. In such an instance, approval can be solicited through the mails by a "memorandum of action" that would be prepared by your attorney. There are many responsibilities associated with attendance and the activities of a board of directors that require legal advice.

The head of the organization or enterprise is usually chairman of the board. As chairman, you should have a prepared agenda of the subjects to be covered at each meeting. A copy of the proposed agenda and any pertinent data that will be helpful in preparing for the meeting should be sent to each board member before the meeting so that there is time to study it. In some instances, it is wise for you to discuss such topics over the phone before the meeting. It is acceptable for you to state your opinions but inappropriate to try to influence the opinion of others. A director's team attitude can be affected adversely on discovering that, at the point his input should be solicited, the decision has already been made.

Before or at each meeting, your *board* should be given current financial and operational data. As you grow, such data should become more sophisticated. A good board will have people on it who can provide financial advice. Guidelines for board participation should be established. For example, it might require that you solicit board approval for actions that exceed a specified commitment of money, any major change in marketing procedure, or a revision to your product line.

Keeping your banker advised of the composition of your board and its actions will increase his confidence in you as a manager. Being a sole proprietorship, or unincorporated, does not prevent you from having a board of directors. In fact, it could be easier for you to recruit board members since there would be a lower level of fiduciary responsibility. If the *board* thinks it may be liable as a result of exercising its fiduciary responsibilities to the company, it may ask that the company provide insurance coverage for such risk.

57 • The Union

If all the benefits claimed for professional management techniques are valid, *stealth management* will give you and your employees a feeling of being on the same team. "What purpose then would a union serve?" The answer to that question is worthy of discussion and will be addressed later in this topic.

If your organization is unionized and you contemplate implementing *stealth management*, you certainly must take the union into consideration when formulating your plans. It is vital that you and the union do not have an adversarial relationship because of your intentions to revise your management style. It would be well to arrange an in-depth discussion with the head of the union about your desire for such change. You should indicate that you have no intention of interfering, in any manner, with the good relationships now prevalent between your employees and the union. Make it clear that your reasons for wanting to change are your concerns for long range business success, and your growing awareness that contented employees who sense a team atmosphere can have a tremendous impact on the company's and their own future. Be candid enough to convey to him the background for coming to this new thinking and ask for his cooperation and help in the implementation process. Explain how the employees will benefit, not only as an indirect result of the company's success, but also from being happier in their jobs. Offer to acquaint him with the process of *stealth management* and review for him the results of such change in other companies. Even invite him to sit in on the early planning meetings, unless that makes you very uncomfortable.

In 1988, Mr. John Mariotti, then president of Huffy Bicycle, a subsidiary of Huffy Bicycle Co., was interviewed about the unique success of his company. It had been able to retain its share in a very difficult market in which manufacturers from both Japan and Korea had become dominant competitors. In the process of optimizing performance by his company, he sought and received much beneficial cooperation from their union, the United Steel Workers. They held retreats with union leaders for the purpose of discussing problems and involved the union in the company's planning process. This story may serve to qualify the attitude, which is so prevalent, that the typical union is intractable and anti-management.

Certainly, it is possible to have either a bad relationship with your union or incompatibility with the people within the union. In such case your ingenuity and tact may be tested severely, and you may feel totally thwarted in your effort. If the job can be done, however, it is best done in a spirit of mutual respect for the long term benefit of both the company and its employees.

If you seem unable to achieve any semblance of cooperation from the union, perhaps you should consider a direct approach to the employees. By this, I do not mean that you should seek help from employees in influencing the union; whatever is done must permit the union leaders to be persuaded to change their minds without embarrassment. With this approach, proceed as outlined in the implementation process, without regard for the union — but be careful not to alienate them! When you feel that the employees notice the changes being made and that you are taking them into the planning process, those who are not inherently adversarial in their attitude toward the company should welcome the changes. The union leaders should soon become aware of such sentiment and establish contact with you about "What's happening?" That will give you a new chance at soliciting their cooperation. Because you are striving for change that is in the long term interest of both the company and the employees, there has to be a way of establishing acceptance by the union. Yes, it could try your patience and your ingenuity, but in most such instances the desired end results are worth the effort. Even so strong a union as the United Automobile Workers has cooperated with Ford, Chrysler, and General Motors in this manner, albeit reluctantly in some instances.

The question remains: "What purpose will the union serve if we have ideal management in which the interests of the worker and the company are both served equitably?" Many possible functions could surface if a union established its own strategic planning group and introduced professional management into its operations. They might begin as suggested for any organization and address the questions "What is our business?" and "What is our mission?"

Just to speculate where this might lead, consider the function of unions in Japan. In Japan, unions do exist but rarely have occasion to exert their muscle as in the United States. Instead, they are involved in every day cooperation between the interests of the workers and the company. They make a concerted effort to prevent criminal and communistic influences. On the rare occasion that a union finds it necessary to resort to strike tactics, it does so almost with embarrassment and with a sincere effort to achieve a cooperative and fair settlement as soon as possible. Such a strike might last but a day or two, long enough to show resolve and then end, allowing management an opportunity to respond. After settlement is reached, the union tries in every manner possible to minimize the cost and disruption suffered as a result of the strike. They view any cost to the company as being harmful to the workers as well.

Although I am unaware of a mission statement or a definition of its business that has been developed by any union, the inconsistency of their actions suggests that such professionalism is often lacking — just as is the case with most businesses. Today, unions frequently are operating with the short term goals of "staying in business" and "maximizing wages". Would it not be more constructive, instead, to plan for the long-term in which unions would become a viable and valuable addition to the business community at large? Suppose we were to define the business of a union that serves the automobile industry, as an example:

> We are in the non-profit business of promoting long term common goals between employees and management within the automobile industry. We organize workers to participate as members in our organization, and aid them when necessary in negotiations having to do with working conditions, safety, wages, employment security, and social benefits. When such aid is unnecessary, we serve to monitor these factors and keep them in perspective with regard to industry at large and changes within our society.

With this rather simple definition of activity, how might the union do all it can in the interest of the industry and the automobile company? To answer this question, the union needs to do some brainstorming on the subject. The following additional activities deserve consideration.

- Occasionally report to the company the results of employee polls on morale
- Serve as an impartial grievance department
- Act as an insurance department, to handle those kinds of insurance that all companies served by the union have in common and, by so doing, help to keep premiums and claims to a minimum
- Help to develop improved safety standards

The list could be much longer and include many of the duties of management that do not directly concern the hard skills of purchasing, manufacturing, and marketing. In fact, were this type of mission possible for the union, it might have to expand its activities rather than struggle for existence. The study of its mission is probably a good idea for most unions with the paramount consideration that business and unions can and should be good for each other.

58 · Quality and The Quest For Perfection

"The success of our company and attainment of its goals is important to me; after all, I participated in establishing those goals." Such motivational thinking should prevail and unconsciously promote overall team effort. Dr. W. Edwards Deming has repeatedly proven this claim in his work, first with the Japanese and since with many companies in the United Sates. Dr. Deming was largely responsible for the transformation of quality in Japan to a level of pride. After experiencing frustration trying to sell his theories in the United States, he successfully convinced the Japanese to apply them — a major factor in the economic success of Japanese manufacturers. There is no substitute for quality.

If you are a manufacturer or a seller of service, quality standards and quality controls are necessary, but when the working climate and motivational levels are proper, quality becomes a prominent part of each participant's working objectives. There will be less evidence of poor quality and lower rejection rates. The proper place to achieve quality is in the process of doing work; the inspection process can only approve or reject work and accumulate statistical data.

When we referred to product quality, a few years ago, we had two considerations in mind:

1. The product should be free of flaws that would cause inconvenience or harm to the customer and have a negative impact on future sales.
2. The product shall, through good design, function for the customer with a competitive level of convenience and superior styling.

In order to obtain *state of the art* quality, in the future, designers will have to think differently to be competitive. For example, the purpose of providing an automobile with a front passenger seat that may be tilted back is to permit the passenger to relax. Many cars have cruise control, a valuable convenience when driving long distances, but most do not provide a comfortable space in which to rest the right leg when using automatic cruise control. It would not be difficult to improve a car in this regard, and doing so would gain the attention of many traveling salespeople. Anticipating the value of such convenience improves the customer's perception of quality.

The Japanese include such thinking in their approach to quality. While American car manufacturers are improving rapidly in eliminating manufacturing flaws, in the area of more subtle improvements in quality, they still are followers. We are aware that two good violinists can perform the same music, but one may sound much better than the other due to a subtle quality called *presence*. Perhaps that word could be appropriately applied to quality and a third consideration added to the two previously mentioned:

3. The product should project a high degree of *quality* presence.

Examples of quality presence are the inclusion of a "redial last number" feature on many telephones, and the automatic seat belt which applies itself when the car door is closed. Perfection is virtually unachievable. To think otherwise would permit, at some point, concluding that there is no further improvement possible. How well, then, should work be done? How good must product design be? These are not simple questions, but they must be answered constantly by managers in their leadership roles. Seeking perfection can have a very negative impact when carried too far. For example, rust proofing a product which has a life cycle of 10 years, to a degree that permits resisting corrosion for 25 years, could increase the cost unnecessarily and make the product uncompetitive in price.

When relating quality and perfection to a service oriented business, the evaluation process is the same. It usually comes down to: "Will the client be willing to pay for the additional effort toward perfection."

When safety problems are involved with design or quality control, decisions can become complex. No set of standards can be established which could be applied universally. Each industry, through an evolutionary process, must establish its own standards and there is always compromise. For example, a car can be made as rugged as a military tank, but it would be priced out of the market.

The following questions should be asked when establishing how near perfect a product should be made, how safe it should be, or how well work should be done:

- Is there potential for harm if used as directed?
- Does the safety level equal or surpass the industry standard?
- Can you improve the product further without increasing cost?
- Can you improve the product further with a reasonable cost increase — one that would be acceptable to the consumer because of the value added?
- Is the level of quality as good as that expected by the recipient or user?

When a new service is being established or a new product is being designed, at some point further refinement or improvement must be put "on hold" and the product or service must be marketed. Doing so may afford you marketing advantage, whereas a delay to further improve the product may allow a competitor to introduce a similar product or service before you. Good judgment in such decision making is sometimes the difference between success and failure. At the point in the development of a new product, when the design seems satisfactory in terms of safety, marketability, and economics, any further improvement that cannot be realized quickly might best be held until a later date. Meanwhile, freezing the design to permit manufacture and marketing as soon as possible would probably prove to be a wise economic decision. Sometimes, permitting limited sales of a new product or service will indicate shortcomings or the need for desirable changes much more rapidly than continued engineering or research effort. Also, by carefully selecting customers for such limited marketing exposure, and openly involving them in your desire to "debug" a product or service, you can further your relationship with them.

The question of *how well work is to be done* is an important consideration which becomes part of the process of assigning work. The person to whom the assignment is given should be made aware of what are considered practical and acceptable limits of work quality as they apply to the assignment. In a well managed organization, such limits usually become rote through the standards and practices established by management. However, a manager must always be alert to those instances where company policy, customer expectations, or engineering specifications do not sufficiently define how well work is to be done and take action to establish the optimum level.

59 · Innovation

The old adage, "Necessity is the mother of invention", is as valid as ever. Designers, scientists, and engineers usually respond very well to necessity as a basis for innovation. It is true of workers in all vocations who sense a need for and the value of improvement. The more basic types of creativity are very difficult to stimulate, however. Examples would include the Zerox copier, the Poloroid camera, computer chips, and atomic energy.

The books, "In Search of Excellence", and "A Passion for Excellence" (see suggested reading list), cite numerous examples of innovation, each resulting from one or more individuals working on a *pet project* or idea in a near secret environment. They refer to such clandestine projects as "skunk works". Usually, a company is aware of such *secret* projects, but tactfully gives such awareness a low profile in deference to the initiative being shown. This attitude caters to the desire of the innovators for freedom from controls and what they deem as excessive accountability. The project proceeds more rapidly, with lower cost, and little, if any, short term involvement by management.

Skunk works usually connive to find needed materials and resources without upsetting inventories or other on-going work. They arrange for needed labor without causing incursions into other projects or departments. The absence of formality plus the surreptitious nature of the project seems to amplify the motivational level of the participants and creativity reaches a higher plateau. Lest we conclude that *skunk works* are the exception and that most innovation is highly structured, the evidence is very strong that virtually every major development by private industry in the past decade has been the result of a *skunk works* type of operation. Such experience suggests that, as a manager, you should be aware that encouraging innovation frequently requires a company *skunk works.*

In our company, our sales manager, who also had some engineering education, connived with our tool and die maker to sneak through a model of a new type check valve. After they had it ready for testing, they proudly brought it to me with a request for permission to test it. I complemented its appearance and granted permission. The tests indicated the design would not achieve their objectives and it was summarily put "on the shelf". About two years later, our chief engineer came to me with an improvement in our sales manager's design that he had already tested successfully, and the few who had been in on the project were all very enthusiastic about its sales potential. I asked them if it was patentable, but they could not think of any patentable feature. I pointed out that for our small company to try to compete in the big marketplace with a valve that was not unique might be so costly that it could prove disastrous. I challenged them to brainstorm the project further to determine a basis for patentability. The end result was a unique valve design that was patented and forced us to redefine our business. It had major impact on our future planning.

It should be pointed out that patents are "a dime a dozen" in that it often is easier to obtain a patent than to make money on the subsequent marketing of the idea or product. Many companies, especially those having their own patent attorneys, seem to delight in obtaining as many patents as they can. For the smaller company, this can be very costly especially with recently escalating charges by the patent office and patent attorneys. It usually is important to be reasonably sure of the potential profitability of a patent before spending the money to obtain it. It also is important to consider the potential cost of legally defending a patent. These factors cause some companies to adopt the attitude of staying ahead of the pack and by so doing eliminate the need for obtaining a patent.

Creativity manifests itself in many ways. Some people are very good at problem solving but would not be adept participating in basic research. Some people are much more creative working alone and feel very frustrated working with a group. Some people seem to *dream-up* new applications of old and well known concepts without external pressure or influence. Some people, who otherwise seem uncreative, become very creative within a brainstorming environment. Some people are able to broadly conceptualize in terms of time and strategic influences. You as a manager can improve company performance by recognizing such traits in your people and by encouraging creativity through proper climate setting, appropriate job descriptions, and good reward systems. The importance of innovation in the small company cannot be over emphasized; often it is the *lifeblood of success.*

Not all creativity stems from *skunk works.* Much of it results from conventional research and development effort or from university research. The latter is usually sponsored by government or private industry. There could be some benefit derived from your organization delegating and funding research by a university on a project of your choosing. Before proceeding with such an arrangement, it would be well to become acquainted with the experience of others and the typical agreement that would apply. Just as large companies often support a research and development department from funding provided by some small percentage of overall sales volume, so should a small company continually be involved in the type research and/or development that will keep your service or product line up-to-date and competitive. In the small company, specifying a fixed percentage of sales to fund such research is often impractical and as manager, you must find some other means of achieving the same result. Too often, if you are doing the same things in the same manner as five years earlier, your company is not progressive and may suffer reverses as a result.

Minnesota Mining and Manufacturing Co. exemplifies a company with a superior approach to encouraging creativity. They permit their employees to spend up to fifteen percent of their time each week in any manner they choose so long as it is product related. This encouraging attitude toward *creative dreaming* has resulted in a continuing flow of new products. Often, with the acceptance of a new product, their policy provides for the establishment of a new division and an entrepreneurial opportunity for the innovator.

60 · Your Customer

The likelihood that your business will be successful without customer appreciation is very slim, and it is becoming less likely in the current business environment. Only with a high demand product or service and no competition would this be possible, and then it might only be temporarily so. With ever-increasing competition in most types of business, managers are constantly being admonished for not being more *customer oriented.* The wide range of misunderstanding about "being customer oriented" and "being user friendly" on the part of business executives is in need of change. The guideline for such change, where it is needed, is as simple as "treat the customer as you would have him treat you were your roles reversed." It is said that a good secretary gives you back a completed letter that says what you would have said if you had known how to say it. In the same vein, treating the customer well requires definition and perspective. The fact that your customer feels you are treating him well could promptly become of little significance were a competitor to treat him appreciably better.

Sales and/or marketing have not been discussed here because in the small to medium size business expertise and policy in that area usually evolve with experience, especially if your sales/marketing approach is *customer oriented.* This area of management is certainly a big part of planning.

A test was given to a group of people who were involved in communications, the object of which was to show whether or not they could be sufficiently sensitive and articulate to write instructions on how to use the common telephone. They were cautioned to consider that they were writing for potential users who had never used a telephone before. Every one of them failed the test — they were unable to imagine themselves as never having used a telephone before. This same type of communication problem is prevalent in business among writers of product usage manuals or documentation. It seems especially true of computer software.

As a manager, you may very well be involved directly or indirectly with product oriented communication problems of this sort. Making these communications truly *customer friendly* can give your product a distinct marketing advantage. You cannot do that in most cases merely by having someone familiar with the service or product critique the documentation, although as a first step that is helpful. After making the instructions as clear as you can, have them reviewed by one or more people who would be typical users from whom you will gain much insight. Next, after making appropriate changes, submit your documentation to another group of typical users for criticism. You will often find them able to make further constructive suggestions. Continue this process until you observe that the criticisms are becoming few in number and insignificant in terms of importance. This approach also can be used with internal communications to be sure that your employees are properly informed. The only other good approach is to have the same task performed by a unique individual who has the very rare talent to be able to apply language in a near perfect manner that can be interpreted only as intended from the vantage point of the intended reader or user. They are "few and far between"!

Being properly customer oriented requires in-depth knowledge of his business and his requirements. This sometimes requires a lengthy period of familiarization and research. Effective marketing demands such customer familiarity for the purpose of being better able to serve. Suppose, as an example, you found that your product was being partially disassembled by the customer to permit applying a customizing revision that was desirable for his application. You could then offer to deliver the product in the desired disassembled condition, perhaps at a lower cost, or to install the customer's revision before shipping. With such an approach, you would obviously be a more valuable supplier , but if your only contact with the customer is through his purchasing agent you might never become aware of the opportunity to help in this manner.

Several years ago, I became aware that one of our customers was spending many man-hours inspecting our products before reshipping them. I chanced to discover this while personally delivering the last item needed to complete an order on which we were late. Near our customer's receiving department, I observed our product being re-inspected and that the operation required much space and several in-

251

spectors. We subsequently talked to the concerned manager in their organization and arranged to have their quality assurance engineer study our in-house quality control department. It was our intent to make necessary changes to reach a performance level that would permit them to eliminate the re-inspection. We accomplished that goal and extended them the privilege of reviewing our quality control, as it applied to them, at any time. As a result of this cooperative effort, not only did the customer save cost, but from the input received by us from their quality assurance engineer, we were able to improve quality to all our customers.

There is no substitute for end-user or customer contact, especially by managers but also by employees at all levels. Many manufacturers of consumer products have found great benefit in requiring employees to spend time with the customer and/or the end-user of their product. For example, with permission from a retailer, the manufacturer might occasionally have one of its engineers or managers spend a day in the department that sells its product to the consumer. You can learn the consumer's attitudes toward the product and frequently gain insight into how to make improvements. At the same time, you will establish good-will between your company and the retailer.

Suppose you encouraged your employees who have contact with customers to submit a report each month on some act of consideration for a customer that they initiated and devise some type of recognition for such deeds. Your employees would soon learn how pleasing this can be to the customer and how this attitude can become ingrained in your marketing style. If, when you went to pick up your car after having it serviced, the driver delivering it took time to clean your windshield, would you not appreciate it; and, if a few days later, the "customer's man" who wrote up the repair order on your car called you to see if the car was performing well, would you not be pleased with that car dealership? I have never had such courtesies extended to me, but I would gladly pay a little more when purchasing my car from such a dealer. Certainly he would have happier customers, his employees would enjoy their work more, and the business should be more successful. Integrated throughout the entire business world, such customer consideration would provide inestimable benefits to society-at-large.

Customer relationships require occasional creativity if they are to develop well. The perception that you are treating your customer well and that your relationship with him is excellent can fade rather rapidly if a competitor begins to treat him better. Just as life-styles and social mores change, so do supplier to customer relationships. Not only must you be alert to such change, but when practical you should initiate change. It would be wise to review all your major customers at least once each year with these considerations in mind. Each department that might be involved should conduct an in-depth study of that customer relationship and how it can be improved. Often the results of such studies can be applied beneficially to small customers as well. If you are marketing commodity-like products (sugar, tires, clothing, etc.), perhaps the only manner in which you can be the supplier of choice is by having a superior relationship based on courtesy, good delivery, and service. Being *above the pack* rather than the seller with the lowest price usually requires much creativity. A small business should have an advantage because it is more flexible and can change more rapidly.

Be participative with your customers!

61 • Be a Generalist

In his book "The Knowledge Executive", Harlan Cleveland refers to people highly trained in one field of expertise as specialists. Examples are accountants, lawyers, doctors, machinists, welders, and computer programmers — just to name a few. He refers to people who also have knowledge in the arts, science, and politics and who can think, study, and express themselves in those fields plus other fields of specialty as *generalists*. He says of them, "They are the people who furnish the glue that holds people together and the executive imagination around which people mobilize".

If you are an entrepreneur of a young, growing, successful business, the time will come when you no longer have enough time to devote to being a specialist in your field of expertise. At that time, you will find it necessary to be a leader of a wide variety of expertise necessary to your business — everything from design to production, from purchasing to marketing and, in the case of a manufacturing company, personnel and accounting. Every manager will experience this problem as his responsibilities broaden.

Assuming that you are not a highly educated, well read person, expert in many fields of expertise, how can you transpose yourself from being a specialist to being a generalist? Certainly it can not happen overnight, and only very gradually. It can happen only if you have a genuine interest in those other fields of expertise associated with your business. It is not difficult to acquire an understanding of accounting, marketing, production, quality control, human resource management, or engineering. Wouldn't you prefer working for a person with whom you could discuss your work intelligently, and in depth, as opposed to superficially? Devoting some of your time at home studying or reading on any of these subjects will help immensely. Show interest and persistence toward *overall* understanding of the activities and decision-making by your associates; this must be done, of course, in a manner that is not perceived by them as being intrusive. Participate in an occasional seminar on one of those subjects in which you seek further knowledge, probably at least every other year.

It is also of value to be knowledgeable in fields other than those used in your business. It is a rare business that is doing the same things today that it was doing 10 years ago. Many would say that substantial change is common every 5 years. More often than not, the cause for change relates to external influences and the decision-making that follows would be aided by such breadth of knowledge. *Broadening* of this kind can be enhanced by participation in public affairs and by studying current events — local, national, and global. It is also aided by general reading of what is regarded as *good books*, usually non-fiction. This practice leads to the kind of knowledge that reduces bias and usually produces better leaders. They are *generalists*. They will find it easier to grow with their business or enterprise, a necessity for the small business man.

62 • Finance

In the normal course of business, as a manager of a small to medium size business, you often will depend on or counsel with others for financial advice, and you will employ an outside professional accounting firm to monitor your financial records and prepare your tax return. If you apply *stealth management* techniques, your operational problems should be minimized, and usually, your experience will teach you how to respond to them. The entrepreneur, however, may suffer from insufficient capital or cash-flow. For the small to medium size business, financial requirements may be categorized as follows:

- Start-up financing
- Operating capital
- Growth capital
- Special project financing
- A good banking relationship

Start-up financing

Given that no business should be started without proper planning, the entrepreneur should automatically plan for all expected financial requirements plus potential contingencies. He also should seek advice from all possible sources such as his accounting advisor. One potential drain of money is time. Rarely does a new organization experience progress in accordance with a planned timetable. Financial strain can result when achieving the goals set by the plan takes appreciably longer than anticipated. During this extended time period, such costly factors as payroll, inventory, and other overhead items continue to accumulate. "Time is money". In the financial planning of a new business venture, it is advisable (if not mandatory), to provide for the *availability* of considerably more funds than seem to be required.

Operating capital

After a business has been established, there usually is an apparent operational pattern indicating seasonal variance in the items that make up a financial balance sheet — inventory requirements, accounts receivable level, and many others. It is important for the entrepreneur or chief executive to be sufficiently aware of accounting principles to understand a balance sheet and the importance of each of its components. He should know what ratios are important and what they should be for his kind of business. Examples of such ratios could include the following (which may not be typical for your business):

- Current assets to Current liabilities — Current assets should exceed current liabilities by 100%.
- Inventory to sales —Inventory should be sufficient for 2 months of sales.
- Accounts receivable to sales — Accounts receivable should not exceed 15% of annual sales.
- Total indebtedness to net worth —Total indebtedness should not exceed 65% of net worth.

The foregoing examples are not meant to be typical for any particular business. Counseling with your accounting advisor is certainly important, and if you have a board of directors, their collective input should be very helpful in this regard.

Keeping these ratios within proper bounds will not only indicate that your business is on track but will probably improve your banking relationship. When your constant monitoring indicates a ratio is improper, unless the cause is temporary and for some good and understandable reason, management should take prompt action to correct the imbalance. Keeping track of such indicators requires up-to-date financial and operational data; finding that inventory has gotten too high six months after the fact can prove very costly. If ratios appropriate for your business are being maintained, it can be assumed that you have sufficient operating capital for the present.

Capital needed for growth or for a special project

Unless you resort to borrowed working capital, growth often is limited by the rate of liquidity increase provided by retained profits. The best way for a small business to finance growth usually is by borrowing from a bank using fixed assets, inventory, or receivables as collateral. Bank borrowing, however, is accompanied by interest expense, the need to submit financial data at frequent intervals, and can be restrictive by requiring minimum bank balances. A big advantage of this type of financing over most others is not having to dilute ownership by selling stock to outside investors. Also, interest expense is tax deductible, whereas dividends to stockholders are not deductible.

You may find that your credit worthiness does not permit the borrowing level necessary. In such case you have several options:

1. Increase capital by the sale of stock
2. Issue long term bonds to present investors or others
3. Borrow from a Small Business Investment Corporation or a Venture Capital Co.
4. Seek a type of bank loan that is guaranteed by the Small Business Administration, a division of the U.S. Department of Commerce
5. Seek help from a customer or supplier with whom you have a close and important relationship

Each of the first four of these options require professional assistance and may entail giving generous stock purchase options to the lending organization. Option number five is an excellent source for financial help during a period of rapid growth or for financing a special project — if you can arrange it. In my former company, we devised a means of controlling the depth of an ocean-deployed streamer cable having a length of up to two miles. Such a cable, used in seismic exploration for oil, would be of considerable value, except that the cost for necessary research and development far exceeded our financial strength. Further, if the development and subsequent marketing effort took too long or required abandonment for any reason, the financial impact could have been disastrous. We asked a major customer who had potential use for such a product to aid us in its development in return for having first purchase rights and a royalty on all sales. They decided to grant us a considerable sum of development funds and assigned an engineer to coordinate the project with us.

In order to take advantage of a very large purchase discount for raw material needed on an order issued to us, we once asked another customer for permission to invoice for the required raw material when received by us. We explained our reason for the request and our financial inability to obtain the large quantity discount without such help. They complied and we were able to save about five percent on a sizable order. If you have previously established a good relationship, there are many ways to gain assistance from customers and suppliers, and usually such cooperation further strengthens the relationship. *The secret is in showing them how they benefit by helping you.*

Good banking relationship

If you anticipate the possible need for borrowing from a bank sometime in the future, it is important to establish a good banking relationship before the need arises.

You should cultivate the relationship with your banker by acquainting him with your organization and providing financial reports to him on a timely basis. Then, if you find it necessary to ask for a loan, his response is more apt to be prompt and with consideration for you and your needs. He may even offer you helpful advice with regard to your expansion plans. A good banking relationship also can be the source of other benefits such as credit information about your customers and introduction to other business people in your community.

Whether or not you are required to put up collateral when borrowing money for your business, the lender will always want to ascertain that you have adequate ability to retire the indebtedness as arranged. Your interest in this appraisal should be even greater, since failure to meet scheduled debt reduction could jeopardize both your collateral and the financial viability of your business. I have found in my own experience, and have observed in the case of other small businesses, that the small business man often must be somewhat daring in financing growth. He must be creative, daring, and prudent — all at the same time, a tough act to perform at best.

Timely financial data

The financial concerns that are important to the small business manager, in addition to cash-flow, mostly concern timely data and financial perspective about his company. Such concerns are certainly as important to the large business C.E.O. In the larger company, however, most of the actual work associated with financial management is handled by others. The small business executive often is unable to delegate such responsibilities. Financial data that is not correct and timely usually proves to be worthless at best or a cover-up of serious problems at worst. Do not let everyday pressures keep you from having up-to-date financial information about your company.

As a manager, you need to be aware of the "break-even point" for each of your product lines or services — the minimum sales volume you must have to avoid losing money. If you have only one product or service that you are selling, this is relatively easy, but with multiple products and/or services, it can become a constantly varying number that is difficult to determine. Seasonal variables can also add to the difficulty. In periods of "slow business" when sales are close to or below your break even point, it is important to be aware also of your "break-even cash flow point". Cash flow in this context is defined as sales less all *out-of-pocket* costs; that is, it does not include provision for indirect costs such as depreciation or mark-down of inventory on hand. If this figure is positive and an up-turn can be realistically forecast within a month or two, precipitous actions like those described in topic 54 (crisis management) often can be avoided. To dwell on such negative aspects of achievement may seem incongruous in a book espousing the positive results of professional management, but in the business life of the typical small business manager or entrepreneur, it is well to be prepared for such conditions. Few of us are without such experience.

Purchasing

It has always seemed unfair to me that small businesses are taken advantage of by the typical pricing policies that apply to so many of their raw materials. You might need a case of special bolts every thirty days and find that there was a marked price advantage in buying five cases. In addition, the five cases would be shipped with freight absorbed by the seller whereas in the one case quantity, not only would you have to absorb the freight, but freight cost would become an appreciable factor in the cost of the case of bolts. It is important that your purchasing people negotiate with available suppliers to get as much of the advantage of big quantity purchasing as possible.

There is usually considerable compromise to be gained from a little shrewd negotiating. For example, you could agree to purchase a year's supply (12 cases) with a scheduled delivery of three cases every ninety days and a five or ten case quantity price to apply. If the normal cost of special bolts was $2,000 per case, the supplier, guaranteed a twelve case production run, might save thirty percent compared to making six or more short production runs. If he gave you a twenty percent price reduction he would still be ahead. Many is the cost reduction our company negotiated with such an approach. Some times it resulted from asking the supplier the question "How might we redesign our part to accommodate to your manufacturing procedures more advantageously?" That question often produced fantastic results.

In small businesses, especially, having a good relationship and negotiating posture with your suppliers can add to your performance substantially. It would not be unusual for a one percent reduction in material costs to translate into a two to four percent increase in pre-tax profits.

63 • An Important Tool

For the 1990's, a most important management tool is your ability to communicate effectively. In utilizing this tool, your challenge will be to properly manage and dispense information. Your personal communications through writing and speech are an important portion of this effort. There is also another aspect of communications known as "information technology" which is becoming a major factor in communications — the use of computers.

Where is information technology applied? Most areas of business including engineering, marketing, quality control, advertising, human resource management, and financial record-keeping may benefit from the application of information technology. An example is the application of computers to improve the marketing effort of a manufacturer. Otis Elevator Co. was able to provide prompt response and anticipate the need for service because of such a revamp of their computer application to customer service. A small "black box" installed in their elevators senses malfunctions and with the application of the proper computer equipment, relays such data to a database which triggers actual response by field service personnel within 30 minutes. This application of information technology serves to improve the company's image and profitability. In addition to providing improved service, it eliminated the need for customers having to call for service. This, in turn, kept other elevator service companies from occasionally receiving business that now automatically goes to Otis.

It is easy to assume that the talent to computerize the financial data of a business is fairly common. However, person "A" might satisfactorily organize it to permit the easy preparation of a tax return; person "B" would so organize it as to also provide the performance data from which the C.E.O. could readily observe the relative performance of each department, each product line, each customer, and the maintenance record of all major equipment. Once established, either system would be operable with very little difference in cost. Which would contribute most to the success of the business? When employing such talent, it is important to be aware of the potential breadth of application of information technology and benefits that it can provide to your business.

PERT, a computer program that streamlines construction, and thereby reduces cost, is a good example of applied information technology. If you establish a new and complex product that historically requires six years from design to production, the proper application of information technology might serve to reduce this cycle considerably. Why is it that the Japanese can produce a new car from conception to delivery in less than four years whereas we take six years or more in the United States? Using *information technology*, major U.S. automobile manufacturers are now attacking this problem.

Ford Motor Co. has reduced the number of employees in their accounts payable department over seventy-five percent by an imaginative use of computers. Instead of issuing purchase orders, the order is executed via computer with the equivalent of paraphrasing applied to ensure that the vendor's computer record agrees with Ford's computer order. When the merchandise is received, the receiving clerk verifies all aspects of the merchandise on the computer. Receipt of the merchandise triggers payment to the vendor, and soon, payment may occur via wire transfer. Note that with this use of computers, there must mutual trust between Ford and their suppliers, but virtually all paperwork has been eliminated.

Computers often are introduced into company operations with the expectation of saving money but, instead, prove frustrating and expensive. Usually, that is because we are inclined to think of the computer either as a word processor or an accounting tool. As we begin to realize that computers can be used to creatively manage and disburse information in heretofore undreamed of ways, they will add substantially to our productivity.

64 • Management Shortcuts

There are management "short-cuts" that can be used, particularly by small business chief executives, providing there is no compromise in the desired level of control and that management has a sufficient and accurate feel of what is happening around them. For example, if your relationships with your customers are close and you are confident that sales projections are not subject to unexpected fluctuations, you could elect to depend on a *bin count* rather than a perpetual inventory to prevent inventory shortages.

A *bin count* refers to taking a periodic count of the inventory in a particular supply bin. It can be made reasonably accurate by using material from the top or outside of the bin. Reordering being triggered when the stock reaches a pre-set low-inventory marker. This marker should be located to assure that the remaining stock will suffice until the reorder is received. In all such short cuts, you must be the judge of the risk/reward relationship. In the example cited, there is the risk that inventory will be improperly wasted or misused; to prevent this requires surveillance on occasion to see that the material purchased does not exceed the amount required for actual production. If ten screws of a given size are required per product assembly, and twelve thousand such screws are consumed over a period of time during which one thousand assemblies are completed, it is necessary to investigate how two thousand of them disappeared.

Another short-cut might be the elimination of a purchasing department or purchasing agent if you and/or various department heads were to assume appropriate portions of the purchasing responsibility. It pretty much depends on how many hours of time are required to do all the purchasing for the company. If that responsibility would occupy but twenty hours a week of one person's time, employing a full-time purchasing agent would be inefficient. It might be that combining purchasing with personnel would be the answer for your organization. They both require similar skills.

If there is an employee, whose normal work gives him reasonable access to the shipping-receiving area and whose job permits frequent interruption, he could possibly handle shipping and receiving effectively. Again, there is the risk/reward factor which must be evaluated, but until your shipping and receiving functions require full time attention, you should devise a way to accomplish the job more economically.

Quality control must never be compromised, but often it can be accomplished more efficiently by spreading the responsibility among shipping/receiving and line production personnel. The Japanese, in fact, believe that high quality is best achieved by developing the ability to do the job properly the first time rather than verifying quality through the use of separate and special inspection procedures. This requires that each employee validate the quality of the previous work done on the product before he begins his contribution. For example, the paint department would not paint a part that is not of high quality, the receiving department would not accept parts that are not up to standard, the assembler would not assemble a part that he knows could be faulty, etc. In such instances, detection of quality flaws must be communicated in a manner that prevents resentment and minimizes scrap expense — all benefits of good team work.

It is just such "short-cuts" that often permit the small business to compete with much larger competitors. Lacking the larger organization's inherent advantage of size, if your organizational structure is as multi-layered and complex as they are, you are unlikely to be able to compete favorably. Operating in this way not only requires good leadership but usually is dependent on effective teamwork. An additional admonition: as your organization grows, you must constantly monitor the need for becoming more sophisticated; waiting too long can be expensive.

65 • Business "Restructuring"

During the early 1990's, in an attempt to become more competitive, it has become commonplace for businesses to streamline their operations — a process which has become known as "restructuring". In practice, restructuring usually involves the elimination of as many layers of management as possible, a stringent analysis of the need for each job, and the dismissal of a large number of employees. Insofar as restructuring eliminates unnecessary jobs, it would seem to be a constructive process. Unfortunately, because it rarely is planned in a participative manner, but instead is done in a very authoritarian manner, experience will show that most restructuring will require a long time before reflecting improved productivity — if ever.

In one instance, of which I am aware, the CEO of a large company called an assembly of employees for the purpose of announcing not only a sizable reduction in work force, but also a reduction in gross pay. The pay reduction would be the same for all, percentage-wise, and prompted the CEO to comment that he had more to lose than "any of you". That insensitive statement caused one employee to ask him how that was possible when the loss of her job would necessitate removing her son from college and prohibit her from keeping up with her house and car payments. Unknown to that CEO, the morale among his employees could not have been much lower.

If you feel that restructuring is needed in your company, go through a planning-like process to define the appropriate changes to be taken. Ask the right questions. For example, if a department has to be eliminated, ask and brainstorm the question "What can we do to otherwise profitably employ the surplus employees now working in that department?" It is a better question than "How many employees can we eliminate?" If the department is not losing money, can a way be found to phase that department into some other area of activity over a reasonable period of time.

If changes of large magnitude are being considered, first address the cause. If overhead is excessive, for example, have the planning group address the problem with a goal of solving it with reasonable speed but without severely impacting the lifestyle of large numbers of employees. Permit understanding of the problem to permeate the organization and welcome suggestions. If the employee group as a whole understands that change is needed to assure the future of the company and the company wants to change in a manner that is sensitive to them, constructive solutions and understanding will occur. It does not make sense to employees, or anyone else for that matter, that a management style which has prevailed for a long time must be changed precipitously when the company is still profitable. How much this type of corporate restructuring contributes to aggravating the social ills of our society and the cost of entitlements to those who are economically disadvantaged is yet to be evaluated. It may be startling to find out.

Your employees can help solve all problems — even those having to do with over-employment and poor productivity.

Section IX

IN CONCLUSION

---

66 • Prioritizing The Steps of Stealth Management

Although you have been presented with a wide variety of management subjects, you may feel that the coverage is incomplete and that you need additional information. If so, consider the advisability of hiring an outside consultant before you start to implement *Stealth Management*. You certainly are encouraged to seek such help as well as continue to study management.

As previously mentioned, if you are not comfortable with the sequence of implementation as recommended, begin with any part that seems appropriate for you and your organization. After reaping the benefit from such a start, perhaps the next step will come easier. For those organizations that have not previously applied this management theory, the following recommended sequence will produce gratifying results.

If yours is a small organization with only one layer of management, you may believe that stealth management has little value for you because many of the management actions suggested are not applicable in your company. Not true! Merely improving your management attitude and philosophy should permit you to accommodate to *stealth management* with understanding and ease as your organization grows. It also will improve your personal relationships and motivational

267

influence. You will be better able to plan and achieve well chosen goals.

You will certainly benefit from the application of any aspect of the *stealth management* program. There are some steps, however, that apply to organizations having three or four levels of management that may not necessarily apply to those having but two levels of management. If you are perceived by your organization as personable with leadership qualities, implementing what you may have learned from this book should help you and your organization achieve its goals and improve productivity. Without that perception you have a real obstacle to such progress. Therefore, your early evaluation should attempt to answer the question, "Do my people have high regard for me as a person and as a manager?" If the answer is yes, you can comfortably proceed with the implementation process in the manner that may seem best to you. If the answer suggests the need to improve your image within your organization, you should re-read sections I through IV and endeavor to make the necessary changes in your management techniques. This may take professional help and, if so, you would be wise to seek such assistance. If you are able to reasonably evaluate your skills with people and be aware of any need for change, you have much of the battle won.

Next you should proceed with the recommendations outlined in topic 39 that concern making your key personnel aware of the planned change in management style, the elimination of hierarchical influences, and the other steps recommended — all intended to set the appropriate climate for *stealth management.*

If the preceding steps result in considerable change in your organization, it would be well to let the dust settle for a few weeks before proceeding further. Often, change that is too rapid can backfire on you. You must be the judge of the proper speed with which to proceed, but erring on the conservative side is best. As soon as you feel comfortable taking further steps, you should define your business and consider the advisability of establishing a mission statement. These steps are described in topics 40 and 41; they sometimes can have a marked effect on your overall business strategy. If such is the case, it would be well to again pause a week or two to let your key people adjust their thinking accordingly.

After those steps you should be ready for both operational and strategic planning as outlined in topic 42. By the time you are well into the planning process, you and your key people should feel exhilarated by the benefits you sense from the overall process. Your feeling of managerial confidence will probably reach a new plateau, and the changes suggested by subsequent topics should be relatively easy. Your organization, and society-at-large will all benefit.

A very important reflection:

Everything you do in the field of management that relates to people, no matter how well intended, can fail or have less than maximum effectiveness if not accompanied by an attitude of sincerity and caring about people. In most such relationships, how you are perceived by others (employees, customers, etc.) is more important than how you think you are doing or how good may be your intentions.

67 • How long will it take

It is difficult to estimate how long it will take to implement the entire management style we call *stealth management*. The more committed you are to creating the necessary climate, the less time it will take. The sooner you make the personnel changes that are needed and convert the team to your way of thinking, the sooner you can begin the planning process.

Do not permit yourself, however, to feel frustration or impatience. The process always takes considerable time, up to six years in a large company. In a smaller company, one having one hundred to two hundred employees, the entire process is not much shorter since real progress seems to be tied to the time it takes to change the *mind set* in your organization. Remember, however, improved performance should make the process seem worthwhile even in the first year.

In my former company, after we had been working on this implementation process for about 6 months, our chief engineer reported to me that a rubber molding die for a new electrical connector did not work even though it produced a marvelous product of novel design that had received accolades from one of our good customers. The only way the part could be removed from the mold, unfortunately, was first to disassemble the mold. The engineer was frustrated and he needed help. I said to him: "Why don't you ask the tool and die maker for his ideas, and if he does not offer a solution, go to the rubber shop foreman and the most experienced rubber molder we have. With each, apply a little self-deprecating humor to the impossible tool we have designed and ask for help in making a good tool of it." It was the rubber shop foreman and his best molder who, together, thought of a simple die change that solved the problem. The point of this story is that 6 months earlier, the engineer might have been reluctant to confess that the design was impractical, I might have shown anger upon finding it out, the shop employee whose help was sought might have laughed at the "dumb engineering department", and the problem might not have been resolved so easily. Not only was the problem readily solved, but in the process, the people involved became a little closer as co-workers and team participants. I observed all this and felt cheered on by such marked evidence of improvement in our company.

The changes in attitudes mentioned in the foregoing story were subtle in their impact, but were indicative of the ongoing change in our company's "culture", the result of implementing *stealth management*. Employees were beginning to realize that their ability to contribute was not only welcomed but more importantly, it was valued. Leadership by top management was more effective because it was applied in this more subtle manner. Such improvement became more striking as the new "culture" was increasingly recognized throughout the organization.

68 · Stealth Management Case Studies

Introduction

There are so many companies who have benefited from the application a style of management which I refer to as *stealth management* that a review of but a few of them would be a subject for another book. I have chosen to refer to two companies, The Teradyne Corporation and Springfield ReManufacturing Corp.

The Teradyne Corp. solicited help from their employees in the design of a new manufacturing facility. They wanted to have a closer team effort between office employees and direct labor manufacturing employees.

Springfield ReManufacturing Corp. was a spin-off from International Harvester Corp., who were losing money on the operation. With the application of *stealth management*, a complete metamorphosis has occurred. The company is now extremely successful.

Teradyne — The New Factory

In the late 1970's, Teradyne wanted to build a new manufacturing facility in Nashua, New Hampshire and move into it from a former facility which they had outgrown. Their old plant was no longer suitable for their operation which had changed in character through the years.

Like most manufacturing companies, they were able to observe a considerable schism between shop and office employees — all part of the typical hierarchy that generally prevailed in most companies at that time. They had taken many steps to eliminate the hierarchy, but the remaining perception, that shop employees were "lower on the totem pole" (socially and educationally) than office employees, still persisted. There is no justification for such an attitude if you properly evaluate the talent and importance of individuals to the organization. How to correct this impediment to better team effort was the problem. How might the physical design of a new factory help solve the problem?

271

Management hired a consulting firm to interview employees in a manner that would ensure privacy but elicit their suggestions for the new factory. I am not aware of the specific questions asked nor the suggestions received. I did, however, visit and tour the new facility and was very impressed with the end result. What worked for them may not be the ideal approach for other companies, in terms of the architecture, and at the time, I wondered how the benefits of their very different facility would stand the test of time.

Their offices completely surrounded the manufacturing shop areas in a manner that suggested continuity instead of the sound proof wall separator typical in all manufacturing companies I had seen previously. The people who had offices immediately adjacent to the manufacturing facilities were those who had frequent reason to relate with shop personnel. Those offices had doors and glass windows that directly opened to shop areas. Shop personnel did not have to go through fancy office and/or reception areas to speak with office employees. Office employees that had lesser need for frequent liaison with manufacturing employees were on the outside of the building, separated by a hall from the offices adjacent to the shop areas.

It is my opinion that this novel arrangement improved communication, but its principle contribution was to employee morale and a better working climate. This was derived from the process of soliciting suggestions from employees and convincing them that management obviously cared. About twelve years later, I had the opportunity of speaking with a long time employee, the secretary of the former vice-president of manufacturing, and asked her to what degree the new factory design contributed to improved morale and communication. It was her opinion that overall esprit de corps was enhanced considerably.

Springfield ReManufacturing Corp.

Springfield ReManufacturing Corp. is a highly successful example of a turnaround situation whose success directly relates to the application of sound professional management. Its unique manner of applying *stealth management* is so soundly based that it has resulted in them being admired and studied by many other companies. The company was a division of International Harvester in 1979, at which time it was losing nearly $2 million a year on sales of $26 million. Its business was rebuilding engines and engine parts. At the young age of 30, Jack Stack was put in charge of the plant to see if he could improve things. By 1981, with employee morale vastly improved, the company earned $1.1 million.

International Harvester was suffering severe financial difficulties and in 1983 decided to sell their Springfield plant.

Jack and 12 other employees arranged to purchase it. Staring with an 89 to 1 debt-to-equity ratio, they renamed it Springfield ReManufacturing Corp. and have watched it grow from less than 200 to over 500 employees. Sales have increased to just under $60 million per year, and profits are a subject of pride. Major customers now include most large automobile and truck manufacturers. They have overcome major obstacles and finally can plan for the future rather than continuing to operate under crisis management.

There is no hierarchy in their company and Jack says, not just for effect, but from a sincere conviction, "I am no better and no worse than anyone else — just a little bit luckier." He provides training to all employees in reading a financial statement and distributes up-to-date financial information about the company each week. Thus, each employee becomes aware of his importance to the financial well-being of the company. Every employee participates in a stock ownership plan and receives a quarterly bonus, assuming one is earned. The overall working climate almost permits each employee to feel self-employed. They are proud of the company and their part in it. Jack feels an important facet of sound management is creating a working atmosphere where people want to come to work in the morning.

Jack does not take near the salary that executives of other companies this size typically draw, even though his organization has told him to be more generous to himself. He feels that his nineteen percent ownership and the relationship he enjoys with the overall company team provide him security, challenge, and job satisfaction. He is happy, he says — what more could he ask for?

The impressive progress made by his company under this management style has resulted in *Inc.* magazine naming Jack Stack as chief operating officer of their "dream management team". Other members of that team include Steven Jobs — former chairman of Apple Computer, H. Ross Perot — founder and former CEO of Electronic Data Systems, and several other high achievers. Jack is teamed with a very prestigious group in this selection by *Inc.* magazine. He is timid about accepting such accolades for himself, because he has truly learned that the power he has is derived from his employees. I feel, however, he is so deserving because he is responsible for establishing the working climate that fosters this team spirit.

I know of no better example of good stealth management than that practiced at Springfield ReManufacturing Corp. Their employees hardly know they are being led, or as Jack might say, they almost are leading themselves.

69 • People — Your Most Important Asset

Throughout this book the importance of people to business has been stressed, but because business managers at-large often find it difficult to put this in full perspective, let us emphasize it one more time — this time, from the vantage point of an investor. Traditionally, investors put high importance on price to earnings ratio and price to book-value ratio in evaluating an investment. If you invest for the long-run, however, unless there is serious financial weakness, people who are both smart and goal oriented will be the most important asset in the organization's success.

The stock of many well known companies such as Merck and Coca Cola sell for very high multiples of earnings and pay but a very small dividend. Excellent people give these companies a quality that produces superior long-range performance. It is too bad that investors do not have a quantitative price-to-people -quality ratio that they can use in their investment decisions.

If you are considering the acquisition of a small company, the quality of its people should not merely be an important consideration. It should be the most important factor. When implementing *Stealth Management*, it is vital to make sure that your people are capable and have potential for growth. There is no room for "Ol' Charley's".

People skills have been stressed throughout the book, but perhaps the following true story will be of important significance to you:

A friend of mine (Marty), while a manager at a very large industrial complex was told by his "boss" to take charge of a group of four maintenance people and get them "straightened out". Marty always had difficulty defining his job because the company saw fit to constantly move him around. He did observe, however, that wherever they moved him always seemed to be fraught with problems.

He called the four maintenance people together to advise them that he had been given responsibility for their department. It was easy to sense their job dissatisfaction and resentment toward him and the company. He said to them: "For reasons I cannot fathom, I have been appointed to manage this department. The reason I can't fathom it is that, with tools, I'm all thumbs and even stand in awe of someone who can change a faucet washer. I've been in this company long enough to totally admire the work that you men do; you don't need a boss, and I promise I won't try to supervise you. I do promise, however, to do every thing I can to help you, so let's try to get along. I will endeavor to meet with each of you on a one-to-one basis from time to time, and we'll try to get together as a group now and then. I'll compile records of the data you give me and pass along any recommendations you have. I'll try to obtain the tools you need to do your job well. I look forward to getting to know you and, for my wife's benefit, I hope to learn a few things from you."

After a few meetings with his new charges, they admitted that the image other people had of them was pretty bad — a condition they would like to change. Marty responded with the question, "What things about other people do you respect?" One of the things that came out of that discussion was that they wish they didn't look like such "slobs" — with dirty clothes, dirty hands, and sloppy looking tool carts. It was apparent that their self-esteem was in need of repair. Marty suggested that if they wanted to improve their appearance, get work smocks, paint their tool carts, or spend more time washing their hands, fine. They could make such decisions on their own and he would help in any way they wished. Meanwhile, Marty was constantly complementing the great work they were doing and managing to obtain the tools they asked for. Slowly, they were starting to be more friendly toward him.

One day, the crew came to work wearing neckties and a week later they had green work jackets with their individual names on them. Marty thought they looked great and asked what they thought about having spare work jackets, in case one got badly soiled during the day. In addition, what would they think about letting people know more about who they were by adding "maintenance engineer" beneath their name. As their self-esteem improved, people began to show respect for them throughout the company. When they would respond to a call for service there often would be a bit of light banter and friendly greetings.

After a few years of being in charge of the "maintenance engineers", Marty's duties were again changed and he was relieved of that job. His four friends were truly sorry he was leaving. He learned soon thereafter that all four of his "engineers" were promoted.

Marty was a good *Stealth Manager*. Not once did he overtly *manage* the people in his department, but the psychological environment he fostered enabled and empowered people toward higher levels of motivation and job satisfaction. He proved that, **given the proper kind of leadership, people will respond with excellent performance and be happier as a result.**

70 • Precepts to Remember

For convenient reference, some of the important precepts of *Stealth Management* are noted below with a page reference. You may find it rewarding to review them from time to time.

- The person we call a manager manages information and things. People manage themselves. p. 15
- If you want to change your organization, you usually must change yourself first. p. 17
- If all managers were to think of themselves as test pilots, with their career lives dependent on their fellow workers, they would be motivated to manage better. p. 22

- A leader induces his followers to want to follow instead of being submissive to his power.   p. 39
- Two basic principles of professional management are: one, the person closest to the action makes the decision, and two, decisions should be made when needed — not delayed until they become less effective.   p. 40
- To communicate well involves transmitting thought, information, or feeling so that it is understood as intended.   p. 48
- Tell me and I may forget, show me and I may remember, but involve me and I will understand.   p. 72
- There are many rewards available in the field of management, and none is more satisfying than the awareness that during your career you have been a beneficial influence on others.   p. 74
- A manager has no power that has not been granted to him by those whose efforts he coordinates — and, the spirit with which that power is granted greatly affects both the manager's and the organization's potential for success.   p. 119
- A good leader inspires his followers to have confidence in him. A great leader inspires his followers to have confidence in themselves.   p. 119
- Every part of managing is something you do with people, not to people.   p. 125

If you are faithfully applying *Stealth Management,* your organizational culture should reflect managers acting as employees and employees acting as managers, all working toward shared goals.

Recommended Attitude Tests

Employee Attitude — Test #1

If the perception employees have about your company and its management is negative and you are oblivious of such a condition, many of the good things you do to promote progress and growth will lack effectiveness. Unhappy employees often will convert your deeds from good to bad with the thought that you are only trying to manipulate them. A less than healthy employee attitude usually festers in a manner that severely inhibits performance.

It is extremely important for top management to know what the attitude of its employees is toward the company and its management. The following questionnaire can be a very useful tool. It should be given to every employee other than the C.E.O., including managers and supervisors. A sealed collection box should be provided for employees to deposit their response to provide privacy, and the responses ought not be reviewed until they all have been received. The test forms should be reviewed by an appointed committee and the summary given to the C.E.O. The questionnaire should include the following questions but may be modified to fit your organization:

* * * * * *

Dear Employee: In reviewing our operations and our company progress, it seems appropriate that we seek your individual thoughts. You probably have ideas that will be a big help and perhaps we have not properly solicited your input in the past. If you will please answer this questionnaire for us and deposit it in the sealed box provided, after all the responses have be received, a committee has been appointed to review and summarize them. Your privacy is assured. After the company has had the opportunity to digest the results and consider responses based on your suggestions, we will bring you up to date. Thank you very much for your cooperation.

Please place a check beneath the letter of your choice, with "A" indicating your highest evaluation and "E" indicating your lowest evaluation.

	A	B	C	D	E
Good team effort exists in our company					
Our management has a good attitude toward its employees					
There is a high level of trust in our company					
You enjoy your job					
You like your supervisor					
Your supervisor seems well trained					
Our pay scales are competitive					
Our personnel policies including benefits are good					
You have confidence in the future of the company					
There is good communication. You feel free to express your ideas, and the company keeps you aware of "what's happening"					

I wish to make the following suggestions: (please print)

Thank you very much for your response to this questionnaire.

Analysis of Top Management Team Analysis — Test #2

(intended for CEO and those reporting to him)

It has been recommended that our top two tiers of managers, which includes you and me, go through the exercise of individually evaluating each of the others in our group as managers by filling out these forms. If you will cooperate in this exercise and deposit the forms you complete in the sealed box provided, I have asked _____ (your company's public accounting firm or lawyer, for example) to summarize them and report to each of us individually without disclosing the results to anyone other than that individual.

After each of us has had a week to digest the results, I will discuss with you what I have learned about myself at one of our management meetings and evaluate the benefit for me. I then will welcome such individual discussion by you but will not obligate you to participate. Other companies have found that a deeper understanding among top management and an enhanced sense of team commitment results from such an exercise. Please cooperate in your usual constructive manner.

*   *   *   *   *   *

Please evaluate _____ by placing a check un-
der the grade letter you find best describes him or her. "A" is highest
and "E" is lowest. "C" would be checked if your evaluation is *average*.

	A	B	C	D	E
Has reasonably even temperament					
Is a diligent worker					
Is dependable					
Is cooperative					
Has good job competence					
Exhibits commendable ethics					
Is flexible					
Is caring and sensitive					
Is willing to take risks					
Communicates well					

You will note that you have been provided one extra form. It is
for you to fill out with your own appraisal of yourself. Keep it and later
compare it to how others perceive these traits in you. Thank you very
much for your participating in this exercise.

* * * * * *

*There are consulting organizations who will conduct employee sur-
veys like those suggested herein. Usually they are more detailed and can
serve to afford you a deeper analysis. In the smaller organization, it is often
easier to gain employee cooperation with the shorter approach that does not
involve outside consultants.*

Suggested reading list

- Drucker, Peter F., *Managing In Turbulent Times*, Harper and Row, 1980
- Goble, Frank G., *The Third Force*, Grossman Publishers, New York 1970
- Goldratt and Cox, *The Goal*, Gower Publishing Co.
- Hawken, Paul, *Growing a Business*, Simon and Schuster, 1988
- Ouchi, William G., *Theory Z*, Avon Books 1982
- Peters and Waterman, *In Search of Excellence*, Harper and Row
- VanGrundy, Arthur B., *Managing Group Activity*, American Management Associations, publications group, 1984
- Senge, Peter M., *The Fifth Discipline*, Doubleday, 1990

*   *   *   *   *   *

INDEX

Reflections

Those who have reviewed this book have been the source of many interesting observations which may have induced you to read it or added to your perspective after having read it. Included among them are the following:

"excellent financial and crisis management advice"
Richard Bednar — Partner, Deloitte & Touche, one of the largest international CPA firms

"pragmatic and very readable"
Dean DeVore — formerly president of medium sized manufacturing company, a management consultant, and now a managing director of a career consulting service company

"illuminating stories"
Anthony J. Eccles — Director of the Sloan Programme, London Graduate School of Business

*"it is not textbook – like in character, I have
difficulty putting it down"*
Dr. John W. Bonge — professor in the school of management, Lehigh University

"section VIII should be required reading for every MBA"
Gene Engleman — a successful banker-businessman who, in the spirit of helping American business has given generously of his time as a lecturer for the American Management Assn.

"very enriching"
Dr. Nancy G. Feldman — a former professor and management consultant

*"should be a bonanza for small manufacturing
company owners and key managers"*
Louis Gelfand — formerly Director of Corp. Relations for a Fortune 100 company, a published author, and ombudsman of a metropolitan newspaper

"the author's practical experience really comes through"
Professor Benjamin Litt — professor in the school of management, Lehigh University

*"what Will Rogers might have written had he
gone to Harvard Business School"*
Martin Mazner — former Director of Marketing for Ashton Tate Corp. and now a group publisher for Ziff-Davis Publishing Co.

(Continued Next Page)

"the intimate style, in an interesting way, addresses problem of persuading managers that they do need to adopt professional techniques"
Dr. Bruce Merrifield — Asst. Sec'y for Productivity, Technology, and Innovation, U.S. Dept. of Commerce

"the most practical management text I have seen"
Donald R. Newlun — A former manufacturing company executive, now a Professor in the Technology Department of a state university

"you are providing practicality not just theory. It is also easy to read with appropriate anecdotes"
F.G. "Buck" Rodgers — Former Corporate V.P. of I.B.M. in charge of world-wide marketing

"I particularly liked the section on implementation"
Carol Rorschach — manager of a small electronics manufacturing company who also has considerable experience in technical writing

"Very practical! I am already applying much of it in my business"
H.T. Sears, Jr. — former vice-pres. of a major oil company. He took early retirement and now is the C.E.O. of a small manufacturing co.

"clearly organized, thorough, and extremely readable"
Richard Silverman — former manager of human resources for a Fortune 100 company and now a management consultant

"a wonderful management book. I particularly like the practical philosophical aspects of it"
Desmond Sides — formerly in managerial services dept. of a big eight acctg. firm, now comptroller and office mgr. of a large non-profit organization

"I like your book"
Jack Stack — President of Springfield ReManufacturing Corp. His success and management style prompted Inc. magazine to name him C.E.O of their management "dream team".

"all my former management training was fragmented in its effect. You put it all together for me"
George Stone — formerly vice-president of a large department store chain and now a management consultant